Also by Tom Cooper and Adrien Fontanellaz in the Africa@War series:
Wars and Insurgencies of Uganda, 1971-1994 (Volume 23)
The Rwandan Patriotic Front, 1990-1994 (Volume 24)
Ethiopian-Eritrean Wars, Volume 1 (Volume 29)
Ethiopian-Eritrean Wars, Volume2 (Volume 30)

Published in 2018 by:
Helion & Company Limited
Unit 8 Amherst Business Centre
Budbrooke Road
Warwick
CV34 5WE
England
Tel. 01926 499 619
Fax 0121 711 4075
Email: info@helion.co.uk
Website: www.helion.co.uk

Designed & typeset by Farr out Publications, Wokingham, Berkshire
Cover design by Paul Hewitt, Battlefield Design (www.battlefield-design.co.uk)
Printed for Helion & Co by Henry Ling Ltd., Dorchester, Dorset

ISBN 978-1-911628-19-4

British Library Cataloguing-in-Publication Data
A catalogue record for this book is available from the British Library

CONTENTS

Note: In order to simplify the use of this book, all names, locations and geographic designations are as provided in *The Times World Atlas*, or other traditionally accepted major sources of reference, as of the time of described events.

ABBREVIATIONS

AAG Armée de l'Air Guinée (Air Force of Guinea [Guinea-Conakry])
AB Air Base
ANA/DAA Armadas Nacional Aérea/Defesa Anti-Aérea (National Air Force and Air Defence [Guinea-Bissau])
ANC African National Congress (South Africa)
APC armoured personnel carrier
ATGM anti-tank guided missile
BOSS Bureau for State Security (South Africa)
CAP Combat Air Patrol
CAS Close Air Support
CIR Centro de Instrução Revolucionária (Revolutionary Training Centre, MPLA/FAPLA, Angola)
CO Commanding Officer
DAA/FAR Defensa Antiaérea y Fuerza Aérea Revolucionaria (Revolutionary Air Defence and Air Force, Cuba)
DITRAC Division des Troupes Aéroportées Renforcées de Choc (Reinforced Airborne Shock-Troops Division, Congo/Zaire).
DRC Democratic Republic of the Congo (Congo-Kinshasa, also Zaire)
DTA Divisão dos Transportes Aéreos (Division of Air Transports, 1938-1973)
ELNA Exército de Libertação Nacional de Angola (Angola National Liberation Army)
EPLA Exército Popular de Libertação de Angola (Popular Army for the Liberation of Angola)
FAC Forças Armadas Cabindesas (Cabinda Armed Forces)
FALA Forças Armadas de Libertação de Angola (Angola Liberation Armed Forces)
FAP Força Aérea Portuguesa (Portuguese Air Force)
FAPA/DAA Força Aérea Popular de Angola/Defesa Anti-Aviones (Angola People's Air Force and Anti-Aircraft Defence)
FAPLA The new name of EPLA since 1974
FAR Fuerzas Armadas Revolucionarias (Revolutionary Armed Forces, of Cuba)
FAZ Forces Armées Zaïroises (Zairian Armed Forces)
FLEC Frente para a Libertação do Enclave de Cabinda (Front for the Liberation of the Enclave of Cabinda, Angola)
FNLA Frente Nacional de Libertação de Angola (Angola National Liberation Front)
FNLC Front National pour la Libération du Congo (National Front for the Liberation of the Congo)
FRA Frente de Resistência Angolana (Angolan Resistance Front)
HQ headquarters
MANPAD man-portable air defence (system)
MBT main battle tank
MGR Marina de Guerra Revolucionaria (Revolutionary Navy, Cuba)
MiG Mikoyan i Gurevich (the design bureau led by Artyom Ivanovich Mikoyan and Mikhail Iosifovich Gurevich, also known as OKB-155 or MMZ' "Zenit")
MINFAR Ministerio de las Fuerzas Armadas Revolucionarias (Ministry of the Revolutionary Armed Forces, Cuba)
MININT Ministerio del Interior (Ministry of Interior, Cuba)
MMCA Misión Militar de Cuba en Angola (Cuban Military Mission in Angola)
MMCG Misión Militar Cubana en Guinea y Guinea-Bissau (Cuban Military Mission in Guinea and Guinea-Bissau)
MNR (Milicias Nacionales Revolucionarias (National Revolutionary Militias, Cuba)
MPLA Movimento Popular de Libertacao de Angola (People's Movement for the Liberation of Angola)
NGO non-governmental organisation
OPVDC Organizaçao Provincial de Voluntérios e Defesa Civil (Provincial Organisation of Volunteers and Civil Defence)
PAIGC Partido Africano para a Independencia da Guiné e Cabo Verde (African Party for the Independence of Guinea and Cape Verde, Portuguese Guiné, later Guinea-Bissau)
PIDE Policia Internacional e de Defesa do Estado (International and State Defence Police)
RPG rocket-propelled grenade (launcher)
SAAF South African Air Force
SADF South African Defence Forces
SDECE Service de documentation Extérieure et de contre-espionnage (External Documentation and Counter-Intelligence Service, France)
SWA South West Africa (nowadays Namibia)
SWAPO South West African People's Organisation (insurgency in the former South West Africa)
TAAG Transportes Aéreos Angolanos (Angolan Air Transport, later TAAG Angola Airlines)
UNITA União Nacional para a Independência Total de Angola (National Union for the Total Independence of Angola)
UNRWA United Nations Relief and Works Agency
UPA Uniao das Populações de Angola (Angola's People's Union)
USAF US Air Force

INTRODUCTION

The silence with regards to the reporting of military-related affairs from Angola in our time is outright amazing – especially for the authors that grew up accustomed to a steady flow of reports about the newest military operations in and around this country. Back in the 1970s and 1980s, hardly a month passed without a major media outlet bringing a report from one of the multiple battlefields of Angola. Of course, the impressions about what exactly was going on were extremely diverse – depending on the part of the world where one grew up. At first, there were reports about a bitter and brutal war between Portuguese forces and diverse 'leftist rebels'. Then the usual story in the West switched to that of a country that had been subjected to an outright invasion of 'Communist forces', whether native (which were usually ignored in the coverage), of Cuban, Soviet, East German, Romanian or of whatever other origin. Reportedly, these forces were in the process of 'exporting the leftist revolutionary ideology' into the territory of what was then South West Africa, defended by 'pro-Western' forces of South Africa, a country with close links to Great Britain and widely perceived as one of most important – even though not especially popular in the public – allies of the North Atlantic Treaty Organisation (NATO). Correspondingly, reports about the South African military launching repeated 'externals' into Angola, with the aim of destroying communist military bases, were a matter of at least monthly coverage.

The usual story in the East, but also in certain parts of the Western hemisphere, and then in much of Latin America, was that of Angola being one of many battlefields in the 'heroic struggle against Imperialism'. Correspondingly, South Africa was not only seen as one of worst imaginable examples for violent oppression of African people, but also a tool of reactionary interventions against progressive governments that emerged in multiple neighbouring countries of the 1960s and 1970s. Certainly enough, precise details on the military forces involved, or the conduct of their operations, were rather scarce.

Over time, a more comprehensive picture began emerging, indicating that a series of three successive wars were fought in Angola in the period from 1961 until 2002. The first of these – variously known as the 'Angolan War of Independence', or 'I Angolan War' – went on from 1961 until 1974, and saw insurgencies by multiple Angolan nationalist movements fighting against the Portuguese colonial rule. It ended with the Portuguese withdrawal and nominal independence of Angola.

Even before that conflict was over, a 'civil' war erupted between three major Angolan insurgent movements and their foreign backers. Lasting until 1992, and including military interventions by Cuba and South Africa, and discrete meddling by the United States of America (USA) and even China, this conflict is colloquially known as the 'Angolan Civil War' or the 'II Angolan War'. Almost uniformly, it is declared as an element of the Cold War – a major struggle for global dominance between the Western 'capitalist', and Eastern 'communist' power blocks. According to that legend, the 'Communists', spearheaded by Cuba, and supported by the Union of Soviet Socialist Republics (USSR, also 'Soviet Union') launched a major military intervention with the aim of establishing themselves in a position of dominance over Angola, but also in neighbouring parts of Africa. In reaction, the Republic of South Africa (RSA) felt forced to launch multiple, limited invasions of Angola – so-called 'externals' – with the aim of destroying the government in Luanda, the capitol of the country, and then with the aim of stopping the spread of Communism. The Cubans and South Africans withdrew in the 1989-1991 period. Combined with political changes at home and abroad this then prompted the government in Luanda into a 'transition' – from a nominally 'communist' state to a nominally 'democratic' one. This enabled the cease-fire of May 1991, which brought an end to the fighting between the government and the last major armed opposition faction.

The reconciliation process, that was to include free elections, collapsed in October 1992, and the third conflict erupted – known either as a continuation of the 'Angolan Civil War', or a new conflict, the 'III Angolan War'. This was to last until the ultimate destruction of the last major insurgent movement in 2002.

The first two of the wars in Angola were widely published on in the West: articles and books about the Portuguese military's involvement of the 1960s and 1970s, and on the South African Operation Savannah can easily fill a well-sized private library. Indeed, the military history of these conflicts is getting ever better coverage thanks to a host of publications from South African sources, and an increasing number of Portuguese- and English-language books. The coverage of Cuban operations – usually available in Spanish language only – is slowly gaining traction, too. There is even more coverage of operations by diverse mercenary outfits – especially those sponsored by the USA and France. However, detailed coverage of native parties that became involved in the diverse of wars fought in Angola over the last 50 years remains scarce: there are less than a handful of detailed studies of the Angolan military forces at all. A comprehensive cross-examination of operations by all the involved parties is thus non-existent. Furthermore, and although dozens of excellent, very detailed reconstructions of specific operations are provided by different Cuban and South African, but also a few neutral sources, operations that did not end well for one or the other party have never been reconstructed in detail, nor subjected to an objective study. Finally, many of the published accounts leave the impression that virtually 'nothing happened' in Angola between the end of Operation Savannah and the battle of Cuito Cuanavale – while, in reality, virtually not one of the involved parties ever ceased fighting.

Therefore, the primary purpose of this volume is a study of Angolan and Cuban military operations in 1975 and 1976: at the end of the Angolan Liberation War, and at the start of the Angolan Civil War, at the time when the situation in this country could only be compared with that of a giant carcass, swirled by plenty of vultures. Initially at least, the military campaigns in question were conducted by miniature forces that ran manoeuvring operations over huge areas. During the weeks prior to the official declaration of independence of the country, a coalition of Angolan insurgents, Zairian forces, and foreign mercenaries advanced for hundreds of kilometres in the north, while in the south a coalition of South African and Angolan insurgent forces came forward at an even higher pace. At several points in time, it appeared as if Luanda would fall at any time. However, due to international pressure, and then the Cuban military intervention, the South Africans were forced to withdraw, while the alliance of Angolan insurgent forces, Zairians and foreign mercenaries was effectively destroyed. Finally, combined Angolan and Cuban forces recovered nearly all of the south of the country, virtually destroying the last large insurgent movement.

The reconstruction of all these operations – and especially the (largely ignored until now) involvement of Angolan forces – has required the consultation of hundreds of diverse sources of reference, and several interviews with participants. The resulting account is certainly far from being flawless. Nevertheless, we do hope that it can offer new insights into how diverse Angolan parties and the Cubans fought.

For our work on this project, the authors have depended on precious help from several participants and numerous colleagues. Foremost amongst these are Teniente-Coronel Eduardo González Sarría, former MiG-21 and MiG-23 pilot of the Cuban air force, Albert Grandolini from France, Pit Weinert from Germany, Mark Lepko and Tom Long from the USA, José Matos from Portugal and Johnatan Kyzer from South Africa. In this place, we would like to express our special gratitude for their friendship, help, encouragement, and generous sharing of numerous photographs over the years. Last but not least, we would like to thank our beloved wives for their endless patience, love and selfless support all the while through this project.

CHAPTER 1
ANGOLAN ARMED FACTIONS

Angola is a beautiful country in south-western Africa. As the seventh largest nation on this continent, it includes a huge area with very diverse geography and population. Crucial for the developments in this country during the period 1975-1976 were a number of armed nationalist groups that had emerged during the last decade of more than 400 years of Portuguese colonial rule. This chapter therefore provides a review of the country, its geography and the population, and the four crucial armed groups existent as of 1975-1976.

Work underway on the Benguela Railway, constructed by the Portuguese in the 1930s. (Mark Lepko Collection)

Geography and People of Angola

Although having a rich history of inhabitation dating back to the Palaeolithic Era, next to nothing is known about this area before it was carved into its modern-day form by the Portuguese conquests, starting in 1483. While the natives initially welcomed the newcomers, and in 1491 the most powerful local ruler – Manikongo ('king') Nzinga Nkuwu – converted to Christianity and accepted foreign guidance in the administration of his realm, the Portuguese were exclusively interested in extracting profit from a booming trade in slaves. Aided by local chiefs, the slave traffic gradually undermined the authority of the manikongo, and resulted in the collapse of the native state. All that was left from earlier periods was the title of the local ruler, 'ngola' – which eventually transformed into the name of the area. Subsequently, the Portuguese had extended their reach southward from the area of present-day Luanda, founded in 1575, and started claiming colonial authority. Luanda was briefly held by the Dutch, in the 17th Century, but with the slave trade dominating the local economy the Portuguese quickly re-established themselves in the dominating position. Nevertheless, no European settlement took place even as of the 19th Century: on the contrary, an estimated *three million people* had been taken away and sold off across the Atlantic, primarily to North America, by that time.

The geography, and thus the terrain, of Angola can be divided into three major regions. From west to east, these are the coastal plain, a transition zone, and the (vast) inland 'plateau'. The low-lying coastal plain is between 50 and 150 kilometres (30-90 miles) wide. The transition zone – dominated by terraces or escarpments – is about 150 kilometres (90 miles) wide in the north, but narrows down to about 30 kilometres (20 miles) further south. The vast Angolan plateau covers approximately two thirds of the country and has an average elevation of 1,100 to 1,520 metres (3,300 to 5,000ft) above sea level.

While having no sizeable lakes, Angola is rich with water resources. Most of the rivers – foremost the Cuanza and the Cunene – rise in the central mountains before draining to the Atlantic Ocean, while the Kwango River drains into the huge Congo River system. The climate in most of the country is tropical, with a dry season from September to April, but the cool Benguela Current moderates the temperatures in the coastal region, and brings most of the rainfall. On the contrary, the cooler central plateau receives much less water. Vegetation varies with the climate: there are thick tropical rain forests around the north and in the Cabinda enclave; savannah and a few rain forests in the centre, and a land of mixed trees and grasses in the south and the east. Wildlife is as diverse and includes many of the larger African mammals, from elephants and rhinoceroses, to giraffes, hippopotamuses, zebras, various antelopes, lions and even gorillas. Angola is immensely rich in mineral resources, foremost including petroleum and diamonds, but also iron ore, manganese, copper, uranium, phosphates, and salt. [1]

Although usually perceived as 'monolithic' by foreigners, the composition of the population of Angola is at least as diverse: it is made up of more than 90 different ethnic groups. Just five of these groups make up more than 90% of the population though: Ovimbunda (37%), Mbundu (25%), BaKongo (15%), Lunda-Chokwe (8%) and Nganguela (6%). The distribution of the population was just as uneven: nearly 70% used to live in the coastal regions, especially in the north; even as of today, only about 35% of Angolans live in the urban areas. Perhaps more importantly, for decades after Angolan independence, for the majority of the country's population there was no 'Angola' as one unified nation and a country: all that mattered was the ethnic group in control of the nearby area, and what their tribal chiefs said.

While easily suppressing any forms of native resistance, Portugal

The City Hall of Luanda in the 1960s. (Mark Lepko Collection)

gained full control of Angola's interior only in the early 20th Century. Henceforth, the country was governed under the so-called *regime do indigenato*, an invidious system of economic exploitation, educational neglect, and political repression. Certainly enough, in 1951 the colony's official status was changed to that of an overseas province and then the policy of an accelerated European settlement was adopted. Over the following 20 years, up to 400,000 Portuguese colonists moved in, and especially cities and major towns experienced rapid development. Luanda grew into a bristling metropolis with a major port and airport, and similar happened in Novoa Lisboa (Huambo), Porto Amboim (Benguela Velha), the port of Lobito and Sa de Bandeira (Lubango) (for a review of colonial and post-independence names for local cities, see Table 1). It was during the same period that most of about 51,400 kilometres (around 32,000 miles) of roads existent as of our times were constructed – of which fewer than one tenth were ever paved. Furthermore, the Portuguese constructed about 2,950 kilometres (1,835 miles) of railroad track – including the principal line – the 'Benguela Railway' – linking mineral-rich Zambia and the Katanga Regions of the Democratic Republic of the Congo, with the port of Lobito on the coast of the Atlantic Ocean. Nevertheless, the road and railroad networks of Angola remain seriously inadequate for a country of this size until this day, and were thus largely supplemented by relatively well-developed internal air services by the early 1960s, by when at least a dirt strip was constructed next to every larger settlement.

However, this was little other than an attempt to stave off the inevitable: local nationalist movements were meanwhile experiencing rapid growth, and in 1961 a guerrilla war against the Portuguese was initiated. Contrary to Mozambique and Guiné, and from the onset of their struggle for independence, the Angolan nationalists were divided into several rival movements. Differences between these often reached such dimensions that some of the movements in question preferred to collaborate with the Portuguese against each other. Despite several attempts at political unification, combatants from diverse factions preferred to fight each other rather than cooperate. Thus, although the conflict of the 1960s and 1970s is usually called the Angolan War of Liberation, and as such separated from the subsequent Angolan Civil War, the matter of fact is that the Angolan civil war had been going on already since the 1960s: this intra-nationalist power struggle only remained unknown to the wider public because the Portuguese war against the nationalists attracted most attention. Unsurprisingly, and for all practical purposes, a full-fledged conflict was clearly in the making already at the time the Portuguese announced their withdrawal in 1974. The principal issue was that – because of successful Portuguese counter-insurgency (COIN) campaigns – all three major nationalist movements existent at the time were weakened to a degree where none was capable of launching and running a conventional, or at least semi-conventional, military operation to bring the huge country under its control.

Table 1: List of City/Town/Locality Names of which have changed since 1975

Colonial Name	New Name
Amboim	Gabela
Ambrizete	N'Zeto
Benguella	Benguela
Carmona	Uige
Gago Coutinho	Lumbala
Henrique de Carvalho	Saurimo
Luso	Luena
Mocamedes	Namibe
Nova Lisboa	Huambo
Novo Redondo	Sumbe
Porto Amboim	Gunza
Pereira de Eça	Ongiva
Porto Alexandre	Tombwe/Tombua
Roçades	Xangongo
Vila Robert Williams	Caála
Sá de Bandeira	Lubango
Salazar	N'Dalatando
Santa Comba/Cela	Waku-Kungo
Santo Antonio de Zaire	Soyo
Sao Salvador	M'banza-Kongo
Serpa Pinto	Menongue
Silva Porto	Kuito
Teixeira da Silva	Bailundo/Bailunda
Teixeira de Sousa	Luau
Xamindele	Toto
Vila Luso	Luena
Vila Salazar	N'dalatando

FNLA (and ELNA)

One of the first movements of Angolan nationalists – the Angola's People's Union (*Uniao das Populações de Angola*, UPA) – was established in 1954. The leader of the UPA was Holden Roberto – a youngster from the BaKongo tribe, educated in the Democratic Republic of the Congo (DRC), where he subsequently worked as a clerk for the Belgian colonial administration. Maintaining a very tight grip on 'his' movement and making virtually all of the important decisions, Roberto thus turned the UPA into a movement of the BaKongo, while failing to make it attractive for other ethnic groups. Furthermore, his movement placed very little emphasis on political work, while his cadre became renowned for their corrupt practices: amongst others, Roberto is known to have diverted funding for financing various of his private ventures. Despite such shortcomings, the UPA – which was reorganized as the Angola National Liberation Front (*Frente Nacional de Libertação de Angola*, FNLA), on 27 March 1962, soon after a merger with a smaller BaKongo political movement – remained the most powerful national movement of the mid-1960s. One reason is that Roberto managed to maintain close relations to the successive Congolese (and then Zairian) heads of state, including Patrice Lumumba, Cyril Adoula, and Major-General Joseph Mobutu. Indeed, Roberto even had family ties with the latter, who seized power in 1965. Correspondingly, the FNLA could always count on steady support from Congo/Zaire, and was even permitted to make use of that country as its base. In turn, Roberto grew over-dependent on Mobutu, and thus found himself outside the position to act without his consent. Furthermore, the FNLA experienced a number of setbacks on the international plan during the late 1960s, because numerous foreign governments began supporting other insurgent movements instead.[2]

The armed wing of the FNLA was the Angola National Liberation Army (*Exército de Libertação Nacional de Angola*, ELNA). Ironically, this was officially established just a few months after the movement triggered the beginning of the Angolan War of Liberation by launching its most successful operation against the Portuguese ever. In mid-March 1961, thousands of UPA's untrained and poorly-armed combatants penetrated northern Angola – left virtually undefended by the Portuguese, who were thus taken by surprise – and destroyed hundreds of administrative posts, farms and coffee plantations, killing hundreds of European settlers and thousands of Africans. In a matter of weeks, the UPA – which reinforced its ranks through forceful recruitment of the local villagers – then established itself in control of nearly all of the BaKongo-populated parts of Angola. Only hastily created settler militias managed to protect the various settlements from being overrun by insurgents. With a mere handful of the insurgents having any kind of military training (most of these were defectors from the Portuguese Army), the UNLA had no means of preventing the colonial military from deploying reinforcements and then recovering all of northern Angola before launchung their own ruthless repression in May 1961.[3]

Following its expulsion from Angola, the remnants of the UPA were re-organized as the ENLA and benefitted – immensely – from the support of the Congolese authorities. In August 1962, it established its most important base near Kinkulu, while its headquarters (HQ) was located in Leopoldville (re-named to Kinshasa, in 1966). The movement began benefiting from support provided by Algeria, Tunisia and Morocco too and had some of its cadre trained abroad during the following years. Furthermore, in addition to receiving around 70 tonnes of arms and ammunition from Algeria and Tunisia in 1963, it received some financial support from private US associations, such as the American Committee on Africa.

Although the combination of safe bases in the DRC and the jungle-covered northern Angola was offering ideal terrain for an insurgency, the ELNA limited itself to small scale, hit-and-run operations across the border. These usually involved groups of between 15 and 30 combatants, and as many porters carrying the necessary supplies. As well as launching a few attacks into the Cabinda enclave, in 1968 it made attempts to open a new frontline in eastern Angola, by launching forays from the Katanga Province of the DRC (later re-named to Shaba) – in an attempt to contest the spread of rival nationalist groups. However, such enterprises remained rather limited. As of 1970, Portuguese military intelligence estimated that the number of ELNA guerrillas active in eastern Angola to have peaked at around 300. Overall, Holden Roberto's fighters were primarily attacking 'soft targets', laying mines, setting up small-scale ambushes, and excelling at avoiding

One of the native guerrilla groups of the 1960s: poorly trained and equipped, they were hopelessly outclassed by the Portuguese colonial authorities. (Albert Grandolini Collection)

direct confrontations with the Portuguese troops. Nevertheless, they did manage to kill 617 members of the security forces between February 1961 and late 1963.

This relative 'lack of activity' was not only a result of Roberto's own decisions, but also the consequence of his overdependence on Mobutu. While eager to have a stake in the Angolan future, the Congolese strongman was also not willing to provoke the Portuguese: indeed, he feared their military retaliation – even more so because much of the mineral exports from Katanga depended on trans-shipment via Angola. Therefore, Mobutu always paid attention to keep Roberto on the short leash: the bulk of the ELNA was always concentrated within its bases in the DRC, where it was suffering from chronic lack of discipline and training. Unsurprisingly, these proved devastating for the movement: a delegation from one befriended insurgent movement from South-West Africa that visited ELNA's camps in the DRC, in 1963, concluded that deploying its own fighters for training there would be counterproductive for its interests. Similarly, in 1969, an official of the Central Intelligence Agency (CIA) of the USA, noticed worn-out uniforms, rusty rifles, lack of sanitary facilities and similar issues while touring various bases.

The ELNA was experiencing immense problems related to its relations with the Angolan population, and thus to recruiting, too. When operating inside its homeland, its fighters tended to steal food from the locals, without ever offering compensation. Indeed, they became involved in frequent actions of forced extraction – and, generally, extracted support by sheer force, instead by political action or other means of persuasion. Furthermore, the ELNA experienced immense problems caused by its – de-facto – mono-ethnic composition. The first mutiny of non-BaKongo combatants erupted in 1963, and required an intervention of Congolese troops. Indeed, Alexandry Taty – one of ELNA's top cadre – launched a coup attempt against Roberto, a year later, before being forced to flee to the Cabinda Enclave with about 1,200 followers. Once in Angola, his troops were integrated into the Portuguese colonial army as the *Tropas Especiais* – which was to prove highly effective during subsequent fighting against their former comrades. Another large-scale mutiny was triggered by shortages of food and clothing in March 1972, in the Kunkuzu camp – and once again had to be put down by Congolese troops.[4]

It was only after this affair that Roberto reorganised his military apparatus. The ELNA was broken down into several numerically designated 'fronts', which in turn included a number of zones (see Table 2 for details). It established several larger tactical units,

The FNLA prided itself with having the best-trained and most disciplined fighters of all the armed nationalist movements in Angola of 1974-1975. The ELNA included a squad of Military Police, troops of which are visible on this still from a contemporary video. (Mark Lepko Collection)

Holden Roberto (foreground) with a group of FNLA/ELNA combatants, in the early 1970s. (Mark Lepko Collection)

battalion-sized *quarteis*, each of which had a HQ and a support-company, two combat companies, and military police, medical, and supply elements, for a total of about 360 officers and other ranks. These were usually armed with Type-56 assault rifles (Chinese-made variants of AK-47s), and Chinese variants of such Soviet firearms like Simonov SKS semi-automatic carabines, DShK heavy machine guns, RPG-2 rocket launchers, and 81mm mortars– in addition to such weapons captured form the Portuguese as Mauser rifles, Heckler & Koch G-3 assault rifles, and FN FAL assault rifles donated by Zaire. For operations inside Angola, the ELNA continued deploying smaller units, usually 75-strong 'independent companies', and even smaller 'mobile companies'. Overall, as of 1972, about 2,500 of ELNA's combatants were active inside Angola, while another 4,000 were near-permanently based inside Zaire.[5]

MPLA (and EPLA)

The MPLA came into being in 1956, when a few small, leftist parties – including the Communist Party of Angola – merged to create the People's Movement for the Liberation of Angola (*Movimento Popular de Libertacao de Angola*, MPLA). Since its inception, this union recruited its followers mostly among the native elites and the Mbundu ethnic group, and its influence was thus restricted to Luanda and the surrounding areas. Furthermore, the nascent party immediately attracted the attention of the International and State Defence Police (*Policia Internacional e de Defesa do Estado*, PIDE), of Portugal, the repression of which forced its activists underground or into emigration. Nevertheless, 52 of the MPLA's top members were arrested, in June 1960, including Agostinho Neto and the brother of Mário de Andrade (leader of the MPLA living in exile in Conakry, in the Republic of Guinea, also 'Guinea-Conakry'), two highly-respected and influential figures.

The MPLA reacted by trying to open an insurrection in Luanda, on 4 February 1961, when dozens of militants armed with clubs and knives attacked two prisons, a radio station, and military barracks. However, these assaults failed: although seven police officers were killed, so were 40 attackers. Furthermore, this action triggered a widespread repression by the Portuguese security forces and colonial militias, during which about 3,000 Angolans were killed in the following days.[6]

The failure of the uprising in Luanda marked the beginning of a years-long period of harsh times for the MPLA, which was thus easily overshadowed by the UPA and then the FNLA. Indeed, surviving activists and militants were forced to flee abroad while others sought refuge in the Dembos area – a hilly zone covered with forests, populated by Mbundu, about 180 kilometres (100 miles) north of Luanda. In September 1961, the MPLA moved its HQ from Conakry to Leopoldville, while in July 1962 Neto escaped house arrest in Portugal and resumed the leadership. A few months later, the movement reorganized itself and created a 'management committee', consisting of ten members, which in turn supervised the establishment of a dedicated armed branch – the Popular Army for the Liberation of Angola (*Exército Popular de Libertação de Angola*, EPLA) – created (roughly) around the same time. Initially at least, the EPLA was a force of between 250 and 300, most of whom had been trained and based abroad. Only a few small groups of it were active inside Angola, primarily in the Dembos forests. In October 1961, a group of 21 were deployed from the HQ in Leopoldville in an attempt to reinforce the survivors, but this was intercepted by guerrillas of the UPC, and its members arrested and then executed. Thus, the first serious operation of the EPLA against the Portuguese took place only on 20 January 1963, when it attacked a small administrative post in the Cabinda enclave.[7]

Subsequent development of the MPLA was impeded by the lack of support at home and from abroad. The UPA/FNLA refused all the overtures to create a common front against the Portuguese. Worse still, the government of the DRC – already busy fighting multiple leftist insurgencies – was very suspicious of the MPLA's Marxist-orientation and banned it from its territory on 2 November 1963. Finally, fierce rivalries developed between different leaders, causing deep rifts within the entire movement and threatening to implode it. Fortunately for the MPLA, a new – and Marxist-oriented – government led by Alphonse Massamba-Débat came to power in the neighbouring Republic of the Congo (Congo-Brazzaville), in August 1963, and promptly allowed the movement to establish its HQ in that country, close to the border to the Cabinda Enclave. Arguably, the Massamba-Débat's decision thus saved the day for the MPLA. However, it should be kept in mind that the FNLA's failure to grow and capitalise on its early international recognition was at least as important for the subsequent development of the MPLA: it created a sort of political vacuum, which enabled the leftists to attract international support.

While the availability of bases in Congo-Brazzaville was most welcome, it still meant that the MPLA's insurgents had to cross the

A squad of MPLA combatants in the early 1970s, some of them armed with Soviet-made PPSh submachine guns. (Albert Grandolini Collection)

Training of MPLA recruits at one of the CIRs in the 1974-1975 period. (Al J Venter Collection)

territory of the DRC – and thus that controlled by the FNLA – to reach Angola. This problem was solved only on 24 November 1964, when Northern Rhodesia was released into independence by Great Britain – to become the Republic of Zambia. Presided over by Kenneth Kaunda, the government of the new republic was quite quick in granting permission for the MPLA to establish its bases in this country and thus open its 'Eastern Front', in 1966. Nevertheless, the movement remained vulnerable to rivalries and disputes. For example, in 1964 a faction led by Viriato da Cruz defected and joined the FNLA.[8]

Beefed up by growing foreign support, and the ability to operate in Angola with more freedom, the MPLA became the most efficient insurgent movement of Angola of the early 1970s. However, even then, its fighters in the sanctuary of the Dembos forest were still isolated from bases in the Congo-Brazzaville, while those operating in the Cabinda Enclave never posed a serious threat for the Portuguese. Additional problems were caused by the local terrain – as well as the population, which never proved really keen to support the insurgents. Finally, once the exploitation of local oil and gas sources began, the Portuguese became able to significantly expand their military presence. Overall, the MPLA's operations out of the Congo-Brazzaville remained limited to cross-border, hit-and-run attacks of short duration. On the other hand, the MPLA did the best out of opportunities offering themselves in Zambia. It began deploying political activists inside eastern Angola, and gradually built up its reputation within the local population. The area proved particularly easy to infiltrate because of its geographic isolation and secondary importance for the Portuguese. Correspondingly, after the first clash with the colonial military, in May 1966, the insurgent activity continued to grow. By 1970, the MPLA – meanwhile under the command of its most effective military commander, Nito Alves – was in control of multiple 'liberated areas', and had created a network of small supply bases, camps and infiltration routes (the best-known one was the so-called 'Rota Agostinho Neto'), which allowed them to gradually expand their operations further south, towards the Benguela Railway, but also in a northern direction, along the borders to the DRC, and in a western direction – towards central Angola. Ultimately, the movement managed to establish a presence in 10 out of 15 districts of Angola, including several areas previously under the influence of the FNLA and other movements. As well as ten major 'Revolutionary Training Centres' (*Centro de Instrução Revolucionária*, CIR), the insurgents established as many as 150 action committees, which resulted in an attempt to create their own para-state, including farmer cooperatives, local associations, and even a few medical clinics. In this fashion, the MPLA became the most powerful nationalist movement in the country. Correspondingly, in 1970 the movement felt confident enough to increase the size of its standard formations through the establishment of multiple companies and then small, battalion-sized semi-regular units, suitable for mobile warfare.

The basic military unit of the MPLA were the groups of 10-12 fighters. Three or four such groups could form a Section, which in turn served as the basis for a Squadron (between three and five groups), while a combination of three to five squadrons was designated a Column with a maximum of about 750 combatants. While initially depending upon captured vintage firearms from Portuguese stocks, including rifles made by Mauser and Steyr, the MPLA's combatants of the early 1970s were armed with a mix of firearms of – primarily – Soviet and Chinese origin. This included Tokarev pistols, PPSh-41 and SKS sub-machine guns, AKM assault rifles, Degtyaryov and RPK light machine guns, DShK heavy machine guns, 82mm mortars, RPG-2s and RPG-7s.[9]

However, the bulk of the EPLA operations remained small-scaled by nature. Since 1966, its insurgents made extensive use of mines, which offered the advantage of limiting their exposition to the Portuguese reactions, while complicating the movement of the enemy. Numerous harassment attacks took place, but usually remained limited to a few shots. Ambushes of truck convoys were conducted too, usually in combination with mining operations, but rarely followed by more than a brief fire-fight before withdrawal. In ambush operations, the insurgents were usually organized in two elements: one armed with automatic weapons and providing fire-support, while the other lobbed hand grenades from short range. On a few occasions, the ambush party was supported by a mortar team that would fire a few bombs before withdrawing. On rare occasions, the EPLA conducted stand-off bombardments of enemy positions by the means of mortars, recoilless guns and its first few Grad-1P rocket launchers.

Overall, the insurgents gained lots of experience in small-scale guerrilla operations over the years, but never developed the capability to deploy and operate battalion-sized forces in manoeuvre warfare, or to combine infantry with fire-support weapons in mobile or siege operations. Foremost, due to its complex command structure, the MPLA always had immense difficulties in the coordination of its widely dispersed units. Finally, the movement grossly underestimated the Portuguese which, under the new leadership of General Costa Gomes, rose to the challenge through adapting a much more aggressive strategy, starting in the early 1970s. Aiming to separate the population from the insurgency, the Portuguese authorities introduced the strategy of constructing protected settlements. Simultaneously, the military started deploying defoliants outside government-controlled areas, running intensive patrolling activity (often supported by helicopters), and launching large-scale offensives against major support bases of the guerrillas. Particularly effective proved Operation Siroco which targeted the MPLA's infrastructure in the Moxico District during the dry season from July to October 1970. The combination of such measures not only made the population in insurgent-controlled areas unable to feed the MPLA guerrillas, but brought it to the verge of starvation and forced thousands to flee to Zambia. By 1972, the movement's strength in eastern Angola had been halved: indeed, most of the insurgents were forced to withdraw to Zambia, from where they could only launch relatively ineffective cross-border raids.

Nevertheless, the blow that nearly caused the ultimate collapse of the MPLA was never delivered by the Portuguese. On the contrary: the military defeat only exacerbated the latent division within the movement. The insurgents from eastern Angola felt that their defeat resulted from ill-advised decisions made by the leadership while others strongly opposed Agostinho Neto's attempts to enter an alliance with the FNLA. To make matters worse, militants from different ethnic groups – first and foremost the Ovimbundu – felt that the Mbundu and domestic leaders were unwilling to share power with them. Discontents coalesced around Daniel Chipenda, a highly charismatic and efficient figure who had been in charge of the Eastern Front. In 1973, after the execution of several of his followers, and after being branded as a 'traitor', Chipenda defected with the bulk of the EPLA's fighting force in Zambia in what became known as the Eastern Revolt Faction. Worse yet: Chipenda was supported by at least a part of the Zambian political establishment, which in turn resulted in the government in Lusaka threatening to expel the MPLA from the country. To add salt to the injury, another faction – nick-named the Active Revolt – then followed in 1974, when Mario de Andrade, the first president of the MPLA, defected together with dozens of other members. Because of such rifts, the movement of

Contrary to various of his other commanders, Agostinho Neto never re-entered Angola during the liberation war. This photograph shows him with a group of MPLA guerrillas on his return in 1975. (Mark Lepko Collection)

leftist nationalists of Angola as of mid-1974 was a mere shadow of its former self: although still estimated at between 3,000 and 5,000 combatants, it lost about 2,000 in combat with the Portuguese, in 1971-1972, and thousands of experienced insurgents – including nearly a half of its leadership inside Angola – to defections.[10]

Table 2: Geographic Commands of the EPLA, 1970

Designation	HQ	Geographic Area
1st Military Region	Congo-Brazzaville	Uige, Luanda, Kwanza-Norte, est. 1961
2nd Military Region	Congo-Brazzaville	Cabinda, est. 1964
3rd Military Region	Zambia	Moxico, Lunda, Malange, est. 1966
4th Military Region	Zambia	Bie, Huambo, southern Kwanza, Benguela, est. 1968
5th Military Region	Zambia	Namibe, Huila, Cunene, Kwando-Kubango

Foreign Support for the MPLA

Traditionally, the extent of foreign help for the MPLA coincided with that movement's ups and downs. The first contacts between the USSR and the MPLA were made in 1958, but it was only three years later that Moscow invited representatives of the Angolan movement to visit the USSR, and then provided funding for the first time – in the form of allocating US$ 25,000 annually (subsequently increased to US$ 50,000). During the same year – 1961 – Czechoslovakia began providing support as well, allocating CZK300 a month, and providing training for 20 insurgents. Bulgaria joined the party in 1962, through provision of firearms, with Algeria following in November of the same year, when the MPLA opened its office in Algiers.[11]

By the mid-1960s, Moscow faced a major competitor within the 'progressive camp' – in the form of the People's Republic of China (PRC). Anxious to challenge the Soviet position as the leader of the communist bloc, Beijing began providing support for numerous liberation movements all over Africa. To make matters worse, Cuba then became extremely active too, and proved willing to help virtually any leftist movement that requested its support. This enticed the Soviets to expand their aid for the MPLA too: the annual allocation was increased to US$100,000 and included ever larger deliveries of arms and ammunition – usually via Congo-Brazzaville. Starting in 1964, significant numbers of MPLA insurgents underwent training at a facility near Perevalnoye, in Crimea. However, this support proved effective only because the leftist Angolan insurgent movement proved a much more effective force than its rivals – and managed to completely reverse the stance of various major African powers, all of which originally favoured the FNLA. Not only that the availability of bases in Zambia proved of crucial importance for the further growth of the MPLA: at least as important was the 3,000 kilometres (1864 miles) long logistic trail connecting these bases with ports in Tanzania, where most shipments were unloaded – enabled by Tanzanian president Julius Nyerere.

The cooperation between Moscow and the MPLA was anything but flawless. Although usually seen as a 'typical Soviet-supported Marxist movement' by all too many that monitored the developments in Angola solely through the prism of the Cold War, the movement was foremost nationalist in essence. Indeed, to their great displeasure, his Soviet contacts considered Agostinho Neto as 'very independent-minded'. The Angolan guerrilla leader then went

Tanzanian President Julius Nyerere (third from left) granted permission for the transhipment of huge amounts of weapons, provided by foreign supporters of diverse African insurgent groups, to pass through the port of Dar-es-Salaam in the 1960s. (Photo by Al J Venter)

a step further by refusing to take sides in regards of the rift between Moscow and Beijing, and outright offended the Soviets when sending 12 of his commanders for training in the People's Republic of China in 1971, and allowing Chinese advisors to provide courses to his combatants in Zambia.[12] Eventually, Moscow concluded that – provided he would be given the opportunity to do so – Neto would prefer to rely on the support of such non-aligned countries as the former Yugoslavia. While limited in scale and scope, Belgrade's commitment to support of the MPLA was highly appreciated by the insurgents, because it never wavered even during the movement's most severe crisis, nor demanded any commitments in return. 'Worst of all' – at least from the standpoint of the USSR – was the fact that the MPLA even made openings to the USA, although without results. Eventually, the MPLA's patiently built-up network of foreign supporters began to unravel during its crises of 1970-1973. It was during this period that the Soviets decided that the ideology had to take secondary place, with priority being that of supporting the movement that was most efficient in the struggle against the Portuguese. Correspondingly, they prepared themselves to switch their support to any other movement as soon as the MPLA began showing signs of weakness and factionalism. Correspondingly, when the insurgency was on the verge of self-destruction, during the Eastern and Active revolts, Moscow not only suspended its financial aid, but almost recognized the FNLA instead.[13]

Early Cuban Involvement

Links between the Cubans and the MPLA were established in the period 1962-1964, when six Angolan insurgents received training in Cuba, while others were trained by Cuban advisors in Algeria. In January 1965, Che Guevara visited Congo-Brazzaville where, amongst others, he met the top leaders of the MPLA and promised additional help. This promise was actually a part of a grand scheme Che was in the process of developing. Correspondingly, he intended to deploy one group of Cuban advisors at bases in Tanzania to support insurgents in the DRC, while another was to be stationed in Congo-Brazzaville and support insurgents in Angola. The latter group – about 250 men led by Rolando Kindelán Bles and Jorge Risquet – was to have a triple mission: acting as a supporting force, helping the MPLA, and protecting the Alphonse Massamba-Débat government – foremost through training a new militia that was to act as a counterweight to the shaky and small military ofthe Congo-Brazzaville, which at the time numbered barely 1,350 officers and other ranks. Furthermore, the presence of Cubans in the country was to serve as deterrent against a possible military intervention by the DRC. The Cuban advisory group arrived in Congo-Brazzaville on 20 May 1965, and was followed by a shipment of arms and ammunition, communication equipment, and supplies carried by the merchant *El Uvero*, which unloaded parts of its load in Guinea-Conakry, Congo-Brazzaville, and in Tanzania. The bulk of the Cuban team arrived in Pointe Noire on 21 August 1965, aboard the merchant ship *Felix Dzerzhinskiy*.[14]

The first six Cuban advisors reached the MPLA's camp in Dolisie – the primary EPLA training facility, positioned about 50 kilometres (roughly 30 miles) from the border between the Cabinda Enclave and Congo-Brazzaville – in late May 1965. The camp in Dolisie included not only the HQ of the 2nd Military Region but also its major supply depot, and housed most of about 300 insurgents assigned to this command at the time. The Cubans immediately started training EPLA fighters in the handling of individual weapons, setting up ambushes, and the use of 75mm recoilless rifles, which the Cubans had brought with them. Starting in June 1965, the advisors also began training their students in small-scale operations of units of up to 30 combatants. The latter training session resulted in the birth of the idea for a relatively ambitious enterprise, the operation code-named Macaco. This was to include a squadron of 100 Angolan insurgents, supported by 50 Cubans, launching an attack on the Portuguese outposts at Sanga Planicie, and then ambushing any reinforcements that would be sent in that direction. This operation was launched in late December 1965, but went awry when the insurgents were ambushed about one mile short of the planned starting point for their own operation. The resulting fire-fight panicked not only the MPLA, but even the Cuban crews left behind four of their recoilless rifles. After this failure, the MPLA significantly downgraded the importance of its 2nd Military Region: this command was henceforth assigned only a bare minimum of men and resources, from which only desultory, hit-and-run attacks were launched. Instead, the bulk of the EPLA was moved to Congo-Brazzaville, from where it was used to reinforce the 1st Military Region, and then establish the Eastern Front.[15]

In need of a new mission, the Cuban team of advisors was then assigned the task of reinforcing insurgents beleaguered within the Dembos forests. This task was particularly daunting because this meant they first had to cross the DRC, and then march for 300 kilometres (190 miles) deep into Angola. After two months of intensive training, about 100 hand-picked EPLA combatants were organized into the Camilo Cienfuegos Squadron.[16] Moving in small groups, this unit successfully infiltrated the DRC before gathering in the border town of Songololo. Once there, they retrieved around 150 firearms – mostly SKS rifles and PPSh sub-machine guns – hidden in several caches beforehand. The Squadron then crossed the border to Angola, on 16 August 1966, and – after successfully avoiding detection by the FNLA and the Portuguese forces – arrived in the Dembos area on 23 September. For the first time in years, reinforcements thus reached the beleaguered 1st Military Region MPLA.

The success of the Camilo Cienfuegos Squadron enticed the insurgents to order similar attempts. Correspondingly, the Kamy Squadron – consisting of 127 men and women – infiltrated the country in mid-January 1967. However, its operation soon turned into an outright nightmare: several insurgents died of starvation, while others were killed in multiple ambushes set up by the FNLA. Finally, most of the rivers the squadron had to cross turned into major obstacles because they were swollen by the rain. Finally, on 10 February 1967, the commander of the unit decided to split his command into two: the weakest elements were to return to the Congo-Brazzaville, while the other would continue the journey in direction of the Dembos forests. Ultimately, only 21 entirely exhausted men had managed to reach the 1st Military Region on 1 April 1967, while only 15 managed to reach the border of the Congo-Kinshasa – where they were quickly denounced by the FNLA, and most of them arrested and executed.[17]

Che Guevara with local comrades during his mission to the DR Congo in 1965. (Al Venter Collection)

Despite this setback, another attempt was made in June 1967, this time by the 180-strong Bomboko Squadron. To secure safe passage numerous Congolese officials were bribed, and thus the unit entered the DRC in a single column, while its arms and equipment were carried in trucks. However, when the column reached Singololo, it found itself surrounded by the Congolese troops, supported by armoured vehicles: the insurgents were left without a choice but to surrender. Although all were later released by Kinshasa, the operation of the Bomboko Squadron was an unmitigated disaster that marked the beginning of the end of the Cuban involvement in the Congo-Brazzaville. Certainly enough, a few additional attempts to reinforce the 1st Military Region were launched subsequently, but the MPLA meanwhile decided to concentrate most of its resources on the Eastern Front instead. Correspondingly, the bulk of its forces was re-deployed to Zambia, which promptly vetoed the deployment of Cuban advisors.

The subsequent fate of the Cuban military mission to the Congo-Brazzaville was nothing better. Although their sheer presence had contributed to counter a coup d'etat by the military against President Massamba-Débat, in 1966, the latter lost power in 1968, and his successor proved not particularly keen in tolerating their presence. Furthermore, by that time Havana came under tremendous Soviet presence to scale-down its unilateral support for diverse 'revolutionary' movements. Correspondingly, on 22 September 1968, the last Cuban advisors left the Congo-Brazzaville. Nevertheless, the close association between Cuba and the MPLA was to prove decisive in 1975.[18]

UNITA

The smallest of the three armed Angolan nationalist movements of the 1960s and 1970s was the National Union for the Total Independence of Angola (*União Nacional para a Independência Total de Angola*, UNITA). UNITA was also the last one to come into being: indeed, its founder, Jonas Savimbi, had first served as the Minister of Foreign Affairs of the FNLA, before growing disappointed by Holden Roberto. In 1965, Savimbi defected together with a group of followers – including the ELNA's Chief-of-Staff, but mostly including militants from the Ovimbundu ethnic groups, like himself – and travelled abroad to negotiate support, all the while refusing invitations to join the MPLA. Eventually, Savimbi found a powerful ally in the PRC, willing to provide support in the form of training. Correspondingly, 11 of his closest associates (see Table 3 for details) underwent a nine-month guerrilla warfare course at the Nanking Military Academy, starting in September 1965, while their leader underwent similar training in the Maoist strategy of People's Warfare.

Furthermore, in early 1966, Savimbi deployed a team from Zambia to eastern Angola, with the aim of conducting political work. This mission proved highly successful and on 15 March 1966 UNITA was officially established during a gathering of 67 local chiefs and delegates. By the end of the same year, the movement had established a permanent 'Central Committee', led by a President (Savimbi), and three vice-presidents, and controlling its armed branch, the Angola Liberation Armed Forces (*Forças Armadas de Libertação de Angola*, FALA). Starting with August 1969, the FALA came under the command of Samuel Chiwale, assisted by David Chingungi, who also acted as the Chief-of-Staff.

The FALA was organized into numbered geographic zones, of which there should have been eight already as of 1968. Each of these controlled a different number of units of variable size. The Portuguese military intelligence is known to have identified three of these, although details are available only about two:

- the Xassengue-Alto Chicapa-Dala-Mona Quimbundo Zone, with 61 insurgents in three groups;
- the Muriege-Casage-Caifuche-Teixeira de Sousa Zone, with 161 fighters in seven groups.

Gradually, the FALA was expanded and included numerous, 100-man strong companies, until establishing its first, 300-strong battalion, on 10 July 1970. Even then, this unit was dispersed most of the time, and its elements served foremost for personal protection of Jonas Savimbi – who, starting in 1968, was the only Angolan insurgent-leader permanently present in the country.[19] Over time, the FALA further established its own military police – dubbed 'The Dragons'. Nevertheless, the movement actually remained very limited in size. The Portuguese military intelligence estimated it at about 500 regulars as of 1968, and only around 1,500 as of late 1974.[20]

Table 3: UNITA Cadres trained in the PRC, 1965

Name
Jonas Savimbi
Jose Kalundungo
Samuel Chiwale
David 'Samwibila' Chingungi
Tiago Sachilombo
Jeremias Kussiya
Nicolau Chiyuka
Mateus Banda
Paulino Moises
Samuel 'Mwanangola' Chivala
Isaias Massumba
Jacob Inacio

A still from a video showing a scene from one of meetings organized by UNITA, in 1975, together with the flag of that movement. (Mark Lepko Collection)

Embattled Maoists

The most-publicised combat operation by the FALA took place on 4 December 1966, when around 60 of its combatants attacked the small Portuguese outpost in Cassamba. Due to inadequate reconnaissance, the insurgents were repulsed, suffering one killed and several wounded, without any success in return. A much larger operation was launched by several hundred insurgents commanded by Samuel Chiwale and Samuel 'Mwanangola' Chivala, at dawn of 25 December 1965, against the Portuguese garrison of Teixeira de Sousa. The FALA lost at least 25 killed, while the Portuguese suffered around a dozen casualties – including the local officer of their secret police.[21]

Drawing lessons from these failures, the movement gave up running large-scale operations against well-prepared defensive positions and instead limited its activity to hit-and-run attacks against lightly protected targets. For example, in March 1969, it claimed that 125 of its combatants had successfully ambushed a Portuguese truck convoy and seized a huge bounty of arms and ammunition.[22]

Actually, even UNITA was never in any better position but to run mere harassment attacks. Completely dependent on support from Zambia – which favoured the MPLA, and actually never authorised the establishment of FALA's bases on its property – UNITA operated in distant parts of Angola, and was de-facto cut-off from the outside world. Most arms shipments from China were seized either by the Tanzanian or Zambian authorities and thus it possessed only very few modern firearms – like FN FAL assault rifles acquired clandestinely from the DRC. Furthermore, its operations had threatened the Benguela Railway, used to export Zambia's copper ore, which incensed Lusaka to the point where Savimbi was arrested on at least one occasion while transiting the country. Indeed, the movement was officially banned in Zambia, starting in 1967, and survived only because the local authorities looked away from its activities – on condition for these to remain low-key by their scope and nature. Later on, UNITA entered limited cooperation with the South West African People's Organisation (SWAPO), and authorised the latter to use parts of Angola under its control as an avenue of approach to what, since 1991, is now Namibia. In return for this favour, the better-equipped SWAPO started providing UNITA with some arms, including a consignment of RPG-7s. The amount of financial support provided to Savimbi was also limited. Beijing provided two instalments – one for US$15,000 and another for US$30,000 – in period 1964-1966, while other funding came from diverse non-governmental organisations (NGOs) in the USA, including The World Council of Churches (US$37,500 in the period 1970-1974), and the US African Liberation Support Committee.[23]

Early during its existence, UNITA experienced significant organisational issues. Several of its local commanders tended to rule over their areas of responsibilities as their own fiefdoms, and many were divided by fierce rivalries. Unsurprisingly, it took Savimbi lots of effort and time to assert central control – which, combined with lack of arms and support – only caused further disagreement: in March 1969, Samuel 'Mwanangola' Chivala defectd to the FNLA with 144 men and 40 firearms. However, following the Maoist doctrine of 'People's War', UNITA went to great extents to provide political training to its cadre – including that of the FALA – and had these working on a build-up of a support base among the local population, and establishment of 'bush hospitals' and schools. Indeed, it went a step further through provision of political indoctrination of the local population, in turn helping the movement collect the basic supplies and recruit the manpower necessary for its survival. Unsurprisingly, the few foreign journalists that managed to visit UNITA-controlled areas before the end of the Portuguese rule, found a poorly-armed – and fed – insurgency, most of the combatants had no shoes, for example – but also one that was well-disciplined and organised. Nevertheless, the movement proved not only vulnerable to increasingly effective COIN operations of the Portuguese, but also to the growing presence of the MPLA in eastern Angola, starting in 1968. Indeed, the rival organisation caused some of the heaviest losses to UNITA. Things only got worse once the FNLA entered the area. Squeezed between the rock and a hard place, Savimbi entered negotiations with the Portuguese and agreed a truce that was in effect between early 1972 and September 1973. Concluding this was only favouring the Maoist insurgency in the long haul, the Portuguese subsequently resumed their operations against UNITA – but, by then it was actually too late.[24]

Portuguese 'Local Forces'

One legacy left by the Portuguese once they withdrew from Angola was the presence of thousands of native troops with a good military education. Indeed, confronted with a near-simultaneous uprisings in Guiné, Angola, and Mozambique, the military of the former colonial super-power was forced to heavily 'tax' all of its available resources – so also in regards of the manpower. Eventually, the Portuguese war effort grew to far more extensive dimensions than that of the USA in Vietnam, and it became unavoidable to recruit native troops. These were not only 'cheaper' to maintain than metropolitan troops, but also provided specific 'extra' capabilities – like that of intimate knowledge of the local terrain, fluency in all local languages and dialects, or the ability to melt in with the local population. Moreover, recruitment of native troops curtailed the possibility of these joining the FNLA, MPLA, or UNITA instead. Unsurprisingly, the proportion of native troops within the Portuguese military grew from about 14.9% in 1961, to 42.4% in 1973 – and this despite the fact that the number of metropolitan troops deployed in Angola increased from 28,477 to 37,773 in the same period.[25]

Initially, native troops were organized into militias tasked with defence of villages, until most of these were raised in status to that of auxiliaries, and placed under the aegis of the Provincial Organisation of Volunteers and Civil Defence (*Organizaçao Provincial de Voluntérios e Defesa Civil*, OPVDC). However, as more redoubtable units came into being – whether under the aegis of the OPVDC, the PIDE, or the Army – they grew in importance and were officially run as the Special Troops (*Tropas Especiais*). The first group of Special Troops came into being when the PIDE reorganized several hundred, of about 1,200, former insurgents led by Alexanadre Tarly that defected to the Portuguese side in the Cabinda enclave in 1965. They were grouped into units of 31 men each, divided into three sections of 10. By 1974, the Special Troops totalled around 800, organised into four small battalions, each of six groups. Wearing the same uniforms as the insurgents, and armed with similar weapons of Soviet design, these units operated independently – first in the Cabinda Enclave, and then in northern Angola.[26]

Next, the PIDE began experimenting with recruitment of the Bushmen as scouts. Already the first series of related tests proved highly successful, because these proved highly skilled as trackers, and capable of surviving in even the roughest terrain. Initially armed with bows and arrows only, the Bushmen were organized into small scouting parties, named Arrows (*Flechas*), they began receiving commando-type training, and were armed with AKMs and M-16s. By the 1970, the Flechas were usually organized in the form of platoons, which were either attached to regular army formations or operated independently, and excelled in long-range patrols. Their recruitment was expanded to a degree where – combined with defectors from the MPLA – the Flechas totalled more than 2,000, in 1974. Meanwhile, in 1968, the Portuguese army activated its first Special Groups (*Grupos Especiais*), which – like the Special Troops – were usually organized into 31-strong groups, mostly manned by local volunteers, but also by re-trained defectors from the MPLA and FNLA. One or two such groups – no less than 99 had been activated by 1974, including around 3,200 troops – was usually assigned to every battalion of the army.[27]

Katangese Gendarmes

The Katangese Gendarmerie came into being during the ill-fated Katangese secessionist attempt in the DRC of the mid-1960s – during which, despite their defeat, the native gendarmerie had proved itself as a force to be reckoned with. Although they were later integrated into the Congolese armed forces while maintaining their distinct identities, they found themselves on the losing end of various power struggles. Following the failure of the mercenary revolt of 1967 and the demise of Moïse Tshombe, their political leader, they were targeted by waves of repression launched by the regime of Joseph Mobutu. As a result, around 4,600 Katangese Gendarmes and civilians fled to Angola in 1967. The following year, Nathanaël Mbumba, a former policeman, emerged as their new leader and ended the power vacuum created by the disappearance of Moise Tshombe, while a dedicated political wing, the National Front for the Liberation of the Congo (*Front National pour la Libération du Congo*, FNLC) was created in June 1969.

The Portuguese colonial authorities almost immediately concluded that these exiles could be useful, noticeably as a lever against the government in Kinshasa that was supporting the FNLA. Hence, a deal was swiftly concluded between the PIDE and the FLNC, according to which the Portuguese would allow the Katangese to stay in Angola and provide a degree of support for their struggle against Mobutu, and the exiles were to be engaged in counter-insurgency operations in Angola. Thus, around 2,300 ex-Gendarmes were reorganised in 15 companies, forming three battalions with Portuguese support. Indeed, from March 1971 on, 14 of these companies received dedicated commando training, and their men became nicknamed 'Tigers' as a result. Although trained, paid and supplied by the Portuguese armed forces, which called them the Faithfuls (*Fiéis*), the Katangese units kept their own officers and NCOs. The Tigers were used to protect diamond mines and roads and, from 1970 on, were engaged in offensive operations against the insurgents and soon became reputed for their fighting skills, suffering from relatively low losses, with a total of 31 KIA by 1972, while conducted hundreds of operations, either in coordination with Portuguese troops or independently. In 1968, the PIDE also raised, under a similar agreement, around ten 45-men strong platoons drawn from Zambian opponents who had found refuge in Angola, and which were named *Leais* (the loyal ones). The Portuguese also raised units mixing African and European recruits, including five 125 men strong Commando companies.[28]

CHAPTER 2
FOREIGN ARMIES

Other than native armed groups, armed forces of numerous neighbouring countries and foreign powers also became involved in the conflict in Angola of 1975-1976. This chapter is therefore dedicated to providing a review of the militaries in question, their equipment, organisation, and earlier combat experiences.

Fuerzas Armadas Revolucionarias

The Revolutionary Armed Forces (*Fuerzas Armadas Revolucionarias*, FAR) – of Cuba – were the direct descendant of the Rebel Army (*Ejército Rebelde*) that had entered Havana on 1 January 1959, toppling the regime of the dictator Fulgencio Bautista in the process. Bautista's military was then quickly disbanded: only a small number of its officers and other ranks – especially pilots and technical personnel – were integrated into the new army, the establishment of which officially began on 16 October 1959, when the Ministry of the Revolutionary Armed Forces (*Ministerio de las Fuerzas Armadas Revolucionarrias*, MINFAR) was set up. Initially at least, the MINFAR oversaw the operations of the Rebel Army, the Rebel Air Force (*Fuerza Aérea Rebelde*), and the Navy (*Marina de Guerra Rebelde*), though the official titles of all three services were soon after changed to the Revolutionary Army (*Ejército Revolucionario*), the Revolutionary Air Force and Air Defence (*Defensa Antiaérea y Fuerza Aérea Revolucionaria*, DAA/FAR), and the Revolutionary Navy (*Marina de Guerra Revolucionaria*, MGR). Furthermore, the ministry controlled the National Revolutionary Militias (*Milicias Nacionales Revolucionarias*, MNR) – but the importance of the same greatly diminished after November 1963, when universal conscription became mandatory.[29]

The Revolutionary Army was reorganized into three commands: Centre, Eastern and Western, effective from 4 April, 21 April and 14 June 1961 respectively, and its units expanded exponentially – thanks to massive support from the USSR and Czechoslovakia. Already in April of the same year, the FAR had established its first large unit, the 50th Division, while by the end of the year it totalled around 20,000 officers and other ranks, organised into nine small infantry divisions, each including two brigades with two battalions, an anti-tank battery, and artillery battery, a reconnaissance company, and a machine gun squad. Nevertheless, most of the troops deployed in reaction to the Bay of Pigs invasion of 1961, were still poorly-trained militiamen, supported by few – and equally ill-trained – regular units operating heavy weapons.[30]

On 22 October 1962, at the height of the Cuban Missile Crisis, Havana mobilised all of the FAR, including a total of 27 divisions: three of these were regular, permanent units, while the rest were 'reduced' divisions, activated only in cases of emergency. Notable is that neither regular nor reduced divisions had any kind of headquarters at regimental level: instead, the divisional HQ controlled six infantry battalions. Furthermore, many of the divisions in question lacked their artillery components (usually totalling between 18 and 30 tubes). Indeed, most of support and specialised units were controlled by Corps and Army headquarters, while the sole Tank Brigade, the 1st and 4th Artillery Brigades (including 12 RM-51 and BM-13 MRLs each, plus the majority of about 2,530 artillery pieces and 120mm mortars) were held back as a strategic reserve.[31]

Following a period during which it primarily received older Soviet weapons – including 500 Czech-built T-34/85 medium tanks (delivered in 1960-1961), and SU-100 tank hunters, but also BM-13 and BM-21 MRLs, Cuba became one of the first foreign recipients of modern Soviet equipment, including T-55 MBTs (in 1963), or 9K53 Luna surface-to-surface (or ballistic) missiles (in 1964). The FAR's armoured corps was thus rapidly expanded: from the original '26 de Julio Motorized Regiment' equipped with a few M4 Shermans and British-made Comet tanks, to an armoured brigade (UM2600, established on 3 August 1961), and then to three armoured brigades (including the UM1688, established on 23 November 1963, and UM1448, established on 15 May 1964). In turn, these three brigades, two motorised divisions, and a dedicated artillery regiment (the UM2055) were put under the control of the Armoured Corps, established in 1967. By early 1970s, the FAR's order of battle included a full Armoured Division (UM1011), which was an element of the Armoured Corps, that still served as a strategic reserve and was subjected to the direct control of the FAR HQ.[32]

Meanwhile, the Cuban ground forces were reorganized to correspond more closely to the model of the Soviet armed forces. Correspondingly, some of the socio-economic duties of the military – such as providing manpower to help with the harvest – were reduced, or taken over by other paramilitary organisations (foremost the Youth Labor Army, the *Ejército Juvenil del Trabajo*, EJT, established in 1973). Around the same time, the DAA/FAR and the MGR were given increased autonomy in their operations, and their HQs liaised directly with the MINFAR, instead of remaining subjected to the control of the FAR. Although the flow of deliveries of Soviet military material remained constant through this period, the total size of the active Cuban armed forces was greatly reduced between 1970 and 1975, to around 120,000 officers and other ranks. In other words: the Cubans placed greater emphasis on quality over quantity, replaced most of the older Soviet arms with such designs as T-55 MBTs and BM-21 MRLs, and paid more attention to the operational preparation and combat effectiveness of their military. Although remaining a predominantly infantry force, the FAR of this time placed the great emphasis on massive use of artillery along pre-planned fire-plans and a – generally – offensive and very aggressive

A group of Cuban officers and other ranks, with Commander Alberlo Colome Ibara (centre, with glasses), in Angola of late 1975. (Albert Grandolini Collection)

use of armour and mechanised forces. On the defensive, its officers were trained to systematically delay their opponent by establishing forward positions, while deploying their units for the defence in depth, and keeping a mobile reserve – usually a reinforced platoon in the case of a battalion, or a reinforced company in the case of a regiment – for the purpose of a counterattack. The adherence to Soviet practices had flaws, too, relatively rigid limitation of autonomy allowed to the junior officers and NCOs. Similarly, soldiers were trained to master only their own speciality, and thus could not be relied upon to accomplish any other functions or tasks.[33]

Meanwhile, in the mid-1960s, the Ministry of Interior (*Ministerio del Interior*, MININT) created the first dedicated commando force on Cuba, the Special Troops (*Tropas Especiales*). Including no fewer than 1,000 officers and other ranks formed into a single battalion, this unit received a crucial role because of its responsibility for the protection of high-ranking officials.[34]

DAA/FAR and MGR

The DAA/FAR was originally built around a miscellany of left-overs, and thus included aircraft of US and British origin, like Douglas B-26 Invaders, Hawker Sea Fury, and Lockheed T-33s. The first 20 MiG-15bis and 4 MiG-15UTI had been delivered in late May 1961, and assembled at San Antonio de los Banos AB, with the help of Soviet technicians. The first MiG-equipped fighter jet unit, the Carlos Ulloa Squadron, was formed around a nucleus of six pilots trained in Czechoslovakia, and declared operational in November of the same year. Deliveries of additional MiG-15bis, MiG-15UTI, a few MiG-15Rs, and then the first 12 MiG-19Ps (in November 1961), enabled the DAA/FAR to establish three additional squadrons, including those nick-named 'Chinos' and 'Checo' – according to the countries in which their personnel were trained.[35]

Due to their poor mechanical reliability and three crashes (in which at least two pilots were killed), MiG-19s were to prove great disappointment. Correspondingly, the type was quickly replaced by 40 MiG-21F-13s, deployed to Cuba in September 1963 by the 32nd Guards 'Vilensky' Fighter Aviation Regiment of the Soviet Air Force. The Soviet personnel withdrew after converting Cuban pilots and ground personnel to the new type, but henceforth, pilots of the DAA/FAR underwent regular air combat training in the USSR. More advanced variants of this type followed through the next few years, including MiG-21PFSs in 1964, MiG-21PFMs in 1965, and MiG-21Ms and MiG-21Rs in 1968. Meanwhile, Cuba acquired additional MiG-17s from the Czech production, and then several batches of MiG-17Fs: these replaced the hopelessly obsolete MiG-15bis', but about 36 MiG-15UTIs remained in service as jet trainers well into the early 1980s. By 1974, the CIA thus estimated the DAA/FAR's frontline strength at 87 MiG-21s of diverse variants (including 23 MiG-21Ms), operated by six squadrons, and around 30 MiG-17s operated by three units. These were attached to three different brigades – one of which was responsible for the support of each of the major ground commands (Western, Central, and Eastern). The primary focus in training of DAA/FAR pilots – nearly all of which underwent training courses in the USSR – was air defence under strict ground control. Ground attack received relatively little attention because the Cubans concluded that if their pilots could master air combat to perfection, they could easily perform ground attacks, too. Their tactical procedures were essentially the same as those of the Soviets, with those of ground attack remaining quite simple: the pilots were trained to approach the target area at low

One of the relatively unusual weapons operated by the DAA/FAR, were Czechoslovak-made, self-propelled 30mm cannons, installed atop a modified chassis of the BTR-60 APC, visible behind Fidel Castro on this photograph. (Albert Grandolini Collection)

altitude and high speed, before pulling up, identifying the target, and either executing a steep or a shallow dive, and finally firing their rockets or releasing bombs. Only pilots of the MiG-17s received extensive training in anti-ship attack, and became reputed for their proficiency in such operations.[36]

The MGR remained the smallest of the Cuban armed services and was primarily in charge of coastal defence. Correspondingly, it operated a large number of patrol, torpedo, and missile-boats – foremost such as the 24 Project 183 and Project 205 fast missile craft (armed with P-15 Termit anti-ship missiles, better known under their NATO designation, SS-N-2 Styx), and 21 Project 122bis- and Project 201 sub-chasers. Organised into squadrons, these were distributed between three naval commands, and totalled about 5,000 officers and other ranks.[37]

Cuban Combat Experiences

As well as the destruction of the CIA-established and trained 'Brigade 2506' during the Bay of Pigs invasion in 1961, the FAR became involved in running multiple operations against anti-Castro insurgents active primarily in the east of the country. While relatively ill-organised, some of these groups did benefit from clandestine US-support – amongst others in the form of para-drops of arms and supplies. At the height of this little-known insurgency, the FAR launched several large-scale COIN operations. For example, in 1961, Operation Jail (*Jaula*), included the staggering number of 80 battalions, with around 60,000 troops, mostly militias. Subsequent COIN operations usually saw the deployment of MININT operatives tasked with collecting intelligence, with regular FAR officers commanding local militias. While most details remain obscure, it is known that by the end of 1964, no fewer than 500 members of the Cuban security forces had been killed: in turn, up to 3,500 insurgents were either killed or captured. A year later, Havana claimed to have defeated the insurgency. However, several small, hopelessly isolated anti-Castrist groups remained active for a while longer. Thus, and ironically, many of FAR commanders who had been insurgents of the late 1950s, had collected extensive COIN experiences in the 1960s.[38]

The deployment of the Cuban military instructors to the Congo-Brazzaville, and in the DRC of 1965-1967, was thus a logical extension of this experience: Havana was offering services of highly-experienced troops to virtually any movement whose ideologies were at least roughly similar to its own. Furthermore, the FAR went as far as to establish a dedicated military school for diverse militants in Cuba, the UM1546. The Congo-Brazzaville episode was also no exception in regards of deployment of FAR advisors abroad – rather a pattern that became a rule. Additional teams were deployed to Guinea-Conakry, Sierra Leone, Equatorial Guinea, South Yemen, and even to Somalia during the following years.[39] In September 1963, when Algeria found itself on the receiving end of a Moroccan military aggression, the FAR formed the Special Training Group (*Grupo Especial de Instrucción*, GEI), of 686, commanded by Efigenio Ameijeiras, and deployed this to Algiers together with enough arms and equipment for a full armoured battalion (including 22 T-34/85s), two artillery battalions (one including 18 D-30 howitzers, and another with 18 120mm mortars), and a battery of 57mm recoilless rifles. Upon their arrival in Algeria, the Cubans not only trained 926 Algerian soldiers, but began planning a counteroffensive against the Moroccan troops (Operation Dignidad). Although no such enterprise ever materialised, Ameijeiras was subsequently bitterly disappointed over not being given the opportunity to train many more Algerian soldiers.[40]

The next major overseas deployment of the FAR took place in 1966, when the African Party for the Independence of Guinea and Cape Verde (*Partido Africano para a Independencia da Guiné e Cabo Verde*, PAIGC) was running a highly effective insurgency against the Portuguese forces in Guiné (Guinea-Bissau) – usually from secure bases in Guinea-Conakry. The PAIGC had already proven itself as the deadliest of all the guerrilla movements active in Portugal's overseas provinces. However, it lacked the time and know-how with regards to operating artillery and mortars. Correspondingly, Amilcar Cabral, the leader of the PAIGC, requested Cuban advice in this regard. The first team of the Cuban Military Mission in Guinea and Guinea-Bissau (*Misión Militar Cubana en Guinea y Guinea-Bissau*, MMCG) – including 50-60 experienced artillerymen – arrived in Conakry on 8 May 1967. Subsequently, this team became responsible for training PAIGC's insurgents on different artillery systems provided by the USSR and other countries. That aside, Cuban advisors crossed the border to Guiné on a number of occasions, in order to help their 'students' deploy indirect-fire weapons.[41]

MiGs in the Jungle

Positive experiences from the deployment of the MMCG in Guinea-Conakry led to the expansion of this mission. The deployment in question was indirectly prompted by the appointment of General António Sebastião Ribeiro de Spinola to the position of the military governor of Guiné in 1968. Finding this 'overseas territory' of Portugal terribly under-developed – even most basic roads were non-existent – de Spinola launched an intensive campaign of building hospitals, schools, housing, and communications, with the aim of improving the living conditions of the local population. Simultaneously, he launched a campaign of more intensive and energetic COIN operation than ever before, with the result of moving the fighting against the PAIGC into the areas controlled by the insurgency. Finally, de Spinola attempted to negotiate with Sekou Touré, president of Guinea-Conakry, with the aim of effecting the release of the Portuguese prisoners of war and hostages held in that country. When these negotiations failed, the Portuguese general ordered a series of devastating attacks on PAIGC-controlled areas along the border to Guinea-Conakry, resulting in serious reverses for the insurgency.

This campaign peaked with the Operation Mar Verde, a daring raid on Conakry launched during the night of 21 to 22 November 1971 with the aim of liberating some of the Portuguese prisoners and hostages held in Guinea-Conakry, destroying fighter jets of the Air Force of Guinea (*Armée de l'Air Guinéenne*, AAG), and demonstrating de Spinola's willingness to hit back at any of PAIGC's allies. Operation Mar Verde made it clear to the members of the MMCG, that the AAG was hopelessly outclassed by the units of the Portuguese Air Force (*Forca Aérea Portuguesa*, FAP) deployed in Guinea. Originally established in 1959-1960, and supplied by 10 MiG-17s and 2 MiG-15UTIs provided by the USSR, the Guinean air force became involved in internal unrest and a near-mutiny in 1969, which prompted President Sekou Touré to purge the military and develop a militia from political organisations supporting him, as a counter-weight. Although the Portuguese failed to find and destroy any MiGs during Operation Mar Verde – by sheer accident, all six that were still operational had been re-deployed at another airfield – the AAG proved unable to retaliate: the pilot of the sole MiG-17 that was scrambled the following morning failed to find and attack even one of the warships involved in the raid. Furthermore, the Portuguese attack destabilised the government in Conakry: amid reports about another coup attempt, Touré's militias purged the

The only available photograph to depict an intact AAG MiG-17 was taken in the mid-1970s, and shows an aircraft that apparently received a coat of green overall, with light admiralty grey on undersurfaces, and marked with a big red serial, 513. Of interest are the application of the fin-flash and underwing hardpoints. (Albert Grandolini Collection)

One of five MiG-17Fs delivered by the Soviets to Guinea-Conakry for the PAIGC's nascent air force (and the future ANA/DAA), in 1973, was this example, photographed inside a hangar at the military side of Bissau International, in 1991. (Photo by Jacques Guillem)

military again. The resulting removal of 900 officers and other ranks left the entire military of Guinea-Conakry in tatters: the air force was down to a mere 200 airmen. Unsurprisingly, it took the AAG two days to react to the Portuguese attack: on 24 November 1971, a lone MiG-17 made a single pass high over the Governor's Palace in Bissau, and then disappeared before the FAP could scramble one of its Fiat G.91Rs from the nearby air base.[42]

Once he secured his position, Touré launched a project of reconstructing the air force. Correspondingly, at least four MiG-17Fs were acquired from Nigeria in 1972, while Havana deployed two teams – including a total of eight pilots – of the DAA/FAR to Conakry, between February and May 1973. Thus expanded, the MMCG now had a dual mission: on one hand, it was to help rebuild the AAG, and on the other, it was to help establish an air force of the PAIGC. Working feverishly, the Cubans helped extend the runways of airports at Conakry, Kankan, and Labé; made several P-12 and P-37 early warning radars operational, and helped train not only new Guinean crews, but converted a team of 11 insurgents that were fresh from basic flight training in the USSR, to a total of five MiG-17Fs and two MiG-15UTIs provided by Moscow. The result was, essentially, the reestablishment of the AAG, but also the establishment of the future National Air Force and Air

A row of Fiat G.91Rs of the FAP, as seen at the airport of Bissalanca in the late 1960s. (Jose Matos Collection)

Defence Force (*Armadas Nacional Aérea/Defesa Anti-Aérea*, ANA/DAA) – of Guinea-Bissau. Moreover, the combination of improved bases, operational MiGs, and functional radars soon enabled them to establish a reasonably good control of airspace over Guinea-Conakry, and start flying combat air patrols (CAPs) along the coast and along the border to Guiné. Furthermore, in March 1973, two MiG – flown by a Cuban and a Guinean – flew a mission of visual reconnaissance over Bissalanca. The overflight took the Portuguese by surprise and the two MiGs distanced long before any G.91Rs could get airborne. Furthermore, it caused grave concerns within the ranks of the FAP at Bissalanca, because it was now obvious that the Portuguese air base there could be raided by Guinean MiG-17s.[43]

Overstretched DAA/FAR

The early 1970s were a busy period for the DAA/FAR community elsewhere, too. In 1971, Cuban advisors trained a team of ten North Vietnamese pilots to fly anti-ship attacks with their MiG-17s: two of these flew the famous attack on USS *Higbee* (DD-806) on 19 April 1972, during which the latter was hit by a single 250kg bomb, which destroyed its rear dual 127mm gun turret.[44] Immediately afterwards, a group of around 100 pilots and ground personnel was deployed to the People's Democratic Republic of Yemen (PDRY, also 'South Yemen') to help work-up the local air force. They remained in the country until late 1977, when the entire team was re-deployed to Ethiopia and saw intensive involvement in the final phase of the Ogaden War against Somalia.[45] Another example of a high-intensity Cuban military intervention occurred during the Arab-Israeli War of October 1973, when – after suffering heavy losses during the attempted re-conquest of the Israel-occupied Golan Heights – Damascus requested Havana for a group of DAA/FAR pilots that could reinforce its battered air force. Not willing to further weaken their air defences – already busy in Guinea-Conakry and Yemen – the Cubans reacted by deploying experienced tank crews instead. Correspondingly, 746 of their soldiers were flown to Syria in utmost secrecy, arriving on 28 October 1973. They not only formed a full tank regiment equipped with (Syrian-owned) T-54s and T-55s, but were integrated into the 47th Tank Brigade of the Syrian Arab Army, and became involved in several skirmishes with the Israelis. The Cuban military deployment in Syria ended only in February 1975, after the US-negotiated cease-fire between Damascus and Tel Aviv, and after Moscow imposed a de-facto arms embargo upon Syria over differences related to the politics towards the Palestinian Liberation Organisation.[46]

Overall, by 1975 the FAR was thus in a contradictive position. On one hand, it possessed extensive experience in the conduct of COIN operations, in working-up foreign air forces, and even some experience in expeditionary operations – yet, all of that paled in comparison to what was awaiting the Cubans in Angola. On the other hand, with its raison d'être remaining that of defence of Cuba, and due to restrictions left behind from the times of the Cuban Missile Crisis of 1962, the FAR lacked the necessary military transport aircraft and had no bomber aircraft. Moreover, Moscow was not the least keen to provide the Cubans with equipment that would have enabled them to deploy their expeditionary forces independently from support of the USSR: indeed, the Soviets often found themselves incensed by Havana launching military interventions abroad without any consultation or coordination, and sometimes contrary to Soviet interests.

Table 4: An Overview of Cuban Military Interventions

Country	Period	Notes
Algeria	1963-1964	686 troops
Congo-Brazzaville	1965-1967	250 troops
Congo-Kinshasa	1965-1966	
Guinea-Conakry	1967-1975	60 troops (on average)
North Vietnam	1970-1971	extent and period unclear
Sierra Leone	1972-1973	20 troops
Yemen	1972-1977	100 troops
Syria	1973-1974	746 troops
Somalia	1974	
Ethiopia	1977-1989	

Forces Armées Zaïroises

As of the mid-1970s, Zaire (former DR Congo) had the second-largest standing military in Sub-Saharan Africa, right after that of the South Africa. Although primarily designed, equipped and trained to conduct COIN operations, its armed forces were well-suited for conventional warfare, too. Indeed, Zaire was, until 1975, benefiting from high prices of copper and could afford spending up to US$90 million a year – approximately 14% of the national budget – for defence purposes.

The bulk of the Zairian Armed Forces (*Forces Armées Zaïroises*, FAZ) was composed of ground forces. Headquartered in Kinshasa, these were organized into seven numbered military regions, each of which controlled a varying number of combat and combat-support units, at least one signals company, a transport company, and a logistical base. Furthermore, the HQs of the 3rd, 4th, and 7th Military Regions had a reconnaissance squadron attached, equipped with light armoured vehicles. A separate command, the Sector Tanganyika, was tasked with combating the insurgency of the People's Revolutionary Party (*Parti de la Révolution Populaire*, PRP), a small leftist movement active in the Fizi region and led by small-time 'revolutionary'-cum-businessmen, Laurent Kabila. Although run from its own HQ in Kalemie, this command was under the nominal control of the 5th Military Region and frequently reinforced to up to nine battalions.

Since 1968, the FAZ maintained a sort of 'strategic reserve' in the form of the Reinforced Airborne Shock-Troops Division (*Division des Troupes Aéroportées Renforcées de Choc*, DITRAC). Originally created in the form of a brigade consisting of two regiments with three battalions each, the DITRAC was expanded to a division through the addition of a third regiment in 1972. Numbered from 1 to 3, its three major units were based in Kinshasa, Kamina, and Kisingani, respectively. They controlled a total of eight commando and para-commando battalions, including the 2nd and the 3rd Para-Commando Battalions, and the 4th and 7th Commando Battalions. Furthermore, a battalion-strong armoured unit equipped with French armoured vehicles was still under training in Mbanza-Ngungu.[47]

The high copper prices of the early 1970s enabled the acquisition of large amounts of heavy equipment in the period 1970-1975. Amongst these were 220 Panhard AML-60 and AML-90 armoured cars, and 60 Panhard M3 APCs from France, 525 mortars in calibres from 60 to 120mm, about 80 artillery pieces (including 40 anti-aircraft guns), and 250 recoilless rifles in calibres from 75 to 106mm. FAZ troops were primarily equipped with FN FAL assault rifles of Belgian origin, FALO light machine guns and MAG medium machine guns, but also Type-56 rifles of Chinese origin. From the USA came such individual weapons as M-16 assault rifles, M-79 grenade launchers, and LAW anti-tank rockets.

Due to never-ending differences with Belgium, President Mobutu Sese Seko meanwhile began seeking solutions for reducing his reliance on military cooperation with that country. Correspondingly, and despite Mobutu's fierce anti-Communist stance, in early 1970s, Kinshasa established diplomatic relations with the PRC. Mobutu paid an official visit to Beijing, in 1973, and before long the FAZ was to benefit from this relationship in the form of orders for 20 Type-63 107mm multiple rocket launchers (MRLs), 70 Type-62 light tanks and Type-59 main battle tanks (MBTs), and 12 Type-63 armoured personnel carriers (APCs) – all of which were delivered between 1974 and 1978. This equipment and Chinese advice was used to expand the original, small armoured unit into an armoured regiment, then a mechanised battalion, and then the 1st Armoured Brigade.[48]

Meanwhile, Zaire turned to North Korea for support in further expansion of the FAZ through the activation of its first regular division of ground forces. Designated the 1st 'Kamanyola' Division – after the location of its original element's first successful COIN operation on 1 June 1964 – this was established in 1974, and included officers and soldiers from all geographic areas and ethnic groups of the country, trained by about 130 North Korean advisors. As well as introducing the typical 'goose-steps' parade march, the North Koreans introduced the function of a political commissar into the command structure (in order to increase the reliability of such units to the country's leader), and provided a full complement of M-46 130mm field guns for the division's artillery battalion. However North Korean doctrine and training practices proved ill-suited to the Zairian context. The harshness of the discipline was unheard-of, while the Zairian officers were not in the least enthusiastic with the North-Korean egalitarian practices: for example, there was no way to convince them to share the same food as provided to their NCOs and other ranks. Unsurprisingly, the training schedules of the 1st Kamanyola Division were repeatedly delayed by several mutinies. These difficulties and the drastically different political stances of the two countries in regards of Angola's independence, resulted in the termination of the North Korean training mission: all the advisors were withdrawn by early 1976, leaving the division only partially established and trained.[49]

In 1972, the FAZ had relinquished its direct control over the six existent Gendarmerie battalions: instead, these were subjected to the control of the National Police. In its place, a new, National Gendarmerie was established under the supervision of the Ministry of Defence, totalling around 30,000, organised into nine regions, and a small Republican Guard (for ceremonial purposes only). The primary mission of all these forces was internal security and law enforcement. However, some of the Gendarmerie units possessed significant combat capabilities.

Overall, by 1975, the FAZ's ground forces were approximately 35,000 strong, including 1,000 officers and 1,500 non-commissioned officers (NCOs), organised into a total of 22 infantry battalions (including eight guard battalions), eight commando and para-commando battalions, and eight support battalions – and structured as listed in Table 5.[50]

Table 5: FAZ Ground Force Structure, early 1975

Military Region	HQ	Notes
1st Military Region	Kananga	
2nd Military Region	Kinshasa	
3rd Military Region	Kisingani	
4th Military Region	Lubumbashi	
5th Military Region	Bukavu	including Sector Tanganyika with HQ in Kalemie
6th Military Region	Mbandaka	
7th Military Region	Boma	
DITRAC	Kinshasa	including 1st, 2nd, and 3rd Regiments
1st Kamanyola Division		undergoing training
1st Armoured Brigade	Mbanza-Ngungu	including one armoured regiment, one mechanized battalion, but still undergoing training

The FAZ included a small naval component, officially established on 25 April 1975 as the Zairian Naval Force (*Force Navale Zaïroise*, ZNF). The ZNF included three naval regions which, in turn, controlled several detachments:

- 1st Naval Region, HQ in Kalemie, responsible for the Great Lakes region.
- 2nd Naval Region, HQ in Kinshasa, responsible for the Congo River Basin.
- 3rd Naval Region, HQ in Banana, responsible for the Congo River estuary and the short coast of the Atlantic Ocean.

Initially, the ZNF was operating a miscellany of small-sized vessels of very diverse origin. In 1972, six US-made Swift-class patrol boats, each armed with an 81mm mortar and two 12.7mm heavy machine guns, were acquired, and 200 sailors trained for their use in the USA. All six of these were deployed on Lake Tanganyika. Finally, by 1976, the ZNF was beefed up through the acquisition of at least six Shanghai II-class and Huchuan-class patrol crafts from the PRC.[51]

However, the appearance of the FAZ was misleading: for numerous reasons, it was no effective military force. Its origins can be traced back to the former Public Force, established by the Belgian colonial authorities. Reorganized as the Congolese National Army, this organisation originally included about 7,600 native NCOs and other ranks – most of which fiercely opposed the idea of being commanded by about 1,000 Belgian officers. Following their mutiny, there was no other option but to promote NCOs to officer ranks. Although hundreds of Zairians underwent military education abroad in the 1960s and 1970s, their presence was insufficient, and the military remained fragile – and all this while forced into action in response to a civil war, a secession attempt of the Katanga Province, multiple large-scale uprisings, and a mercenary revolt of 1967. Partially due to governmental policies – including favouring specific ethnic groups – fierce rivalries developed within the FAZ's officer corps, especially between the veterans of the former Public Force and the new generation trained at foreign military educational facilities. While Mobutu took care to retire most of the veterans, a new rift subsequently developed between officers trained abroad, and those trained at newly-established military educational facilities in Zaire. Furthermore, Mobutu always suspected the loyalty of many officers, and thus saw the FAZ as a threat against his power: a number of highly-promising officers – mostly US-trained – were falsely accused of coup-plotting and jailed in 1975. Meanwhile the military was subjected to a form of 'institutional chaos', caused by frequent reorganisations decreed by the President, while suffering from a general lack of qualified technicians. Further plagued by neglect, corruption, poor standards of living and training, and miserable discipline, and unsurprisingly considering this chaotic environment, the Zairian military remained heavily dependent on foreign advisors – and the presence of foreign mercenaries or official troop contingents – well into the 1970s and even after.[52]

By early 1973, 226 Belgian, 43 US, 9 Israeli, and several British and French advisors were assisting the army. With the arrival of the Chinese and then the North Koreans, the situation became even more complex, because of fundamentally different ideology, doctrine, organisational and tactical backgrounds. To say that this mix proved detrimental for the FAZ's cohesiveness, and thus added a new problem to an already fragile situation, would be an understatement.[53]

FAZA

Although various services effectively pretending to be something like the 'air force' of the DRC and then Zaire had existed at earlier times, the genuine Zairian Air Force (*Forces Aérienne Zairoise*, FAZA) actually came into being only through the training of native personnel in the late 1960s and early 1970s. In 1972, the FAZA established its HQ at Ndolo Airport, in Kinshasa, and was re-organized into three commands:

- Central Operational Command;
- Air Force School Command, and
- Technical and Logistics Command.

Equipped with a miscellany of about 60 assorted aircraft and helicopters left behind from earlier times, the FAZA was a diminutive force of about 760 personnel, including 55 pilots, 16 flight engineers, 10 radio operators, and 81 pilot-trainees. Only 5 out of 36 originally delivered North American T-28s remained, providing advanced training and a limited strike capability. They were in the process of being replaced by 12 SIAI-Marchetti SF.260MC prop-engined, basic and advanced trainers, and 17 Aermacchi MB.326s jet trainers and light strikers (only 15 of which remained intact as of 1975), locally nicknamed Sukisa'. The transport component included a collection of 15 Douglas C-47, Douglas C-54, Fairchild C-118s and Lockheed C-130As of US-origin, while the single helicopter squadron operated a mix of nine SNCA Sud-Est (later Aerospatiale) SE.3150/318C Alouette II and SE.3160/316B Alouette III, and Aerospatiale SA.330C Puma helicopters, organized as listed in Table 6. The Zairians turned to Italy for new equipment and most of the training in the 1960s, and thus most of FAZA's new pilots had been trained there. Nevertheless, French technicians contracted by a dedicated private company, the SODEMAZ – created by Lockheed (nowadays Lockheed-Martin) – provided most of the maintenance for transports and helicopters. However, the air force was plagued by exactly the same problems as FAZ's ground force: standards of conduct and behaviour were miserable, standards of maintenance minimal, officers were heavily corrupt, and regularly selling kerosene and spare parts on the black market, while the pool of native ground personnel (especially technical specialists) was nearly non-existent. For example, as of August 1975 only two C-130s, one DC-4 and two C-47s were operational. Part of the reason for this situation was the rapid expansion: the five SA.330Cs were the first from an order for 12, while the first three C-130As – delivered in 1971 – were followed by a second batch of three, delivered in

1975. Furthermore, because Zaire placed an order for 17 Dassault Mirage M5 supersonic fighter-bombers and interceptors in 1973, many of the native personnel were undergoing conversion training in France.[54]

Table 6: FAZA Flying Units, 1973-1975

Unit Designation	HQ or Base	Equipment
Central Operations Command	Ndolo	
• 11th Squadron	N'Djili	5 T-28, 15 MB.326GB
• 21st Transport Squadron	N'Djili	2 C-54, 2 C-118, 3 C-130A
• 22nd Transport Squadron	N'Djili	8 C-47
• 31st Helicopter Squadron	N'Djili	1 SE.316A, 3 SE.316B, 5 SA.330C
Air Force School Command	Kamina	
Flying School	Kamina	12 SF.260MC

South African Defence Force

With the white minority institutionalising racial segregation and discrimination of the native population in the late 1940s, the Republic of South Africa found itself exposed to massive international condemnation, severe arms embargoes and trade limitations, and increasingly militant resistance. For all practical purposes, the country was considered a pariah in nearly all of Africa in the mid-1970s, and its military forces – South African Defence Force (SADF) – was considered a sort of a regional Juggernaut. Certainly enough, already then, the SADF packed more military capability and experience than all other military forces of Sub-Sahara combined – and it was in the process of rejuvenating its arsenal.

In 1968 the SADF replaced the voluntary military service with universal conscription among the white male population, and in 1972 expanded the service time from 9 to 12 months. About 50,000 were on active duty in 1970. While thus significantly bolstering its manpower, this act imposed severe restrictions too: with most of the soldiers now being conscripts or reservists drawn from a relatively small demographic pool, the SADF was extremely sensitive to casualties, while finding it particularly hard to keep its operations secret from the public, too.

As of 1974, the ground component of the SADF was organized into the 1st South African Corps, consisting of the 7th Infantry and the 8th Armoured Division, each of which consisted of three brigades. Altogether, there were 10 active motorised infantry battalions, one parachute battalion and one parachute regiment, 42 Citizen Force battalions, and a small commando battalion of 200. The primary intervention and COIN force was the 1st Parachute Battalion, established in 1961. Another special forces-type of asset was the 1st Reconnaissance Commando, established eleven years later. While the rest of the units and their tactics were heavily influenced by the British doctrine and organisation dating back to the times of the World War II, the SADF could also draw on traditions of mobile warfare dating back to the times of the Boer War, which proved radically different. Indeed, during the 1960s, officers like Colonel Constand Viljoen concluded that the rather static and inflexible British-inspired doctrine was ill-adapted for warfare in Africa, and the future lay in the use of rather small, combined-arms forces, adapted to the vastness of the local theatres of operations. The work on new concepts was further encouraged by Israeli experiences from the June 1967 War, where highly-mobile operations and decentralised command had proved spectacularly successful against well-fortified, yet static defences. Starting in 1973, the 1st South African Battalion became the laboratory for experimenting with new concepts in mobile warfare – resulting in ideas for a doctrine that was still nascent in 1975, but proved its worth beyond any doubt.

The development of the new doctrine, strategy, and tactics went hand-in-hand with significant modernisation of the SADF's arsenal. By the early 1970s, most of the vintage weaponry from the times of World War II was replaced through the acquisition of 200 British-made Centurion MBTs, 230 Ferret scout cars, and 280 Saracen APCs. However, most of these were soon re-sold abroad, and instead the SADF decided to acquire modifications of the Panhard AML-60 and AML-90 armoured cars, manufactured under licence in South Africa under the designation Eland-60 and Eland-90, respectively. A total of 369 Eland-60s and 13[illegible] Eland-90 had been commissioned into service with reconnaissance squadrons attached to every infantry battalion already by 1970. Furthermore, anti-tank capabilities were strengthened through the purchase of French-made ENTAC anti-tank guided missiles (ATGMs), while infantry weapons like venerable Bren machine guns and Lee-Enfield rifles, were replaced by FN FAL assault rifles, manufactured under licence as R-1s. Only the artillery branch of the SADF remained dependent on old weapons, including 183 famous 25-Pounders (90mm howitzers), 52 5-Inch medium guns, and Sexton self-propelled howitzers.[55]

Officially established on 1 February 1920, the South African Air Force (SAAF) was virtually unrivalled in all of Sub-Saharan Africa. By the 1970s, it had acquired a total of 58 Dassault Mirage III fighter-bombers and interceptors of diverse sub-variants: the type proved highly popular in service, despite a few weak-spots and its relatively short range. Furthermore, South Africa launched licence production of the MB.326 jet trainers – under the designation Impala Mk.I – followed, in 1974, by a dedicated, single-seat attack variant, the Impala Mk.II. A year later, the SAAF placed an order for the first batch of 16 Dassault Mirage F.1CZ interceptors and 32 Mirage F.1AZ fighter-bombers, which were expected to enter service starting in 1976. Meanwhile, the air force maintained a strong bomber component, equipped with eight English Electric (later BAC) Canberra B.Mk 12 and T.Mk 4, and 16 Blackburn Buccaneer S.Mk 60 bombers. If there was any weakness within the SAAF, then it was its transport component: this was equipped with only seven C-130B Hercules and nine C.160Z Transalls, and thus still over-reliant on about 40 aged C-47 and C-54 transports. This was of crucial importance as the near-block-obsolescence of the SAAF's transport fleet was significantly limiting the size of troops it could operate or support far away from its home-bases. On the other hand, the SAAF operated a huge helicopter fleet, including a total of 128 SE.316B Alouette IIIs, 68 SA.330 Pumas, and 16 Aerospatiale SA.321 Super Frelons – and a significant miscellany of assorted light aircraft, some of which could be used for liaison and reconnaissance purposes.

The SAAF began operating over southern Angola in 1967, and collected plenty of experience from joint operations with the Portuguese – who proved keen to let the South Africans attack the SWAPO bases inside Angola. Furthermore, SAAF reconnaissance aircraft conducted extensive aerial mapping and survey operations. Correspondingly, South African liaison officers were attached to the Portuguese command posts at Serpa Pinto and Silva Porto as of 1968, while SAAF Alouette III helicopters became a regular sight over much of southern Angola. Although their crews were instructed to refrain from actively seeking to engage the Angolan

A pair each of ELAND-90s and ELAND-60s of the SADF. These heavily armed armoured scout cars were to prove highly effective during the fighting in Angola in 1975. (Albert Grandolini Collection)

insurgents, before long the South Africans began converting some of their Alouette IIIs into gunships through the installation of Mauser 20mm cannons inside the cabin. Certainly enough, the real extent of their involvement in contemporary COIN operations is unlikely to be ever precisely revealed: many SAAF crews found the way to hide the extent of their involvement through trading bottles of delicious South African wines for 20mm shells with their Portuguese hosts.

The South African Navy was significantly expanded during the late 1960s too – most noticeably through the induction of three destroyers acquired from the Royal Navy, christened the SAS *Jan van Riebeeck*, SAS *Simon van der Stel* and SAS *Vrystaat*, and three Type-12 frigates, the SAS *President Kruger*, SAS *President Steyn* and SAS *President Pretorius*. Moreover, the Navy had ordered three Daphne-class submarines in France: the first of these, the SAS *Maria van Riebeeck*, was delivered in 1970 and was soon followed by its two sister-ships SAS *Emily Hobhouse* and SAS *Johanna van der Merwe*. Finally, the Navy operated a variety of support ships, such as the tugs SAS *De Noorde* and SAS *De Neys*, or the replenishment vessel SAS *Tafelberg*.[56]

CHAPTER 3
THE CARNATION REVOLUTION

The coup d'etat in Portugal of 25 April 1974 – an affair worth its own volume, and also known as the Carnation Revolution – had swift and far-reaching consequences for all of Lisbon's overseas territories. All of a sudden, the end of protracted and seemingly endless wars in Guinea, Angola, and Mozambique became a very real prospect. Indeed, one of the main objectives of the new Portuguese government – presided over by General Antonio de Spinola and established in power on 15 May 1974 – was to end these conflicts, as soon as possible.

Actually, the new government was divided over this issue – at least initially: the moderates wanted to allow various degrees of autonomy to some of the territories, ranging from some form of a federation to a form of a commonwealth system. However, the left-wing Movement of the Armed Forces (*Movimento das Forcas Armadas*, MFA), which had organized the coup and was associated with the Communist Party of Portugal – was advocating the granting of pure and simple independence at the earliest point in time. This faction eventually gained the upper hand. On 30 September 1974, de Spinola resigned and General Costa Gomes took over as president: only a day later, Gomes had announced the goal of granting complete independence to Angola, 'as soon as possible'. At the time, negotiations with the PAIGC in Guinea, and insurgents in Mozambique, had already resulted in the independence of Guinea-Bissau, on 10 September 1974, while that for Mozambique was scheduled for 25 June 1975. The situation in Angola was far more complex, foremost because the country was the home of a sizeable population of Portuguese origin, but also because negotiations had to be undertaken with no fewer than three, fiercely opposed, nationalist movements, and because all the efforts to entice these into forming a united front either failed, or proved short-lived.[57]

General António Sebastião Ribeiro de Spinola proved himself as a highly competent military commander, before becoming involved in the Carnation Revolution of 1974. (Mark Lepko Collection)

Chaos or Cohesive Alliances?

The Carnation Revolution caught virtually every stakeholder in Angola by surprise and unprepared: not only the FNLA, MPLA, and UNITA, but all of their foreign backers too. Having an already long history of mutual conflict, the FNLA and the MPLA began to prepare for a decisive battle expected to determine which one of them would lead the country after independence. The much weaker UNITA could only hope to gamble during the forthcoming elections. Nonetheless, all three movements were hell-bent on attempting to obtain as many weapons, supplies, and as much expertise, as they could get from their respective foreign allies. In the meantime, the vacuum created by the Portuguese disengagement was progressively met by increased commitment of a host of foreign powers: indeed, the dynamics of the Cold War triggered an escalation which made a peaceful transition to independence practically impossible – if for no other reason than because the involvement of foreign powers had guaranteed that the conflict would be fuelled by large amounts of weaponry. Expecting 'others' would do the same, and fearing they might be outdone by each other, powers like the USA, the USSR, the PRC, Zaire, France, Cuba and South Africa all began increasing their involvement through significant expansion of their support for local proxies. To make matters worse, both the Soviets and the Americans initially lacked means to gather intelligence inside Angola and thus had acted on the basis of hopelessly insufficient information. Thus, two ill-fated alliances came into being: the FNLA and UNITA were supported by the 'conservative West', while the MPLA began receiving support from 'progressive' governments like those in Moscow, Havana and Belgrade.

It is almost absurd that not one of the involved powers had anything like a cohesive strategy, and that each acted for its own reasons; indeed, that many of their intentions were diametrically opposite to the interest of some of their closest allies, not to mention the population of Angola. For instance, the FNLA went all out after the aim of seizing power in Luanda, while the primary goal of the USA was a demonstration of its commitment to repulse any Soviet advance – an especially critical factor at the time of the on-going fall of South Vietnam. Things were even more complicated because the US Congress vetoed any large-scale involvement, in turn limiting the overall goal to that of making a possible victory of the MPLA – and thus of the Soviet Union (at least from the US point of view) – as costly as possible. On the other side of the hill, Cuba and the Soviet Union also proved to have very different intentions; Moscow's commitment was quite reluctant, while Cuba's stance was arguably one of 'going all in'.[58]

FNLA in Luanda

The Portuguese Army had suspended all of its offensive operations in Angola immediately after the coup of 25 April 1974. The PIDE and other police forces were instructed to cease hunting the nationalists and permit all three of their movements to come into the open, and thus the insurgents were capable – as far as they had the necessary capabilities – to establish their presence in many of areas from which they were expelled years ago.

Following a brief lull, the FNLA exploited the opportunity to dispatch a large number of its units from bases in Zaire into northern Angola, in order to secure its area of influence and eliminate any semblance of the MPLA's presence there. Correspondingly, in May 1974, ELNA attacked a column of the EPLA that attempted to reinforce the latter's 1st Military District. Furthermore, it repeatedly targeted the Ovimbundu population and sought to ethnically cleanse the same from its area of influence. On 15 October 1974, the FNLA agreed a cease-fire with the Portuguese, and became the first nationalist movement granted permission to deploy its delegation to Luanda. Once there, its activists launched a political campaign among the BaKongo, which represented between 5 and 10% of the population. However, except for its political activists, the FNLA also deployed a 70-strong detachment of the ELNA, which was subsequently reinforced by additional units deployed from their bases in Zaire – sometimes on-board Air Zaire's Douglas DC-10s. Reasonably well-equipped and organised, these troops provided the FNLA with a clear military edge over any of its rivals. Correspondingly, Holden Roberto came to the idea to seize control of Luanda in November 1974. However, the colonial authorities refused to issue permission for landing the necessary airliners at the local airport, forcing the FNLA to abort this idea. With this Roberto's sole hope of seizing power was out of the window knowing that his support base was limited demographically and geographically, he also knew that he had no serious chances in the case of any kind of elections.[59]

This was a particularly painful realisation – even more so considering that its appearance in Luanda made the FNLA a recipient of much more substantial support from abroad. First Romania, and then even the USA began delivering financial aid and military supply to this movement, starting in mid-1974. Indeed, in January 1975, the US government provided US$300,000 to the FNLA. The reasons for this development were relatively complex: the collapse of the MPLA's Eastern Front in 1973, and the success of COIN operations against the FNLA and UNITA, enabled the Portuguese to re-deploy some of their army to Mozambique, where these turned the tide against local insurgents. In turn, because the Mozambican guerrillas operated from bases inside Tanzania President Nyerere requested the PRC to reinforce its support for the FNLA and UNITA, so these could increase their pressure upon the Portuguese in Angola. However, Nyerere's request reached Beijing

FNLA/ELNA troops on the streets of Luanda in late 1974. (Albert Grandolini Collection)

just around the time this was establishing diplomatic connections to Zaire, which was followed by significant Zairian orders for the Chinese arms. Beijing reacted with a positive reply – to all the requests: at the same time, it began shipping armour to Zaire, in September 1974, it also shipped 450 tonnes of arms – reportedly including enough assault rifles, RPGs, mortars and machine guns to arm 10,000 combatants – to the FNLA's bases in the same country. Furthermore, the Chinese deployed 120 military advisers to Zaire, with the task of training ELNA's insurgents. Certainly enough, this 'bonanza' did not last for long: in October 1975, as soon as it became known that the FNLA and UNITA were secretly cooperating with South Africans – which was an 'absolute no-no' for Beijing – all the cooperation with these two Angolan nationalist movements was suspended. However, meanwhile, Chinese arms shipments began reaching their destinations in Zaire, and did so right at the time the MPLA was isolated even from the USSR. Correspondingly, Chinese arms tipped the balance heavily in favour of the FNLA/ELNA.

At the same time, and for reasons similar to those which enticed it to support the FNLA, Beijing provided 70 tonnes of arms to UNITA, while Tanzania provided 100 semi-automatic rifles, stocks of landmines, funding, and a nine-month officer course for 120 combatants of the FALA – although the latter proved totally insufficient to reverse that movement's military inferiority to the FNLA and the MPLA. On the other hand, UNITA – which was the movement the most committed to a peaceful transition to independence – skilfully exploited the Portuguese offer for a cease-fire from 14 June 1974, to expand its political networks among the Ovimbundu, and thus create a stabile basis for further expansion. Finally, Savimbi deployed a small delegation to Luanda, on 10 November 1974. By then, his organisation began benefitting from a drastic change of stance in Zambia, too: because it concluded that UNITA had much better prospects during the planned elections than its rivals, the government in Lusaka ceased supporting other Angolan nationalists, and instead concentrated its full attention on aiding Savimbi's movement. While this resulted in no arms deliveries, it immensely eased UNITA's logistics. Unsurprisingly, by August 1975 the FALA grew to about 4,000 trained and armed fighters, with another 6,000 undergoing training and lacking arms. It's communication system was still rudimentary by nature, and it lacked medium and heavy weapons, but it was rapidly turning into a serious military factor.[60]

Phoenix – Re-Born

As of April 1974, the MPLA was still on the verge of total collapse. Scrambling to save whatever was left of the movement through re-uniting loyalists with delegates from both the Eastern and Active Revolts, Agostinho Neto and Nito Alves organised a congress in Lusaka on 12 August 1974. This effort failed, though: Daniel Chipenda was meanwhile negotiating with Mobutu, and finally moved to Kinshasa, where he entered an alliance with the FNLA. Agostinho Neto thus organized another congress of about 250 of his supporters. Held in Angola from 12 to 21 September 1974, this resulted in the election of a 35-member Central Committee and a Politburo. Foremost, it saw a re-election of Neto as President, thus restoring his legitimacy. However, all of this had preoccupied, and de-facto paralysed the MPLA during a crucial period.

Rather unexpectedly, it was the Portuguese – now governed by a leftist government – that proved crucial for securing the MPLA's position as one of the primary contenders for leadership in an independent Angola. They rushed to conclude a cease-fire with Neto's movement, and helped it deploy its activists and the Maiombe Squadron, led by Nito Alves, to Luanda in October 1974. Meanwhile, the Communist Party of Portugal was doing everything possible in order to convince Moscow to resume its support for the MPLA – and did so at the time when the Soviets were short of shifting their support towards the Chipenda faction (before the latter committed the 'cardinal sin' of entering an alliance with the FNLA). Furthermore, the Portuguese government refused to recognize Chipenda as the leader of the MPLA, while Vice-Admiral António Alva Rosa Coutinho, Governor of Angola from July 1974 until January 1975, not only favoured the MPLA in the public, but even deployed his troops to help the movement establish itself in control of the Cabinda Enclave.

Daniel Chipenda taking a salute. Chipenda used to be the closest of the MPLA's leaders to the Cubans, before his defection of 1974. Survivors of his movement were eventually integrated into the famed 32nd Battalion SADF. (Photo by Al J Venter)

The Alvor Accord

Despite the deep rivalries which opposed them, the three movements were also under tremendous pressure from various countries – foremost African ones – to negotiate. Talks between representatives of the three movements took place on several occasions and in the end, they agreed to cooperate together to negotiate independence with the Portuguese during a meeting in Mombasa in early January 1975. Then, the common talks with the Portuguese were held in the town of Alvor between 10 and 15 January 1975, and an agreement was finally signed – known as the Alvor Accord – by all the parties. Accordingly, an interim government was to lead the country until the election of a constituent assembly which was to take place in late October 1975, and would precede independence, starting with 11 November 1975. This government was to be led by a Portuguese high commissioner, supported by a presidential council including one representative of each movement, which in turn was to control a 16-member cabinet, with four ministers per movement and four Portuguese. The Accord included clauses related to the armed forces, which were to include 48,000 men, of which half were to be Portuguese troops, while the other half was to include 8,000 men provided by each of the three movements armed wings. A police force was to be organised in similar fashion. The Portuguese troops in excess of the 24,000 men mentioned in the Accord had to leave Angola before 30 April 1975, while the last Portuguese troops were planned to follow during the three months after independence. As envisioned in the Alvor Accord, the interim government became active on 31 January 1975.[61]

Rise of the FAPLA

This apparent diplomatic success proved largely illusory. While the FNLA was determined to make the most of its military superiority, the MPLA leadership was preoccupied with efforts to restore and expand its armed branch. On 1 August 1974, Nito Alves gathered 83 of his top officers and reorganised the military wing in order to create the basis for large-scale expansion into a conventional army, named the People's Armed Forces of Liberation of Angola (*Forças Armadas Populares de Libertação de Angola*, FAPLA), commanded by Henrique 'Iko' Carreira. With only 1,500 combatants left at its disposal, this was no easy task. Moreover, in order to train its fast expending number of recruits, the movement also opened new bases on Angolan territory – mostly in the 1st and 4th Military Regions. With the help of these facilities, the FAPLA planned to expand its strength to about 20,000 by early November 1975.

However, MPLA's armed branch never had the opportunity to assemble and operate semi-regular or regular units capable of conventional operations, and thus lacked the corresponding know-how, cadre, and necessary specialists. Thus, while changing little of its organisation, as early as of 1 August 1974, the FAPLA began recruiting Angolans that used to serve in the colonial armed forces. This effort was particularly successful in regards of attracting desperately-needed commandos, lower-ranking officers and quartermasters. The former commandos were used to form six special units named the Valódia, Kwenha, Vietnam, Cambodia, Ho Chi Minch City, and Corvos ao Imbondeiro squadrons. Furthermore, Nito Alves personally led efforts to recruit local militias in Luanda. The units of the so-called People's Power (*Poder Popular*) were of little military value and their worth was highly questionable, but they made the presence of the movement in the Angolan capital 'felt'. The result of this effort was that the FAPLA grew in large numbers and was expected to surpass 6,000 armed and trained combatants by July 1975.[62]

Henrique 'Iko' Carreira, the first commander of the FAPLA and Angola's first defence minister, was another of the Cuban protégés in Luanda. (Al J Venter Collection)

Clearly, this was still far from being sufficient. In comparison, Chipenda's faction of the FNLA alone, meanwhile, grew to between 2,000 and 3,000 fighters, while the ELNA was said to have had up to 21,000 fighters, and the FALA another 4,000.[63]

Correspondingly, a delegation led by Carreira, and his Deputy Logistics, Pedro van Dunem, travelled to Algeria, Yugoslavia and the USSR, in December 1974 and January 1975, with the aim of securing deliveries of arms and aid in regards of training. The mission was successful as the FAPLA officers got promises of weapons and supplies deliveries from Algiers, Belgrade and Moscow, although the expected quantities were estimated as insufficient to completely equip the planned 20,000-strong army. Foremost, all three donors explained that the related shipments could not be dispatched as quickly as requested – regardless of the Portuguese granting permission for ships carrying arms for the FAPLA to dock in Luanda, starting in July 1975. A solution was therefore found by shipping most of the weapons to Pointe Noire, in the Congo-Brazzaville, where the same were re-loaded into smaller boats and then 'smuggled' into Angola. Even then, the related operations experienced significant delays. Not only that the first Soviet shipments began arriving at Pointe Noire only in August 1975, and remained rather small-sized, but the new president of the Congo-Brazzaville, Marien Ngouabi, had his own agendas in mind – foremost related to a seizure of the Cabinda Enclave. The withdrawal of his approval for the Soviet deliveries to Pointe Noire was reversed only after Moscow applied tremendous diplomatic pressure.

Perhaps more importantly, during its visit to Moscow, the FAPLA managed to secure the Soviet support for a project its leadership considered paramount: the establishment of a motorised brigade trained in conventional warfare, and useful for offensive operations. Rather unexpectedly, the Soviets offered to train virtually all the 2,000 officers and other ranks for such a unit. With the FAPLA lacking the necessary troops, an agreement was reached the Soviets to train 200 Angolans that would form its core. The first group of these – about 30 men – underwent training at the Vystrel Officer School, in Solnechnogorsk, near Moscow while the others were trained at Perevalnoye, in the Crimean Peninsula, between February and August 1975.

While the Soviet arms were thus to remain unavailable for a while longer, the resulting situation was not considered as 'critical' or even 'urgent' by the leadership of the MPLA. The reasons were two-fold. Firstly, Algeria and Yugoslavia dispatched several shipments of arms during early 1975. The first major shipment from Algeria – including half a dozen BRDM-2 armoured cars and a few mortars – was unloaded by an Algerian merchant in Caxito, in Angola, in early 1975. Meanwhile, Belgrade wire-transferred US$100,000 to the MPLA, enabling it to pay for transhipment of its arsenal stockpiled in Tanzania, in April of the same year. Moreover, Yugoslavia then dispatched another shipment, including additional armoured cars and recoilless guns aboard the merchant *Postojna*. This reached Angola in April 1975, but was re-routed by the Portuguese to Pointe Noire. Secondly, the MPLA considered the eruption of an all-out 'civil war' rather unlikely – at least as long as the Portuguese troops were still in Angola. Correspondingly, it concluded that it had enough time to complete its build-up, 'by the end of 1975 or early 1976'.[64]

Precisely this sense of complacency is the explanation for the MPLA's leadership not pressing harder to find an alternative source of support – in Cuba, for example. Certainly enough, several delegations visited Havana in 1974, but received no positive replies. It was only in early October 1974, when the MPLA approached the Cuban ambassador to Tanzania with a request for instructors, that some movement came into this affair. This time, Havana reacted by deploying two military officers to Dar-es-Salaam with the task of assessing the situation and finding out what exactly was going on in Angola. After several meetings with top commanders of the MPLA and the FAPLA in late 1974, the two returned to Cuba in March 1975, reporting such of Neto's requests as payment of US$100,000 for transhipping of arms stocks from Tanzania to Luanda, the establishment of an officer school, stocks of arms and uniforms for 10,000 troops, and provision of two pilot instructors and one for mechanics. However, and although the MPLA addressed Havana with similar requests in May and June 1975 again, the Cubans did not move: this changed only in July 1975, during the Battle for Luanda.

Alliance with Tigers

With the Soviets refusing to deploy any instructors to Angola before independence, the MPLA/FAPLA met a delegation of the FNLC and the Portuguese authorities on 17 December 1974. This resulted in an important agreement: in exchange for the MPLA's promise to support the FNLC in its struggle against Mobutu, the Katangese Tigers promised to support Neto's movement should this come under attack from the FNLA or UNITA. In this fashion, the MPLA and the FAPLA – which had no serious war-fighting capability as of late 1974 – were reinforced by four small cohesive battalions including at least 2,000 well-trained, disciplined, and battle-hardened troops. In the context of Angola of 1975, such assets were worth their weight in gold.[65]

CHAPTER 4
ALL-OUT WAR

The first armed clashes between the MPLA/FAPLA and the FNLA/ELNA had occurred in Luanda in November 1974, and usually on the initiative of the latter. They quickly died down, although the atmosphere remained tense, as both groups were seeking to expand their influence in the slums of the city. Another series of – increasingly violent – clashes followed between March and July 1975. It was interrupted by multiple cease-fires mediated by diverse third parties, including the Portuguese and even the President of Kenya. Meanwhile preoccupied with their withdrawal, the Portuguese proved ever less keen to meddle. Indeed, in April 1975, they demobilised most of their militias staffed by the natives, and simply abandoned their stocks of arms: a stock of around 40,000 pistols, rifles, assault rifles, machine guns and associated ammunition was plundered by the activists of the FNLA, MPLA and UNITA. The resulting insecurity triggered a massive exodus of the Portuguese colonists which in turn caused a collapse of the economy. In perfect clarity over the fact that all the agreements of the Alvor Accord were meanwhile null and void, the stage was now set for an all-out showdown between the three Angolan nationalist movements.

Battle for Luanda

On 26 January 1975, the FNLA attacked the Radio Luanda station and destroyed it completely, kidnapping and torturing its assistant director – a member of the MPLA – in the process. On 13 February 1975, the MPLA attacked the HQ of Chipenda's faction, forcing the survivors to flee the capital. Eventually, Daniel Chipenda, who had been undermined by the Portuguese decision to exclude him from the Alvor accords, was left without a choice but to announce a merger with the FNLA on 22 February. As a result, the ELNA was not only reinforced by at least 2,000 combatants, but found itself in control of nearly all of eastern and southern Angola. By March 1975, the FNLA further tightened its grip over Northern Angola, where the MPLA/FAPLA presence was reduced to a few isolated and vulnerable spots. The situation inside Luanda was meanwhile boiling: most of the population was either of mixed origin, or Mbundu, and favoured the MPLA. Thus, the Poder Popular militias experienced a rapid growth, and the balance of power gradually

As of late 1974, the MPLA had little in the form of military forces to confront the FNLA/ELNA. Its activists were soon to change this through intensive 'political education' of the Angolan population. (Albert Grandolini)

Combatants of the MPLA on the streets of Luanda in early 1975. (Albert Grandolini Collection)

shifted in favour of Neto's movement. Indeed, before long, it was the MPLA/FAPLA that began taking the initiative, intending to expel its rivals from the capital by force, as soon as possible.[66]

On 23 March 1975, Holden Robert's combatants attacked several MPLA positions in Luanda, including its HQ in Villa Alice. This signalled the start of a days-long battle in the course of which the ELNA attempted to expel the MPLA from the city slums. A week later, ELNA troops in Luanda were reinforced by the arrival of a motorised battalion dispatched from Zaire, thus doubling its presence in the capital to at least 1,000. Correspondingly, it re-initiated its onslaught – although with limited success. Meanwhile supported by a rapidly-increasing number of Poder Popular militias, the MPLA/FAPLA held most of its positions. The ELNA thus decided to launch its next major operation outside of the city. On 26 March 1975, it attacked the FAPLA's training camp in Caxito and killed around 50 recruits.

Despite the last Portuguese-negotiated cease-fire, which came into force on 1 April, tensions remained high. Indeed, on 28th of the same month, and aiming to spoil its rival's celebrations planned for the 1 May, the ELNA launched a coordinated attack against multiple MPLA offices in Luanda's slums, and the HQ of the MPLA-controlled Trade Union. This triggered days-long fighting in which at least 500 were killed and 700 wounded before a new cease-fire was negotiated, effective from 12 May 1975. By then, not only had the fighting spread to much of northern and southern Angola, but first reports surfaced about the entry of 1,200 FAZ troops into the country, with the aim of reinforcing the ENLA.[67]

After regrouping its available forces, following the arrival of the first shipments of arms from Yugoslavia, and under increasing pressure from its political activists and military commanders alike, the FAPLA launched a counter-offensive in Luanda in late May. At first, it deployed its forces around the city, thus cutting off the ELNA groups inside the capital. Furthermore, on 4 June, the FPLA attacked the sole UNITA camp in Luanda, killing or summarily executing at least 50 FALA recruits.[68] This phase of the battle for Luanda ended with another cease-fire, on 7 June 1975, negotiated by Kenya. This stipulated a de-facto withdrawal of all three movements out of the Angolan capital, and a reduction of their contingents to 500 combatants each. As meanwhile usual, neither the FNLA/ELNA, nor MPLA/FAPLA, or the UNITA/FALA respected this agreement. Although badly shaken, the ELNA's contingent was still

As the fighting between the MPLA and the FNLA in Luanda intensified, scenes like this one – showing the aftermath of one of the fire-fights including burning buses, cars and offices – became ever more frequent. (Albert Grandolini Collection)

anything but defeated. Similarly, UNITA remained keen to retain presence in the city, regardless the circumstances. However, the MPLA was soon reinforced by a group of Katangese Tigers led by Captain Grégoire Mulombo and thus keen to unleash the 'killing blow' against the FNLA.[69]

Supported by Poder Popular militias and a pair of BTR-152 APCs delivered by Algeria or Yugoslavia, on 9 July 1975 its troops assaulted and largely destroyed ELNA positions on the outskirts of the city, before moving towards its main base in downtown

Luanda. Following several days of bitter fighting, the surviving ELNA combatants found themselves besieged in the Fort Sao Pedro da Barra. They were granted permission to evacuate thanks to Portuguese negotiations, on 14 July. Meanwhile, Jonas Savimbi came to the conclusion that the presence of his movement was unsustainable after all. Correspondingly, he negotiated an evacuation of all the surviving militants of UNITA and FALA: the convoy of about 180 trucks carrying several thousands drove away in the direction of Dondo, on the Kwanza River, where it ran into a massive ambush set up by the MPLA/FAPLA, on 12 July. The exact number of casualties remains unknown to this day, but it is certain that Neto's combatants massacred not only most of UNITA/FALA's fighters and activists, but nearly all of the civilians accompanying them, too.[70]

After nearly six months of on-off fighting, and an estimated 40,000 people killed alone between early March and mid-July 1975, the MPLA thus found itself in full control of the Angolan capital.

Red Eyes

Between late July and mid-October 1975, the civil war in Angola expanded to all major parts of the country. Initially at least, the situation appeared 'extremely fluid': 'offensives' of one party were followed by 'counter-offensives' of the other, and numerous localities changed hands multiple times. With the FNLA/ELNA, MPLA/FAPLA, and UNITA/FALA all forced to garrison the localities under their control, their forces became widely dispersed. As the flow of different battles was to show, while all three movements and their military wings shared a number of characteristics, especially the ELNA and then the FAZ were to prove not only the least-disciplined, but also the less-suited to conventional or even semi-conventional operations. This was to become the reason for their eventual failure.

Peculiarities of the Angolan style of war-fighting started influencing the outcome of the fighting, too. At earlier times, the insurgents knew it was better to escape and fight another day, preferably under more favourable circumstances. Nobody expected the Portuguese to remain in Angola forever. However, the three movements involved in this war were all of Angolan origin, and there was no place for all of them to go: they had to stay and fight. Because the bulk of combatants involved in the following battles had next to no combat experience from earlier times, indeed because most of them were only recently recruited, poorly trained, led by inexperienced officers, and thus formed into non-cohesive units, a few crack, seasoned units – like the Katangese Tigers or ELNA's Special Commandos – were in possession of a theoretical capability to exercise an impact entirely out of proportion to their size. Furthermore, units including troops with European backgrounds could benefit from the fact that many Angolans believed that 'white soldiers' could not be killed by bullets. Finally, many native combatants turned out to be entirely unwilling to dig trenches: they considered such an act akin to burying themselves, as 'tombs are only for the dead'. Therefore, fortifications of any sort were rare, and the attackers nearly always had the advantage – especially if supported by heavy weapons. The more 'spectacular' the later were, the more decisive were they to prove for the outcome. Unsurprisingly, weapons like Grad-1P single-tube 122mm rocket launchers, latter dubbed 'Red Eyes' by the South Africans, were soon to prove vital, even if lacking in precision and effectiveness.

Revival of the FNLA

Following its devastating defeat in Luanda, the FNLA set up a new HQ in Ambriz, which had the advantage of being relatively close to the capitol, but also having an airstrip nearby. While this eased the issue of supplies, it did not help recover the image of the ELNA: its reputation as the most effective fighting force in Angola was shattered forever, and scores of its combatants defected in the following weeks. In an attempt to recover the morale of his 'army', Roberto Holden arrived in Ambriz, on 27 July, and took over the command. Meanwhile, his foreign backers arrived at the decision to increase their involvement. Concluding that it could not let the MPLA win, and despite repeated overtures from the new rulers of Luanda (including an order for Boeing 737 airliners for the newly-established national airline), on 18 July 1975, President of the USA, Gerald Ford, approved the transfer of US$6 million to support the FNLA and UNITA. This amount was increased by another US$8 million on 27 July and, finally, US$10.2 million on 20 August 1975. Critical for the related decision was the catastrophe of the final chapter of the US involvement in Vietnam, and the resolve to demonstrate – foremost to NATO partners – Washington's commitment to its allies. However, after 15 years of adventures in Vietnam, the US Congress was not the least anxious to let the USA become involved in new conflicts abroad. The result was a paradox: the USA were to 'intervene' in Angola, but in a very limited, and deniable fashion. Merely the CIA was permitted to support the MPLA's rivals within its operation IAFEATURE.

The first related shipment of arms – around 25 tonnes – left the airport of Charleston aboard a Lockheed C-141 Starlifter transport of the 437th Airlift Wing of the US Air Force (USAF) on 29 July 1975, and arrived via Robertsfield, Monrovia to Kinshasa. It was followed by two flights with similar content in early August. All of the ultimate 25 flights (which delivered a total of 2,800 tonnes) of this nature unloaded their cargoes at N'Djili IAP. From there, the shipments were re-distributed to their destinations on board an entire 'fleet' of lighter aircraft operated by the CIA, including a Piper Aztec, a Cessna 172, a Cessna 180, a Cessna 310 (originally belonging to President Idi Amin of Uganda and stolen at Carmona), a Turbo Commander, two Mooneys, two Fokker F.27 Friendships, and one SE.316B Alouette III helicopter. Moreover, another F.27 and a Vickers Viscount were leased from Air Zaire. All the aircraft were operated by mercenaries.[71]

Most of the arms they carried were vintage – like M1 carbines – because these were available in huge quantities and their relations to the source were easily deniable. It was only later on that the CIA organized an exchange deal along which the Zairians began delivering Belgian-made FN FAL rifles to the FNLA, which were then replaced by US-made M16s. Shipments from Kinshasa were usually transported to Angola on board smaller craft, down the Congo River. The same happened with most of the cargo delivered to the Zairian port of Matadi on board the ship USS *American Champion*, on 12 September 1975. Altogether, during the Operation IAFEATURE, the CIA had delivered to the FNLA and UNITA a total of 52 107mm and 120mm mortars, 100 81mm and 82mm mortars, 319 60mm mortars, 14 106mm recoilless rifles, 22 12.7mm heavy machine guns and 374 7.62mm light machine guns, 115 Bazookas and RPG-7s, 4,210 M72 LAWs, 410 M79 grenade launchers, 19,986 assault rifles and carbines, 66 sub-machine guns, and 283 radio sets, together with a large stock of related ammunition.[72]

The first large consignment of arms from FAZ's stocks – reportedly sufficient to arm two small battalions, and including nine AML-60 and AML-90 armoured cars, together with their Zairian

FNLA/ELNA combatants as seen while undergoing training by US advisors – most already armed by CIA-provided M16 assault rifles. (Albert Grandolini Collection)

crews – reached Ambriz in late July 1975. Further, during July the FNLA was strengthened through entering an alliance with the Angolan Resistance Front (*Frente de Resistência Angolana*, FRA) – a small group of Angolans of Portuguese origin, whose agenda was to create an independent, white-controlled Angola similar to Rhodesia or South Africa. The principal result was that around 40 veterans of the Portuguese military – including several officers and former commando operators – led by Colonel Gilbertos Santos e Castro reinforced the ELNA. They formed the cadre for a new, commando unit consisting of native recruits, the training of which began in late July 1975. The resulting outfit, the so-called Special Commando Company (the soldiers of which wore Red Berets), eventually grew to between 150 and 250 by the time it was ready for combat, in early November 1975. It packed relatively lots of firepower, provided by two AML-60s, one AML-90, two wheeled M3 APCs, and a jeep-mounted 106mm recoilless rifle.

March on Luanda

The rapid influx of new and heavy weaponry, and the presence of the Portuguese and Zairian specialists allowed the FNLA to turn the table on its enemy quite soon following withdrawal from Luanda. On 20 July 1975, the movement announced its intention to march on the capitol and occupy the same before independence day. Unsurprisingly, considering the importance of the control of Luanda on such an important date, the road connecting Ambriz with Luanda rapidly grew in importance: this area was to see some of most intensive fighting during the following weeks.

Initiated on 20 July, the ELNA's offensive jumped off smoothly, with MPLA/FAPLA offering only token resistance – and losing two recently delivered BRDM-2 armoured scout cars in the process. Indeed, three days later, ELNA seized Caxito, a mere 50 kilometres (31 miles) from Luanda – before their further progress was stopped by the FAPLA.[73] After bringing in reinforcements and additional supplies, this offensive was resumed in late August 1975, but this time with entirely different results: it was stopped cold. Worse was to follow when, meanwhile, the HQ of the FAPLA set its own counter-offensive – Operation Black Cyclone (*Operaçáo Ciclone Negro*) – on footing. For this purpose, Henrique 'Iko' Carreira deployed the first operational element of what became known as the 9th Motorized Infantry Brigade (9th BRIM).

A column of ELNA – including mercenary-operated AML-60s – on advance in the direction of Luanda in July 1975. (Albert Grandolini Collection)

Holden Roberto next to a road-sign, 'only 32 kilometres' outside Luanda. (Albert Grandolini Collection)

Around the same time, the MPLA received the first Soviet arms shipments agreed earlier that year. This was unloaded at Pointe Noire, and then forwarded aboard smaller Angolan vessels to Cabo San Braz, around 130 kilometres (80 miles) north of Luanda. Although only a small part of what Moscow actually promised, and except for fire-arms, the shipment in question included 10 BRDM-

One of the first BRDM-2s for the 9th BRIM, as seen while being unloaded at Cabo San Braz in July 1975. (Albert Grandolini Collection)

A mortar team of FAPLA in position about 50 kilometres north of Luanda. (Albert Grandolini Collection)

2s, 12 76mm cannons, 39 82mm mortars, 32 Grad-1P rocket launchers, several ZU-23 23mm anti-aircraft cannons, and 44 ZPU 14.5mm heavy machine guns. As such, it bolstered the firepower of the entire FAPLA by an order of magnitude.[74]

Operation Black Cyclone was unleashed on 7 September 1975. Deploying its Grad-1Ps for the first time ever, and proceeded by six of its BRDM-2s, the 9th BRIM attacked the ELNA in Caxito frontally, and secured the town by the next morning – before pushing the enemy further in the direction of Ambriz. While withdrawing, the defeated combatants provided the MPLA with one of the major propaganda victories of this war – by leaving behind numerous ammunition crates labelled 'USAF', and thus providing evidence for US involvement.[75] Only once one of the more sober ELNA commanders managed to blow up the bridge on the Onzo River was the FAPLA's advance stopped. However, while the 9th BRIM thus benefited immensely from its new fire-power, other MPLA/FAPLA troops involved in this operation proved anything other than reliable or combat effective. Hundreds left the battlefield on their own, before returning at the time of their own choice. Correspondingly, most of the commanders involved had no clear idea how many troops they had under their command at any point in time.

When hearing about the defeat of the ELNA, Mobutu reacted by deploying the best troops the FAZ could offer. On 11 September 1975, the 4th and 7th Commando Battalions were airlifted by FAZA's C-130s to Ambriz. Reinforced by arms delivered a few days later by USS *American Champion* to Matadi, they formed a mixed column, including Zairian Commandos and ELNA's Special Commandos, supported by AMLs and 120mm mortars. This force re-crossed the Onzo River on a bridge laid down by Zairian combat engineers, and recaptured Caxito on 17 September, and then launched a new advance on Luanda. The FAPLA fell back this time, and it was only nine days later – on 26 September – that the 9th BRIM managed to stop this onslaught at Morro da Cal, primarily because the Zairians and ELNA's commandos ran out of fuel. This frontline remained static until late October 1975.[76]

Central and Southern Fronts

The last Portuguese troops evacuated northern Angola on 4 August 1975. With the FNLA eliminating the last few MPLA groups there, this part of the country came entirely under the control of Holden Roberto's movement. Neto and his aides thus switched their attention to southern and eastern Angola, with the aim of establishing themselves in control of the Benguela Railway, but also

US-equipped and South African-trained group of FALA troops in southern Angola in late1975. (Albert Grandolini Collection)

all the ports between Luanda and the border to South-West Africa. Correspondingly, in July 1975, the FAPLA kicked the FNLA out of Novo Redondo (subsequently renamed Sumbe) in a three-day battle, forcing the survivors to withdraw towards Lobito. After bringing in its Kwenya Squadron and some supplies, the FAPLA seized Lobito and Benguela, and then continued its advance on Mocamedes (subsequently renamed Namibe). The latter was of particular importance because the local population proved very supportive for the MPLA.

Encouraged, the MPLA then activated the Central Front – which included the provinces of Huambo, Bié, Benguela and South Kwanza – and the Southern Front, including the provinces of Cunene, Huila, and Namibe. Principal aims of its subsequent campaign were to protect Porto Amboim, Sumbe, Lobito and Benguela along the coast, secure Gabela further inland, and then seize Dondo, and – finally – Novoa Lisboa (renamed Huambo), which housed the HQ of UNITA. However, while the MPLA enjoyed plentiful support of the population along the coast, and enjoyed the upper hand in the fighting, the further inland it moved, the more resistance it encountered. On 30 July, the FAPLA attacked the ELNA-held Luso (subsequently renamed Lueno), and then killed at least 30 FALA fighters based nearby. This proved to be the last straw for UNITA, which declared war on Luanda on 4 August 1975. Correspondingly, the conflict now not only included the struggle between the MPLA and the FNLA, but also one between the MPLA and UNITA. Already the same day, FALA units under the direct command of its top commander, General Chiwale, began to clear an airstrip outside Kuito, and then seized this town. Their attack on Luena, however, was not as successful because the place was under the control of the Katangese Tigers, who fought on the side of the MPLA.[77]

Meanwhile, the FAPLA concentrated six squadrons – including the Valódia, and the crack Cambodia and Vietnam Squadrons – in the Gabela area, where its training camp 'Blood of the People' was located. From there, these advanced in the southern direction with the intention of clearing the area all the way to the border with South Western Africa. However, this offensive only generated several weeks of confused fighting; the FAPLA first seized Kibela and Cela, but then had to abandon both in the face of strong attacks by combined ELNA and FALA forces. The FAPLA reorganized and, in mid-August, launched a two-pronged attack against Kibela: this managed to expel the ELNA's garrison, and eventually seized Cela again, but soon afterwards both places were lost to a counterattack by the FALA. Further attacks were less effective: the FALA's assault of Lobito, in late August, was easily repulsed, and in September 1975 UNITA not only lost Cela again, but then failed to retake it. Subsequently, the FAPLA dispatched a column including several squadrons and supported by three BRDM-2s along the road connecting Benguela with Babera and Huambo, and this seized Mariano Machado and Babera by the end of the September 1975. However, further advances proved impossible due to fierce resistance of the FALA. Similarly, an advance of four squadrons supported by four BRDM-2s along the road connecting Lobito with Balombo, Alto Hama and Huambo resulted in the seizure of Sousa Lara on 29 September, but – and although facing only about 150 FALA – it ended following the capture of Balombo

The next major operation by the FALA was for the first time supported by South African advisors, who helped work-up three AML-90s and AML-60s that arrived in October from Zaire, together with additional mortars. The force involved included one battalion of insurgents, supported by two AML-90s, one AML-60, three jeep-mounted ENTAC ATGM-teams, two 'technicals' with 12.7mm and 14.5mm machine guns, and one 106mm recoilless gun – altogether 14 troops of the SADF.[78] On 5 October 1975, this unit ran into an ambush set up by the FAPLA near a bridge about seven kilometres (four miles) short of Balombo. Finding itself on the receiving end of a barrage by mortars and a few Grad-1P launchers, the insurgents fled the site, covered by the South African AMLs and ENTAC-jeeps that virtually exhausted their ammunition in the process. Although successful, the FAPLA suffered significant losses in this clash, including two BRDM-2s, and once again had to abandon any thoughts about an advance on Huambo.[79]

South African Paradox

The South African involvement in Angola resulted from a rather uneasy compromise within the government in Pretoria. Due to its politics of Apartheid, South Africa was meanwhile more isolated than ever before. In turn, its government grew wary about the threat of 'black' nationalist movements determined to bring about its downfall, all of which were – invariably – defined as 'communists'. South African control of the former German colony of South West Africa (SWA) was contested by SWAPO since the 1960s, and by 1973 reached the point where the SADF had to take over the control of the border areas from the police. Things only worsened once the Portuguese ceased controlling their side of the border in Angola: SWAPO quickly filled the vacuum by setting up a whole string of bases, used as launching points for attacks into SWA and moved its HQ from Lusaka in Zambia, to Luanda.

Still in control of the most powerful economy and armed forces in the region, the government of Prime Minister John Vorster initiated a rather open-handed policy towards pro-Western, African countries such as Ivory Coast, Gabon, Zaire, and Zambia, aiming to strengthen economic ties. Furthermore, it pursued the policy of a negotiated settlement between the Rhodesian government and two major nationalist movements opposed to it. Finally, South Africa entered negotiations with the major insurgent group in Mozambique, offering to recognize its government and provide economic aid, in exchange for the guerrillas restraining themselves from providing any kind of support to such nationalist movements as the African National Congress.

However, Vorster's policy of détente was far from being universally supported in South Africa. If the intelligence service, Bureau for State Security (BOSS), or the Foreign Minister Hilgard Muller largely shared similar views, this was not the case with plenty of other powerful political figures, foremost Pieter Willem Botha, the Defence Minister. Botha was advocating much more aggressive policies, which he considered as necessary against the threat of what was perceived as a powerful and Communist-supported block, dead-intended to seize control over South Africa. Botha's worldview was widely shared among the SADF and the Military Intelligence. Thus, the South African government was divided between 'Doves' and 'Hawks'. Tragically, the latter gained the upper hand in early September 1975, and this is what defined the extent of the South African involvement in Angola for the next 14 years. Certainly enough, the outlook for a possible cooperation with any government of an independent Angola were much more reduced in comparison to the outlook for future cooperation with any government of an independent Mozambique: not only were there three main contenders for power, instead of one, but Pretoria also had no important economic levers upon Luanda, like it had in the case of Maputo. Of course, the idea that appeared the simplest of all was to let the SADF take over in Luanda and install a sympathetic government. However, not one South African politician had any kind of illusions about the credibility of any nationalist movement brought to power with the help of what was widely perceived as the 'military force of Apartheid'. Therefore, the South Africans began searching for an option that would keep their involvement secret.[80]

Preliminary talks between the South Africans, FNLA and UNITA took place in 1974 and were intensified during early 1975. Both movements promptly expressed their will to, in exchange of South-African help, interdict SWAPO activities – if they were in charge after independence. The FNLA was even willing to allow the SADF to launch cross-border raids up to 80 kilometres (49 miles) deep into Angola if needed. As a result, the South Africans provided a trickle of military supplies and funding during the first half of 1975. However, by June, BOSS concluded that the balance was shifting decisively in favour of the MPLA and that much more was necessary to beef-up the FNLA and UNITA. Correspondingly, in early July 1975, high-ranking BOSS officers met with Jonas Savimbi and Roberto Holden to assess their needs in term of military support before drawing-up a report preconizing the delivery arms worth US$14.1, including radios, explosives, vehicles, mortars, machine guns and other weapons. On 14 July, Prime Minister John Vorster approved the BOSS plan, although all the weapons were to be of foreign origin to disguise Pretoria's hand.

FNLA and UNITA began to receive much larger South African shipments than previously at roughly the same time as they began receiving US-aid within Operation IAFEATURE. Furthermore, on 9 August 1975, SADF troops crossed the border to secure the nearby Calueque Dam and the Ruacana power station – largely financed by South Africa, and meanwhile regularly harassed by elements of the FALA. Warships and submarines of the South African Navy began patrolling the sea off Angola, while the SADF launched Operation Sausage II, with the aim of destroying several SWAPO bases. Finally, on 28 August 1975, Botha ordered the SADF to start supplying the FNLA with additional weapons – not included in BOSS's earlier plan.[81]

Meanwhile, SADF officers in contact with the FNLA – such as Lieutenant-Colonel Jan Breytenbach – quickly concluded that arms and equipment would never be sufficient to shift the military balance in Angola: these had to be complemented by training, logistical support, and even military intelligence. Related reports from the SADF were filed roughly around the same time as when the CIA came to similar conclusions and began contacting Pretoria with requests for suitable advisors. Prime Minister Vorster thus approved the deployment of SADF instructors to Angola on 4 September 1975. Two teams were dispatched:

- One, led by Lieutenant-Colonel Breytenbach, responsible for training an ELNA battalion of about 400 at Mpupa, and
- Another, led by Lieutenant-Colonel Kaas van der Waals, responsible for training 700 FALA combatants, organised in four companies, at Capolo.

These two teams were to be followed by other batches of trainees, because the South Africans intended to train about 6,000 recruits for no less than two brigades. According to a SADF plan drafted on 24 September 1975, once their training was completed, the ELNA and FALA were to stop any FAPLA advance and then counterattack, recapture recently lost positions and then seize all the major ports along the southern coast of Angola. After such a string of victories, the South Africans hoped that the Organisation of African Unity (OAU) would have no choice but to strong-arm the MPLA into agreeing to enter into a post-independence national union government including the FNLA and the UNITA.[82]

MMCA

Ironically, around the same time similar plans were drafted on the other side of the Atlantic Ocean – in Cuba. In July 1975, Havana finally came to the decision to answer the MPLA's requests for help in a favourable fashion. The first group of 50 advisors arrived in Brazzaville on 25 July, with the task of helping the movement to accept and tranship arms supplies that were to follow. A few days later, a seven-man detachment under Commandante Raùl Díaz Argüelles arrived in Luanda. Their mission was to assess the situation and evaluate the FAPLA needs. After a series of meetings with the MPLA politico-military leadership, during which Argüelles gave Neto the US$100,000 requested earlier that year, he returned to Cuba to present his conclusions to Fidel and Raúl Castro on 11 August 1975. While the MPLA had requested, beside weapons and uniforms for their trainees, only around one hundred military instructors, which were to be dispersed among a large number of units, the Castros and Argüelles opted for a completely different

Cuban soldier with the flag of the MMCA, in Luanda. (Albert Grandolini Collection)

Advisors of the MMCA with one of first group of FAPLA recruits they had to train: many of the latter were still boys. (Al J Venter Collection)

Cuban advisor training FAPLA recruits in the use of the Soviet-made RPG-7 rocket-propelled launcher. (Albert Grandolini Collection)

solution: the Cuban Military Mission in Angola (*Misión Militar de Cuba en Angola*, MMCA) was to include 480 instructors who would be concentrated in only four main locations. Fidel Castro himself explained the motives behind this decision as follows:

> Why did we want this? Because it's much easier to lead and organize our forces this way [...]. More importantly, it's much safer because in a worst-case scenario a unit of 60-70 Cubans is a respectable force [...]. Seventy men with automatic rifles, mortars, bazookas and antitank and antiaircraft cannons can face any situation. This includes the worst variant, a situation in which there's nobody left in the group but Cubans. Any one of these groups is strong enough to confront any military situation that might arise in the kind of war that's under way there.[83]

The largest Cuban detachment, with 191 men under General Ramón Espinosa Martin, was to be stationed in the highly vulnerable Cabinda enclave. The others were to be distributed to three main training camps in Henrique de Carvalho (Saurimo), Benguela and Salazar (N'Dalatando). The Cuban took the MPLA terminology to name these camps and numbered them as listed in Table 7: with exception of the CIR 4, each of these was to be staffed by 66-67 Cubans, and have an armoury including nine 82mm mortars, seven 75mm recoilless guns, 18 RPG-7s, and six ZPU-4 anti-aircraft guns. The MMCA headquarters with 25 men was to stay in Luanda and its function was crucial as it was to advise the FAPLA's high command. The MMCA also included a small detail of 17 medical personnel, as well as several pilots and specialists in air or shipping control, overall nearly 500 men, all of them volunteers from the FAR, under command of Commandante Raùl Díaz Argüelles (colloquially known as 'Domingo da Silva' in Angola). In turn, the latter answered to the General Abelardo Colomé Ibarra, the First Deputy Minister FAR.

Table 7: MMCA October 1975

Unit Designation	Commander	Number of Advisors
HQ (Luanda)	Raùl Díaz Argülles	25
CIR 1, Salazar/ N'Dalatando	Romárico Sotomayor García	67
CIR 2, Benguela	Eustaquio Nodarse Bonet	66-67
CIR 3, Enrique de Carvalho/Saurimo	Ulises Estrada Reyes	66-67
CIR 4, Cabinda	Ramón Espinosa Martin	191

Despite all the possible threats, the Cubans were expecting their role to be limited to support and training and not include any direct involvement in combat – except if the situation took a turn for the worse, as Castro explained to a group of advisors before their departure:

> ... Circumstances could arise in which one of the schools would

A group of FAPLA troops together with some of their Cuban advisors, seen shortly after their graduation. Most early Angolan units were rushed into combat with their troops never completing even their basic training. (Albert Grandolini Collection)

Merchant *Vietnam Heroico*, which was one of ships used to deploy members of the MMCA to Luanda, in August 1975. (Mark Lepko Collection)

be called upon to support an operation or defend a region. In that case, the school with its Cuban personnel would take part in military operations. [...] Other potential dangers: That troops from Zaire intervene, that regular troops invade the country. In a situation such as that, you will without doubt find yourselves involved in the fighting. There are reports, for example, that South African troops have penetrated into some border regions from the south [...]. If there is an intervention by South African troops, you will have to intervene.[84]

The MMCA expected to train 4,800 FAPLA combatants in six months. The latter were organized into 16 small battalions, and diverse support units including eight batteries each of 82mm mortars, 12.7mm and 14.5mm HMGs and 75mm or 82mm recoilless guns, as well as three 120mm mortar batteries and one 122mm howitzer battery. Each of the CIR was to train two battalions simultaneously for three months, before training another two similar units for another three months.

Once ready, these units were to form a strategic reserve under control of the FAPLA HQ. The Cubans were confident that such a force would be more than enough to crush both FNLA and UNITA. Furthermore, the Cubans were to deliver most of the necessary supplies to equip this force, including 12,000 M52 rifles of Czechoslovak origin, 133 RPG-7s from Bulgaria, and dozens of mortars and machine-guns. Because of the anticipated lack of available vehicles needed to run the operation in Angola, the Cubans were also to provide 134 vehicles. As at this stage, the Soviets were not really supporting the Cuban initiative, and even refused to provide assistance to transport the MMCA and its supplies, or to send their own advisors in Angola. Overall, only a small portion of the weapons delivered by the Cubans to the MPLA were Soviet-produced.[85]

Table 8: MMCA-related Arms Shipments, 1975

Armament Type	Number
Radio sets	93
M52 (rifles)	12,000
Heavy machine guns (14.5mm)	18
Heavy machine guns (12.7mm)	30
RPG-7	133
75mm recoilless guns	48
82mm mortars	51
82mm recoilless guns	18
M-30 howitzers	6
Anti-tank mines	5,040
Anti-personnel mines	30,600

The first elements of the MMCA left for Angola on 21 August, and were followed by several other groups. By the end of September, around 50 men had reached Luanda by commercial flights. This advanced group planned the implementation of the bulk of the mission, which was to arrive in early October. Meanwhile, the merchants *Vietnam Heroico*, *La Plata* and *Coral Island* had left Cuba on 16 and 20 September, with the all the supplies intended for the mission as well as around 300 MMCA members, while other advisors travelled to Angola on board commercial flights. *Vietnam Heroico* and *Coral Island* dropped anchor at Porto Ambroim on 5 and 8 October respectively while *La Plata* arrived at Pointe Noire on 9 October and began to unload her shipment – which was promptly dispatched to Cabinda. By 20 October, all the training camps were up and running, with the exception of Saurimo, which became operational a few days later.[86] Sufficient to say that soon after their arrival, the Cubans were forced into the realisation that most of their recruits were completely inexperienced, even if willing to learn. An officer attached to CIR 2 recalled:

> Our troops were very young boys, but intelligent, disciplined and with desire to learn. They were particularly skilled at handling armament and infantry manoeuvring in close order. We worked cohesively and, as they say, from dawn till dusk. It was a real misfortune not to have had a little more time to prepare them better.[87]

CHAPTER 5
CARLOTA VS SAVANNAH

As of early October 1975, the MPLA's position appeared strong. In addition to Luanda, the movement controlled 11 out of 16 provincial capitals, was in the process of receiving a large training mission from Cuba, and about to receive major shipments of arms from the USSR. Certainly enough, South African and US advisors were active in Angola, and arms shipments were flowing via Zaire, but it was already clear that neither the ELNA nor the FALA would be ready in time to turn the tables before independence day. Pretoria thus found itself without a choice but to increase the involvement of the SADF. In a matter of days, plans were put in motion to organize two combined South African-Angolan forces. The infantrymen were to be of Angolan origin, while the SADF would provide commanders and specialists necessary to handle heavy armament. To hide South African involvement as much as possible, the SADF soldiers were not to wear regular uniforms and the use of standard weaponry was to be kept to an absolute minimum. If asked by any foreigners, the South Africans were to present themselves as 'mercenaries'. Because the use of standard army vehicles was to be avoided, too, civilian trucks owned by Portuguese refugees which had fled to the Namibian border were bought, and immediately dubbed 'vegetable trucks', while the whole operation was code-named Savannah.

SADF's Task Forces

The plan for Savannah envisaged the deployment of multiple 'task forces' and 'battle groups' of the SADF and diverse allies inside Angola:

Task Force Zulu, commanded by Colonel Koos van Heerden, included two battle groups, Alpha and Bravo. Battle Group Alpha (BGA) was led by Commandant Delville Linford, and included Companies A and B. It was exclusively staffed by Bushmen (either former Portuguese Flechas or those recruited in SWA recently), and a small core of former Portuguese Army officers and other ranks, who had been trained for months, and had already seen combat against SWAPO in the Caprivi Strip. Battle Group Bravo (BGB) was led by Commandant Jan Breytenbach and included the ELNA battalion he had trained since September. By mid-October, this included A, B, and C Companies, a machine-gun platoon with 12 Vickers mounted on Land Rovers, and a mortar platoon with 12 3-inch mortars. Altogether, Task Force Zulu counted around 1,000 troops.[88]

Task Force Foxbat, commanded by Commandant Eddie Webb, consisted of a three-companies strong FALA battalion, a FALA-manned platoon of four 81mm mortars, three ENTAC ATGM-teams of the SADF, four heavy machine guns and two recoilless rifles mounted on Land Rovers, and was later reinforced by a full squadron of Eland armoured cars.[89]

Task Force Zulu (TFZ) crossed the border at Katwitwi, on 14 October 1975, and advanced on UNITA-controlled Serpa Pinto (Menongue). After a brief fire-fight with its allies – a blue-on-blue incident in which there were, fortunately, no casualties caused to either side – the column turned south again and dashed for its first objective: Pereira de Eça (Ongiva). Benefitting from the moment of surprise, the TFZ quickly seized this town with a linear advance along its main street, and in face of resistance from a single FAPLA squadron. The party sent around the town to cut-off the enemy withdrawal was delayed by the mud, and thus the defenders managed to retreat to Roçades (Xangongo) after losing their commander, Commander Cowboy. TFZ resumed its advance

SADF Eland armoured cars and UNITA/FALA infantry – a mix that was to become famous during the South African invasion of Angola, starting with October 1975. (Albert Grandolini Collection)

SADF Elands on the streets of Sa da Bandeira (Lubango), early in the morning of 24 October 1975. (Albert Grandolini Collection)

almost immediately afterwards and seized Xangongo on the next day. By then, Colonel van Heerden's command was reinforced by a full squadron of 22 Eland armoured cars organised into five four-vehicles troops, a two-vehicle command-element, and supported by a four-tube strong mortar platoon – all exclusively manned by SADF troops.

On 22 October 1975, the SADF airlifted another full Eland-squadron to Kuito, where it joined Task Force Foxbat (TFF). The original task of this unit was the protection of Huambo and the three roads leading to this town from the north. However, TFF was then ordered into an advance in the direction of the coast, so to form the eastern prong of a 'pincer' movement, completed by the approach of Task Force Zulu from the south. Thus, three days later, Task Force Foxbat – including a combat team under Major Louis Holtzhausen, centred on two FALA companies and three Eland troops – launched its advance in a western direction. It first took Balombo and, on 26 October, it expelled two FAPLA squadrons from Luimbale, inflicting severe casualties. After deploying multiple combined-arms detachments to counter various FAPLA attempts to advance on Huambo, TFF rushed forward two FALA companies supported by 12 Elands and other elements towards Lobito, in early November, in an attempt to cut-off the enemy retreating from TFZ. With the help of a twin-engined Beech B55 Baron, which UNITA found abandoned at Huambo airport, it found and outflanked a strong blocking position held by the Dora Squadron, FAPLA at Caluita (70 kilometres/43 miles north of Benguela), quickly approached to only 200-250 metres range and then annihilated the enemy with concentrated fire from all of its heavy weapons, killing between 63 and 80 in the process. Survivors of the Dora Squadron subsequently claimed to have knocked out two Elands during this clash. While this claim remains unconfirmed, it is certain that the Beech Baron that supported the SADF column was lost in a crash outside Norton de Matos, on 28 October, together with its pilot, Major Piet Uys, and three passengers.[90]

By 6 November 1975, TFF established multiple ambush positions on the road connecting Lobito with Sumba, and destroyed several

A column of SADF armoured cars and trucks carrying UNITA/FALA infantry in Pereira de Eca (Ongiva), early during Operation Savannah. (Albert Grandolini Collection)

FAPLA convoys retreating from the latter town. After mopping up, the force then seized the town, a day later, where it was joined by TFZ.[91]

Meanwhile, TFZ had resumed its advance toward Sa da Bandeira (Lubango), the HQ of the FAPLA Southern Front. Breaking through several ambushes, it stopped to rest in the vicinity of this town on 23 October, and then repulsed a weak counter-attack from Lubango during the night (in the course of which it destroyed three enemy vehicles). On the morning of 24 October, it assaulted the town by the means of BGB attacking the local airport, while BGA drove around the enemy flank to seize the Hill Monte Cristo, before continuing with an attempt to cut-off the road to Namibe. While Battle Group Alpha met no resistance, the airport was fiercely defended by at least one FAPLA squadron, and it took an infantry assault by Battle Group Bravo, supported by Elands, to secure the site – together with a number of civilian aircraft parked there (including one Piper Aztek, and one Beech King Air). At least 84 Angolans were killed and 30 captured in the process. Amongst the dead was the FAPLA commander of Lubango, Commander Dack Doy. Strikingly, he was killed while firing a mortar – because he was the only man trained in the use of such a weapon. While TFZ captured large stocks of supplies inside the FAPLA's base in Lubango, it was subsequently reinforced by two additional platoons of the ELNA, another platoon of 81mm mortars, and a platoon from the 1st Parachute Battalion SADF (the latter subsequently manned three of the captured B-10 recoilless guns). Next, TFZ advanced in the direction of Namibe, deploying each of its battle groups on a different road. Supported by an Eland troop, BGA approached the port on 27 October, quickly overcoming two FAPLA ambush parties, positioned seven and two kilometres short of it. BGB then took over the advance and invested the port on the next day, meeting only weak resistance in the airport area and next to the local HQ of the MPLA. Once in control of Namibe, the South Africans found themselves in control of an immense booty, including several hundred brand-new civilian vehicles stored there because the war prevented their delivery to Zambia. Without wasting any time, both battle groups then returned to Lubango, with the intention of resuming their advance in the northern direction.

By that point in time, TFZ had easily and completely overwhelmed all of the FAPLA's forces in its way – for multiple reasons. It could bring a comparatively tremendous amount of fire-power to bear and its commanders were experts in massing their infantry and armoured cars at the decisive point. Foremost, the South Africans made excellent use of concentrating most of the fire-power at the head of their columns: the combination of Elands with Land Rover-mounted machine guns meant that any enemy ambush party found itself almost immediately on the receiving hand of very intensive fire. Furthermore, the TFZ was advancing at incredible speed, and thus repeatedly took the enemy wrong-footed, or entirely unaware of the incoming threat. Moreover, it did not advance along the only axis available, but nearly always had company-sized elements deployed along secondary axes with the aim of covering the flank or dealing with isolated FAPLA positions. Finally, the SADF's intelligence included a number of former Portuguese intelligence operatives that defected to SWA and provided all the radio frequencies and codes used by the MPLA and FAPLA. Correspondingly, the South Africans found it easy to find, take by surprise and destroy FAPLA's Southern Front's forces in piecemeal battles, one unit after the other. In comparison, the Angolan commanders in the area found themselves in possession of only a few heavy weapons (foremost Grad-1Ps), very little ammunition for these, and next to nobody trained to operate them. Therefore, although ordered to hold Lubango 'at all cost', there was nothing they could have done to prevent its fall.[92]

Battle of Catengue

With the fall of Lubango and Namibe, it became obvious for the FAPLA high command and the MMCA advisors that something was seriously wrong in southern Angola; indeed, that the South Africans must be involved. With Benguela under threat, the decision was made to mobilize the two FAPLA battalions under training and their Cuban instructors at CIR 2, in Benguela – and this even though these two units had received only a few days-worth of training. One of the two battalions, under command of the Cuban Major Gonzalo del Valle Céspedes, and accompanied by more than three dozen other advisors, left the training camp at dawn of 30 October and marched on Catengue, around 70 kilometres (43 miles) from the coastal city, intending to establish a blocking position and prevent any enemy advance on Benguela. The resulting task force included three infantry companies with around 100 troops each, and its Angolan officers all had one Cuban advisor with them. Notable is that contrary to the FAPLA, which usually established positions inside the defended locality, the Cubans followed different tactics: they never attempted to prevent the enemy from

SADF Elands on the streets of Lobito. (Albert Grandolini Collection)

seizing Catengue, but constructed a defensive position 'behind' the town, on the road to Benguela. This tactic was dating back to the times of the insurgency against the Batista Regime, when the enemy proved easier to catch off guard. Correspondingly, the mixed FAPLA/MMCA unit established a strong defensive position on a ridge just behind a bridge, in the form of zig-zagging and carefully camouflaged trenches and fire positions (dug out despite the very hard ground). Gonzalo del Valle Céspedes recalled the problems the units under his command were facing as follows:

> We did not have adequate tools to build fortifications. We used bayonets of our rifles and everything else that could be used to dig. The defences of each company were organized in depth, with two platoons up front and the others some 150-200 metres behind. Our anti-tank weapons [three 75mm recoilless rifles authors' note] were located right behind our forward positions, on each side of the road. Because of the lack of the means of communication, our mortars [three 82mm tubes; authors' note] occupied positions right next to my observation post, 50 or 60 metres behind the frontline, to provide semi-direct support fire. The centre sector was covered by one infantry company, with the second acting as reserve, while the third remained behind us, as a rear-guard....Furthermore, the battalion was reinforced by small FAPLA groups that operated in the area, and who brought with them a single 82mm mortar, and a Grad-1P launcher – though it had only one rocket.[93]

On 2 November 1975, Task Force Zulu entered Catengue without encountering resistance. Battle Group Alpha then deployed it's A Company into a reconnaissance along the road to Huambo, while the B Company advanced along the road to Benguela for similar reasons – and even more so because a lone 122mm rocket was fired from the western direction and landed near the town. Around 0900hrs, C Company – reinforced by an Eland troop and a platoon of 81mm mortars – arrived in front of the bridge, where its ELNA soldiers dismounted and formed an extended line, preparing for the crossing. Precisely at that point in time, the FAPLA and its Cuban instructors opened fire with virtually all the fire-power available. Most of the ELNA Troops panicked and fled towards Catengue: only some 40 troops remained behind, taking cover and returning fire. The four Elands also took cover and returned fire whenever possible, while mortars plastered enemy positions – despite receiving some counter-battery fire. Because TFZ had never previously met this kind of resistance, reinforcements were rushed to the scene in form of two Eland troops, two mortar platoons (one with four 81mm tubes, and other with 12 3-In mortars), the machine-gun platoon, and three Para-manned B-10 recoilless rifles. With all of this firepower on their side, the tide began to turn in favour of the South Africans. Their mortars silenced all the FAPLA mortar teams, and – by the afternoon – all the recoilless guns. Next, B and C Companies of BGB launched a series of frontal attacks and gradually managed to reach the trenches on the top of the hill. The FAPLA did launch a few confused counter-attacks, but by 1800hrs the position had been secured. Meanwhile, BGA had launched a wide flanking move and arrived to the rear of the enemy position, easily scattering its rear-guard along the way. Thus, when the bulk of the Angolan and Cuban forces began to withdraw toward Benguela, the South Africans were in a perfect position to ambush them and inflict further casualties. A large part of the FAPLA force was dispersed, and several Cuban instructors, including Céspedes, found themselves isolated. Most of them reappeared only days later. Out of the 35 to 40 men of the MMCA contingent, between four and eight were killed, and seven wounded. FAPLA acknowledged to have lost a total of 723 men KIA during the Battle of Catengue with Task Force Zulu and the Caluita battle against Task Force Foxbat (both engagements took place on the same day).[94]

Wasting no time, TFZ quickly resumed its advance on Benguela. On 4 November, Battle Group Alpha overran the CIR 2, on the outskirts of the town, and the airport, before being pinned down by FAPLA reinforcements, supported by multiple Grad-1P launchers positioned in the surrounding hills. However, the position of the FAPLA/MMCA was obviously untenable – even more so because the TFF meanwhile resumed its advance in the direction of Lobito, thus threatening to cut it off from northern Angola. Therefore, when Battle Groups Alpha and Bravo began investing the port, on 5 November, they found out that the bulk of the garrison had left. Similarly, when TFZ reached Lobito, a day later, it found it undefended.[95]

Panic in Luanda

By the end of October, it was obvious that ELNA was preparing to breach the frontline at Quifangondo. Furthermore, the defeat at

A shot-up Gaz-66 truck (possibly Cuban), as found by the SADF following the battle of Catengue, on 2 November 1975. (Albert Grandolini Collection)

Poorly-trained and poorly-disciplined youthful troops of the FAPLA proved hopelessly outmatched during the battles for Catengue and Caluita in early November 1975: they suffered horrendous losses on the hands of the SADF. (Albert Grandolini Collection)

Catengue and the loss of Benguela and Lobito came as a shock for both the leaders of the MPLA and the MMCA. Southern Angola had been perceived as a secondary front, and – because of the lack of reliable intelligence – the threat of the SADF was largely overlooked until TFZ reached central Angola. Indeed, until the end of October, the Cubans had failed to identify the presence of SADF elements among the enemy columns which were closing in on Benguela. With the fall of the later city, it became obvious that Luanda would have to defend not only from the ELNA in the north, but also from the SADF in the south. Unsurprisingly, during the MPLA Politburo's meeting of 3 November 1974, the conclusion was drawn that a withdrawal from Luanda to Cabinda might become necessary. To prevent such a disaster, the leadership decided to request increased Cuban support. As in the case of the MPLA, the Cubans were taken by surprise. Until 1 November, the MMCA's reports were invariably optimistic – because of the lack of intelligence about the SADF. Now, Havana was left without a choice if it wanted to avoid a complete failure – and potential annihilation – of its mission in Angola, obviously associated with a major loss of prestige. Therefore, the next day, Fidel Castro and his closest advisors made their decision: to launch a major military intervention in Angola. The operation to save the MPLA government was code-named Carlota – after a slave who led a revolt in a mill in the Mataza region, in Cuba, before being captured and executed by Spaniards on 5 November 1843.

Late on 5 November, 100 artillerymen and heavy weapon specialists from the Artillery School 'Camilio Cienfuegos' boarded a Bristol Britannia airliner of the Cuban national airline, Cubana de Aviación. The aircraft took off at 1845hrs local time and landed in Brazzaville at 1930 on 6 November 1975. From Brazzaville half of this group was sent to Pointe Noir, where they received a crash course in the use of Strela-2M man-portable air defence systems (MANPADS; ASCC code: SA-7 Grail) provided by a Soviet team.[96] Meanwhile, the other part of the team was airlifted to Luanda aboard aircraft crewed by Cuban pilots, arriving there on 7 November. Almost immediately, they began preparing the equipment of the first BM-21 Grad battery that had been delivered to Pointe Noire a few days earlier, before being transhipped to Luanda aboard the Cuban merchant *La Plata*.[97]

Contrary to so many other Cuban military interventions abroad, Operation Carlota was to generate a large-scale mobilisation: not

Training of a Cuban SA-7 team in a camp outside Pointe Noire, in the Congo-Brazzaville, in November 1975. (Albert Grandolini Collection)

In January 1976, Soviet merchant *Metalurg Anosov* – famous for its role during the Cuban Crisis of 1962 – also brought a load of arms to Angola. (CIA)

An Antonov An-12 transport of the Soviet flag airline Aeroflot, as seen on arrival at Luanda IAP, in November 1975. (Albert Grandolini Collection)

Between November 1975 and February 1976, the port of Luanda was full to bursting with merchant ships unloading Cuban troops and Soviet arms. (Mark Lepko Collection)

only that the national airline was put on war footing, but virtually the entire Cuban merchant fleet had to be mobilised to support this enterprise. Due to their relatively small size and slow speed, the ships in question had to make a total of 42 voyages from Cuba and Angola (each of these lasted 20 days on average) during the first six months of the operation. From January 1976, Moscow supported this effort by providing Ilyushin Il-62 passenger aircraft, which made 120 flights between Havana and Angola.[98] The aircraft and ships carried dozens of thousands of Cuban reservists. Namely, the FAR preferred to deploy its reservists instead of newly-conscripted troops because the former had already completed their training and were thus considered for 'seasoned enough' to be deployed in combat. Therefore, the majority of about 36,000 Cuban troops deployed in Angola by the end of March 1976, were reservists.

The Soviet Factor

Despite the mobilization of virtually all available ships and passenger aircraft, Cuban transportation capacities alone were still hopelessly insufficient for carrying a large number of troops and equipment over nearly 11,000 kilometres (roughly 6800 miles) to Angola within the required period of time. Indeed, although the Cuban leadership had decided to launch Carlota without consulting with – and even less so requesting approval from – Moscow, it gambled that the Soviets would feel compelled to support the operation in due time. Time was to prove them right.

By the time Carlota began, the Soviets were already in the process of delivering growing consignments of arms for the MPLA to the Congo-Brazzaville. For this purpose, through November 1975 they began deploying giant Antonov An-22 transports. These delivered BM-21s, 122mm M-30 howitzers, T-34/85 tanks, and BTR-152 armoured personnel carriers intended for the 9th BRIM. Of course, once the Cubans launched their intervention, all of this equipment had to be transhipped to Luanda, too. Although completely unconnected to Operation Carlotta, this task was concluded during the second half of November 1975 – and it immensely eased the

Britannias to the Rescue

One of four Britannia 318s operated by the Cubana as of November 1975. (Albert Grandolini Collection)

At its time considered a landmark in turboprop-powered airliner design, and highly popular with passengers, and known as 'The Whispering Giant' for its quiet exterior noise and smooth flying, the development of the Bristol Type 175 Britannia was initiated on request from the British Overseas Airways Corporation (BOAC), in 1946. The BOAC envisaged it as serving on long-range routes over the British Empire, like London-to-Johannesburg, Cairo, Karachi or Sydney. Protracted development resulted in the first prototype being flown only on 23 December 1953. Further delays were caused by teething problems of the Proteus engines, and by additional testing ordered following three catastrophic crashes of de Havilland Comet jet airliners.

By the time 25 Britannias finally entered service with BOAC, starting in 1957, they emerged in the form of larger transatlantic airliners from Series 200, 310, and 320. However, while an aircraft with performances of this type appearing in 1950 would have put the British at the forefront of commercial aviation, by 1957 turboprop airliners were made obsolete by the appearance of the Boeing 707 jet airliner. Furthermore, BOAC ruined the reputation of the type very early, by exaggerating easily avoidable inlet icing issues. Correspondingly, only 85 Britannias were ever built. The majority were initially operated by BOAC and such of its subsidiaries as Ghana Airways, Cathay Pacific, Central Africa, East African, Nigeria and Malayan airlines, but also Aeronaves de Mexico and El Al of Israel. Twenty-five entered service with the Royal Air Force. Furthermore, Canadair manufactured 75 derivatives in the form of CL-28/CP-107 Argus' maritime patrol and anti-submarine warfare aircraft, the stretched hybrid CL-44 freighters, and CC-106 Yukon maritime patrol aircraft. Overall, a highly promising airliner that proved extremely expensive to develop was to see only limited service in world-wide aviation.

Starting in 1958, Cubana de Aviación acquired the 310 series (in the form of the Model 318), for transatlantic service. Despite the Cuban Revolution, the airline negotiated a special accord with British aircraft manufactures to maintain this model, and continued flying diverse Britannias until 1990.

When, in October 1975, top Cuban military officers considered what transport aircraft to use for hauling troops and equipment to Angola, they were quickly forced into the conclusion that the types then in service with the DAA/FAR were hopelessly insufficient for the task. The old Ilyushin Il-14s and Il-18s had both proven as far too short-legged for the task on hand. Correspondingly, the Cubans opted for the use of Cubana de Aviación's Britannia airliners, which – with their range of 8,600 kilometres (5,344 miles) – were clearly superior. As of 1975, the Cubana was still operating four Britannia 318s – registrations CU-T668, CU-T669, CU-T670, and CU-T671 – and the type proved popular with the crews, especially because of its reliability. The first two flights from Havana via Guinea-Bissau to Brazzaville, flown on 5 and 8 November 1975, were undertaken by the crews of Captains Auerlio Martines Leiro and Orlando Cossio Soto, respectively.[99]

Cuban operation because it saved much of the limited shipping capability: the FAR thus did not have to take care about hauling the same weapons all the way from Cuba.

Originally, Moscow was neither keen nor ready to deploy its military personnel directly to Angola. However, this standpoint 'had to change' as ever larger numbers of Cuban troops arrived there. Indeed, once Carlota began, the Soviets decided to deploy their military instructors to Congo-Brazzaville, too. On 1st November, a small team under Captain Evgeny Lyashenko arrived in Brazzaville aboard an Aeroflot flight. Prior to its arrival at Pointe Noire, the task for Lyashenko's team was to teach FAPLA in the use of Strela MANPADS. Instead, its first group of students consisted of Cuban specialists – those that arrived in Brazzaville on 5 November, as described above.

Due to growing demands for instructors in Angola, the Soviet team was increased to 40 – meanwhile led by Colonel Vassily Trofimenko – and then transferred from Pointe Noire to Luanda with the help of an Antonov An-12 transport of the Aeroflot, on 16 November 1975.[100]

Subsequently, Moscow's stance in regards of Operation Carlota continued changing. Indeed, in January 1976 it experienced a dramatic expansion: insisting all of these were to be used by the FAR troops only, the Soviets delivered 73 additional tanks and 21 BM-21 MRLs, followed by immense stocks of fire-arms, ammunition, equipment and supplies – directly to Angola. Furthermore, and starting with 7 January 1976, Aeroflot launched daily flights on the route Havana – Conakry – Luanda, using Ilyushin Il-62 jet airliners to transport Cuban troops to Angola. With Soviet help, the flow of the Cuban deployment came forward at amazing speed: while the FAR only managed to deploy between 3,500 and 4,000 of its troops in the country by 31 December 1975, three months later it had 36,000 – in great part thanks to Soviet transport aircraft.[101]

Speartip

Because they were limited in their ability to deploy sufficient numbers of troops during the first two months of Carlota, the Cuban commanders in Angola were forced to limit the involvement of their units on the battlefield. Early on, these were foremost deployed to reinforce the beleaguered MMCA. The first unit to do so was the 650-strong MININT Special Troops Battalion, which arrived in Luanda aboard several Britannians: the first company (158 men) aboard two aircraft on 9 November in the evening; the second on 12 November, while the third company and support elements followed on 16 November. Thus, the MMCA was beefed-up to about 1,200 troops. Meanwhile, Commander Leopoldo Cintra Frias arrived in Luanda on 13 November to take over command of the mission, while Commander Díaz Argüelles was put in charge of the units facing the South African task forces.

Furthermore, between 11 and 13 November, the ships *Vietnam Heroico*, *Imías* and *Océano Pacífico* had left Cuba carrying a full 664-strong artillery regiment and its equipment, which were to land in Luanda between 27 November and 1 December.[102] The next major unit to be shipped was a full motorized regiment which left Cuba aboard four ships – including the *Sierra Maestra* and *Jigüe* from 22 November onwards, and landed in Pointe Noire between 9 and 30 December (with the exception of the *Jigüe*, which dropped anchor at Luanda on 16 December). Indeed, while the bulk of the regiment was deployed in Cabinda to defend the enclave against a large-scale Zairian attack, one of its infantry battalions was sent to Luanda. This unit, the Third Motorised Infantry Battalion (*Tercer Battalón de Infanteria Motorizada*, 3 Bon IM) was led by Commandant Raúl Fernández Marrero and had its three infantry companies mounted in BTR-60s, and reinforced by a mortar company equipped with 120mm tubes, and one battery of M-30 howitzers. Thus, by the end of December, between 3,500 and 4,000 Cuban *combat* troops were in Angola, including around 1,000 in the Cabinda enclave. Indeed, the 3 Bon IM became the second completely Cuban-manned unit engaged in combat operations in Angola.[103]

Therefore, the early Cuban military commitment in Angola under Operation Carlota was virtually a mirror-image of the SADF involvement under Savannah. The MININT and FAR concentrated on providing a core of specialized elements, including highly-trained commandos, officers and weapons specialists – foremost artillerymen, to corset and integrate with the FAPLA infantry.

Buena Suerte!

On 20 October 1975, the MPLA gathered a group of 9 pilots of the Flying Club of Angola, and of the former Division of Air Transports (*Divisão dos Transportes Aéreos*, DTA; reorganised as the TAAG Aerial Transports of Angola [TAAG *Transportes Aéreos de Angola*, TAAG], in 1973), and 35 young recruits at Luanda International Airport (IAP). The reason for their meeting was the decision to mobilise all the available aircraft and crews to train a cadre for an air force that could support the FAPLA in the ongoing war.[104] The training of recruits started almost immediately, and was greatly supported by the fact that the original team of nine instructors eventually grew to more than a dozen, including seven Portuguese, three ('white') Angolans, several French and Spaniards. This made it possible to split the experienced personnel into two: one group continued the training of 35 recruits (officially completed on 28 March 1976), while the other flew operational sorties with a total of three Fokker F.27s and six Douglas DC-3s of the TAAG on behalf of the MPLA/FAPLA,

Cuban troops with their flag and the obligatory photograph of Supreme Leader – Fidel Castro – as seen on arrival in Angola. They were to play the crucial role during the battles between November 1975 and March 1976. (Albert Grandolini Collection)

The graveyard of the FAP at Luanda IAP used to contain the wreckage of more than 40 different types of aircraft as of 1975. Visible in this photograph are a Noratlas (foreground left), a C-47 (centre), and at least one Do.27 (lying upside down). (Albert Grandolini Collection)

Cuban troops with one of the B-26 Invaders left behind by the FAP at Luanda IAP. Although apparently intact, the aircraft was worn out and had been abandoned since 1974. (Albert Grandolini Collection)

eventually forming the new national airline, officially the TAAG Angolan Aerial Transports (*Transportes Aéreos Angolanos*, TAAG; later TAAG Angola Airlines). These aircraft hauled vital supplies to troops deployed in remote parts of Angola, such like Luena or Saurimo.[105]

Meanwhile, the Portuguese authorities left members of the MMCA to roam around Luanda IAP, and the Cubans promptly found six Alouette III and two SE.315B Lama helicopters in, disassembled condition, inside one of hangars. Originally the property of the consortium Companhia de Diamantes de Angola DIAMANG, which intended to operate them in eastern Angola, all of these were promptly requisitioned, and the MMCA contracted a Portuguese civilian mechanic to help with their assembly. Havana promptly reacted by deploying nine helicopter-pilots – Francesco Pita Alonso, Jorge Quintana Barbosa, Hases Ramos Negrin, Alberto Ortega Segrera, René Corredera Brito, Circo Vargas Guerra, Raúl Vigo Diaz, Aníbal Cofiño Bombino, and Ramón Herrera Morejón – all with extensive experiences on diverse US and Soviet-made models, to Luanda. After undergoing a crash conversion course on their mounts, these crews – and their Alouette IIIs – were to see very intensive service during the following months.[106]

In addition to transports of the TAAG and helicopters requisitioned by the Cubans, the nascent flying service of the MPLA/FAPLA could reach back upon dozens, if not more than a hundred of diverse aircraft. While withdrawing from Luanda IAP, the FAP left behind at least eight B-26 Invaders, 11 North American T-6 Texans, 4 C-47 and 4 Nord 2501 Noratlas transports, and up to a dozen of Dornier Do.27 light transports. However, not one of these was operational: most were de-facto dumped aside of the tarmac and had been there for years, others had various crucial systems taken away long before the Angolans could put their hands upon them. More importantly, dozens of privately owned Taylorcraft Austers, aircraft of Beech, Cessna and Piper design, a handful of

Giant Antonov An-22 transports – the largest aircraft in world-wide service as of 1975 – of the Soviet (Military) Transport Aviation, like the example in this photograph taken a few years later, were used to deliver MiG-17s and, later on, MiG-21s ordered by Angola, from Moscow to Luanda. (Tom Cooper Collection)

Do.27s, and several Aero Commander 500s, were found intact at different airports that came under the control of the MPLA/FAPLA. Finally, the TAAG was reinforced through additional transports: the government of Congo-Brazzaville sent two ex-FAP Noratlas, while another aircraft of the same type was donated by Mozambique. Correspondingly, in early December 1975 Havana ordered three crews versed in flying transport and passenger aircraft to Luanda. Amongst them were Jimmy Archer Silva, Juan Céspedes Fernández (who became the personal pilot of Díaz Argüelles), Alfredo Armengot Ramos, Francisco García Cuza, Armando Ramos Pagán, Ángel Nenedico, Efraín Munoz Cordovés, Hernán Hernández, Amaury López, Modesto Concepción Pupo, Omar Correa Soler, Erlán Romero Luca, José Raúl Oritz Vega, Agrelio Laridas Sardá, and Tomás Montero Ruiz. Their arrival, followed by that of a team of specialists in air traffic control and handling of cargo at airports – led by Chaime Arcer – greatly lessened the stress to which the original TAAG was exposed, the pilots of which – according to Cuban accounts – were meanwhile flying 'excessive numbers of flight hours'.[107]

Finally, following the decision to launch Operation Carlota, and in the aftermath of the Angolan declaration of independence, on 11 November 1975, Havana decided to deploy two regular units of the DAA/FAR. The first of these was to become a squadron equipped with MiG-17 fighter-bombers, while a unit equipped with MiG-21s was to follow. The selection of pilots and ground crews for this mission is known to have started on 26 December 1975, and was followed by an intensive course in air combat. Rafael del Pino, who subsequently served as the commander of the DAA/FAR contingent in Angola, explained the reasons as follows:

> I knew that in Angola we would be doing a lot of instrument flying, nose dives under complex meteorological conditions, and bomb and attack land targets with missiles and rockets. I decided, however, to train mainly in air combat. I made this decision not only due to time constraints, but because I always thought that any combat pilot who attains absolute command of his aircraft and sets himself firmly behind the enemy plane throughout all the complexities of an air attack is capable of fulfilling any of the three other missions. Being just a pilot is not difficult… But, being a combat pilot is something else, it is the fusion of man/machine/space in one sole element…. The first day of training was how to intercept airborne planes with the help of ground radar control and radio instructions…Soviet tactics have made this type of interception so rigid and inflexible that they found themselves forced to obey the radio instructions from the ground as if they were long-leashed plough horses wearing blinders. Using subsonic MiG-17s exclusively, the second day of training was devoted to planning air combat exercises, "dogfights" to the pilots. From that day onward, we trained only in dogfights between MiG-21sand MiG-17s, so that the pilots become adapted to combat with aircraft of different characteristics. The pilots I had chosen could not have been better, and although they saw me as their teacher, during the training I was able to see that several of them surpassed me in ability and skill. There was only one thing lacking, provided by the implacable passing of time: experience.[108]

Rather by accident than by design, on exactly the same day – 26 December 1975 – Soviet transport aircraft delivered nine MiG-17Fs and one MiG-15UTI, and all the necessary support equipment, together with a team of technicians necessary to assemble them, to Luanda IAP. The aircraft in question were originally requested by the MPLA from Moscow months earlier, quite soon after the negotiations with the US government definitely failed: in the light of the American decision to stick to supporting the FNLA, there was no reason to hold back any more. With there being not a single Angolan to fly or maintain these aircraft, it was on Havana to provide the crews: the pilots in question – amongst them José A Montes (commander of the future MiG-17 unit), Eusebio Carmenate Pedroso, Armando González Nodarse, Felipe González Reyes, Darío Domínguez Melgarejo, Celso Avial Rodríguez, Pedro Luis Casbella Martinez, and Rolando Santiesteban – followed on 7 January 1976 on board an Il-62M of the Aeroflot. Hours before their flight to Luanda, they had gathered in the MINFAR Building in Havana to receive a comprehensive briefing on the situation in Angola, as described by del Pino:

> The blue and red signs and arrows showed the complex situation existing within the African conflict. The Cuban troops had forced the FNLA forces to retreat 80 kilometres from the capital. Nevertheless, the enemy continued strong and held control of the important northern cities of Carmona and Negage. The latter housed a modern air base with all kinds of logistical support. In the south, UNITA covered over half of the country's territory and controlled a series of important cities, Novoa Lisboa (Huambo), Silva Porto (Bie), Benguela, Luso (Luena), Mocamedes (Namibe), Silva Porto (Menongue), and the modern port of Lobito.

Finally, Fidel Castro appeared to explain the latest developments and impress upon his pilots that, '…the MPLA has no forces, that we [the Cubans; authors' note] would become the MPLA army', but also that they were to engage solely on his orders. The 'supreme leader of the Cuban Revolution' concluded his appearance with, 'Buena suerte!' ('good luck').

Unknown to those attending this briefing, but already known to del Pino – who was meanwhile at Luanda IAP – was the fact that two days earlier a major mishap befell the group of Soviet technicians that were working on assembling the newly-delivered MiG-17s. Indeed, the tragedy in question was the cause a significant postponement in the combat deployment of Angolan MiGs, as recalled by del Pino:

> I was asked to rush to the hanger where the MiG-17s were being readied. There had been a catastrophe. At first, I thought a piece of heavy equipment might have fallen on one of the men, but to my amazement, when I got to the hangar, it was horrendous. Almost all of the Soviet engineers and technicians in the assembly brigade were either dead or dying. Two of them were writhing on the floor, in fierce convulsions. I summoned the counter-intelligence officers to find out the cause for such an unexplainable atrocity. Lieutenant Munoz soon returned with the explanation. He took me to a corner of the hangar, pointing at a lidless 55-gallon barrel of wood alcohol, surrounded by empty plastic glasses and remnants of limes and oranges. "Colonel, our big brothers had a bash last night but with the wrong drink!"

Exactly how many Soviets effectively killed themselves by drinking pure alcohol during the night from 6 to 7 January 1976, remains unknown, but it seems that the first Soviet casualties in Angola thus did not die in combat, but during a drinking orgy. Two days later, Soviet An-22s had to fly in a new team of specialists to Luanda. Thus, the first three MiG-17s and the MiG-15UTI were assembled and ready for operations only on 19 January 1976. Only then could the Cubans start flying their first training and orientation flights around Luanda.[109]

Angolan Air Force

Knowing that the appearance of Soviet-made fighter jets at Luanda IAP could not be kept secret for very long, as soon as the Soviet technicians had assembled all nine MiG-17s and the sole MiG-15UTI, Agostinho Neto rushed to officially declare the Angola People's Air Force and Air Defence Force (*Força Aérea Popular de Angola/Defesa Anti-Aviones*, FAPA/DAA) as established, on 21 January 1976. On that morning a big ceremony was held at Luanda IAP, during which an entire row of MiG-17Fs and two C-47s were presented to the public. In his inaugural speech, Neto officially announced the duties of the air force as follows:

- Defence of national airspace against all violations or external aggression;

Taken at Luanda IAP in 1976, this rare photograph shows some of the aircraft left behind by the Portuguese, including one Noratlas (background left), one Lockheed PV-2 Ventura, at least five Do.27s, and two B-26s. Visible in the foreground is one of 'new arrivals' – a MiG-17F painted in light admiralty grey overall, with two underwing drop tanks and its forward fuselage covered in a tarpaulin. (Photo by Gerd Spieß)

Taken at Luanda on 25 January 1976, during celebrations associated with the establishment of the FAPA/DAA, this photograph shows a row of (Cuban-manned) MiG-17Fs, plus two C-47 transports left behind by the Portuguese. (Tom Cooper Collection)

Trio of Cuban-flown MiG-17Fs making a fly-past over Luanda IAP on 25 January 1976. Barely noticeable are 'fin flashes' in the form of the Angolan national colours applied on their rudder and that of the MiG-17F serial 'C25', parked in the foreground. (Mark Lepko Collection)

Cuban ground personnel with some of the Soviet technicians that helped assemble the first fighter jets destined for Angola, in front of the first MiG-15UTI of the FAPA/DAA (serial C21), in early 1976. (Albert Grandolini Collection)

- Support of ground forces on Angolan territory from Cabinda to the Cunene River;
- Monitoring Angolan airspace with the aid of radars based on Angolan territory;
- Support of the economic reconstruction of the country.

Furthermore, he appointed FAPLA's Major Dimbondua as the first commander of the FAPA/DAA. Of course, this was a big masquerade, just like the fact that a single FAPLA soldier was positioned next to one Cuban pilot and the so-called 'plane captain' (top technician responsible for the maintenance) in front of each MiG – in order to 'convince' the journalists present that all of the MiGs would be flown by Angolans. In reality, Dimboundua had nothing to say in the presence of the far more experienced Cuban officers (indeed, according to the latter, he was rarely – if ever – present at his post, and preoccupied with running after women and alcohol). Moreover, Fidel Castro himself imposed a strict ban on any kind of combat activities by DAA/FAR away from Luanda, and thus – although urgently needed – they were to see no action for several weeks following.[110]

The same fate befell the much more potent combat aircraft delivered two days later: on 23 January 1976, Soviet An-22s unloaded the first two MiG-21MF interceptors at Luanda IAP, together with equipment for a battery of S-125 Pechora (ASCC-code 'SA-3 Goa') surface-to-air missiles.[111] Correspondingly, Havana reacted by deploying an additional group of pilots to fly them, including Emer Juan Pita, Benigno González Cortés, Huberto Trujillo Hernández, Alejandro Morejón Gálvez, Albio Córdova Monterón, Antonio Rojas Marrero, Roberto Canar Alvarez, Pedro L. Colmero Lauredo, Evelio Bravo Martin, Fidel Vargas Rabelo, Argelio Cardes Reyes, and Eduardo González Sarría. The latter, then a youngster keen to fly brand-new MiG-21MFs in combat – especially after one of the SAAF's Canberras overflew Luanda IAP on a reconnaissance sortie – recalled:

> The organisation was such that our operational commander was receiving orders from the commander of the MMCA, which meant we were subjected to the army. We had very strict rules of engagement, including a strict prohibition of attacks on the South Africans… Our MiG-21s received serials from C40 to C51.[112]

Finally, an Il-18 transport of Cubana de Aviacion was forward deployed at Luanda: stripped of its seats, it was used to make regular transport flights to Saurimo and Luso, and – once this town was recovered from UNITA (see below for details) – to Huambo.[113]

CHAPTER 6
QUIFANGONDO AND CABINDA – DECISIVE BATTLES

Ironically, not one of the FAR units deployed in a great hurry to Angola early during Operation Carlota took part in either of the two most decisive battles at this point in the war: those of Quifangondo and Cabinda – which broke the back of the FNLA and shattered even some of best units of the FAZ.

Quifangondo

In late October the HQ of the FAPLA concluded that the FNLA was about to resume its offensive on Luanda. By that time, the ELNA had concentrated around 1,200 combatants in the Quifangondo area, including the Special Troops Company. These were supported by two FAZ battalions (about 900 in total), equipped with a dozen jeep-mounted recoilless rifles, and 15 AML-60, AML-90 and M3s, and commanded by Colonel Lama Mamina. By the end of the month, another unit of 300 Zairian troops had landed in Ambriz to act as a reserve force. Not keen to be taken by surprise, the FAPLA opted to head-off the coming offensive and started planning its own pre-emptive attack on 19 October. Planning to reinforce the 9th BRIM, two days later, the CIR 3 dispatched one of its two newly-established 300-strong battalions in this direction. Although barely trained, this unit was reinforced by 36 MMCA advisors – including its commander, Commandant Luis Evelio Vega Romero. Furthermore, it was lavishly equipped for Angolan circumstances, including a battery each of 82mm and 120mm mortars, one battery of ZPU-4 heavy machine guns, a platoon of 12.7mm heavy machine guns, and one battery of 75mm recoilless rifles. The arrival of this unit more than compensated for the withdrawal of two companies of Katangese Tigers redeployed to the south.

The FAPLA made the first move. On 23 October, elements of the 9th BRIM, the mixed battalion, and one company of Katangese Tigers – supported by four BRDM-2s, two mortars, a battery of Grad-1Ps, and a platoon each of ZiS-3s and 75mm recoilless guns – attacked the ELNA. Launched without any reconnaissance beforehand, and suffering from lack of cooperation between the different units involved, this assault quickly collapsed when confronted by a determined counter-attack. The FAPLA infantry left the battlefield in haste, leaving the Katangese and the mixed FAPLA/FAR battalion on their own. To add salt to the injury, the coordination between the artillery of the latter and the 9th BRIM left much to be desired. Eventually, the entire venture turned into chaos and ended when all the involved units returned to their departure lines a few hours later.[114]

On Cuban advice, the FAPLA units then entrenched themselves on a dominating ridge flanked by marshes and a lagoon, where they constructed a number of well-concealed bunkers and protected fire-positions, connected by a network of trenches. Correspondingly, when the ELNA attempted to follow-up on its earlier success and attacked in the direction of Quifangondo, on 23 October, it found itself on the receiving end of a significant barrage and was stopped cold. After licking its wounds, the ELNA re-attacked at 0700hrs in the morning on 5 November, following a two-hour long mortar barrage, and supported by AMLs. Once again, the fire from mortars and Grad-1Ps, and a few ZPU-4s, forced it to withdraw. Despite this failure, and contrary to advice of Brigadier Ben de Wet Roos, SADF – who suggested an alternative route of advance – the ELNA commanders remained committed to their original plan. To a certain degree, they were right: outflanking Quifangondo would have been anything other than easy, as recalled by Commander N'Dalu, the FAPLA's Chief-of-Staff:

> Had they tried taking Luanda from the other more easterly road, which would have been viable, that would have taken them two to three months. Quifangondo looked like the best option, even if it meant they had to pass that 500 metres long corridor, where the road runs along a straight dyke surrounded by the marshes, and where they could not disperse their troops. That was where we had the advantage: we were on the heights.[115]

Concluding that additional fire-power was necessary to soften the enemy position, the FAZ deployed two M-46 130mm cannons on 7 November 1975. However, one of the cannons was damaged by a misfire and blew up immediately upon arrival, while the other was rendered non-operational by a less critical incident. The next evening, two C-130s of the SAAF arrived at Ambriz to unload a troop of the 14th Field Regiment, SADF, commanded by Captain Jacob van Heerden, equipped with three 5.5-In medium guns (one of which was non-operational). These guns were deployed to their firing positions by 9 November 1975, by when the SAAF also agreed to bomb the Angolan-Cuban position with three Canberra bombers.[116]

Carmona

This is not the say that the FNLA did not attempt to advance on a different axis. On 26 October, at least one of its battalions grouped with a battalion of the FAZ in Carmona. Supported by armoured cars, these two units then assaulted Samba Cajú, and – two days later – Quiangombe, threatening to continue all the way to N'Dalatando and Dondo. Alarmed by the prospect of losing a vital crossroad between Luanda, eastern and southern Angola, and a major hydroelectric power plant, the Cubans reinforced the CIR 1 with a battalion from CIR 3. Correspondingly, the MMCA reinforced the CIR 1 with a battalion fresh from training at CIR 3, two companies and one of its squadrons, supported by one platoon each of 12.7mm machine guns, 75mm recoilless guns and 82mm mortars. These ambushed the FNLA/FAZ force on 28 October, and – although

Caption: Foreign mercenaries with one of the ex-Zairian AML-90s marked with title 'ELNA', in northern Angola of November 1975. (Albert Grandolini Collection)

A SADF 5.5-In medium gun in action: as so often in 1975, the crew wore East German-made steel helmets, large supplies of which were captured during the advance into Southern Angola. (Albert Grandolini Collection)

FAZ troops moving up by truck towards the northern front to fight the FAPLA in November 1975. (Albert Grandolini Collection)

Peregrinations of a Grad Battery

One of the first BM-21s (installed on a Ural 375 truck) moving down the streets of Luanda in November 1975. (Albert Grandolini Collection)

As of the mid-1970s, and although in service for more than a decade, and having already earned itself the reputation of being a light, relatively simple-to-use system packing a tremendous amount of fire-power, the BM-21 MRLS was a relatively new and little-known weapon. When, a few weeks before Angolan independence, the Soviet Embassy staff in Brazzaville concluded that the MPLA was in urgent need of heavier weapons to face its rivals, the logical conclusion was to deliver BM-21s – and to do so by the means of airlift. However, such ideas were out of question for Moscow, which had already decided that no Soviet arms were to be delivered directly to Angola before its official independence. Instead, a full battery of six BM-21s was delivered on board three Antonov An-22 transports to Brazzaville. The operation was run in such secrecy that the Soviets risked landings at Pointe Noire airport, although this was cleared for aircraft weighting only up to 90 tonnes, while An-22s in question weighted around 130 tonnes on landing. Fearing they might damage the runway, the Soviets obtained special permission from the Congolese president for this affair.

Once the BM-21s were delivered, the Cubans hurriedly loaded the six vehicles, and all the associated equipment and ammunition, on their merchant La Plata and brought everything to Luanda on 7 November. There, the experts from the Camilio Cienfuegos Artillery School (who arrived the same day) readied all six vehicles for combat – only to realize that the fuses were missing. A related emergency request was promptly sent to Havana, which reacted by dispatching fuses from the FAR's inventory. Finally, on 10 November 1975, the BM-21 battery commanded by Commander Fernandez Gondín was declared operational and – in great secrecy – deployed behind the Quifangondo frontline. It was to play the role of the trump card in the coming battle.[118]

causing only limited casualties – forced the enemy to retreat. Indeed, during the following counter-attack, the Cuban-Angolan force easily retook Samba Cajú. After this defeat, Holden Roberto gave up attempts to launch a multi-prong offensive on Luanda, and concentrated all of FNLA's efforts on the Caxito – Luanda axis.[117]

Death Road

The day on which the ELNA-FAZ-SADF coalition wanted to deliver its decisive blow was 10 November 1975. At 0540hrs in the morning, SADF 5.5-In guns emplaced eleven kilometres from Quifangondo began lobbing shells on to the FAPLA positions. A few minutes later, the three Canberras unloaded their bombs on the same objective after a long flight all the way from Rundu in SWA. However, all of the high explosive unleashed on the combined FAPLA-MMCA positions had next to no effect: the Angolans and the Cubans were meanwhile not only well-entrenched, but their positions were actually unknown to the enemy. The Canberras, for example, released their bombs from a much too high altitude, out of concern they might get hit by ground fire, and thus missed their target. Similarly, a FAZ commando company sent to outflank and infiltrate the enemy defences found itself bogged down in the marshes, unable to advance. Therefore, the sole working element of the new offensive proved to be a repeat of the exercise from three weeks earlier: an advance of the Special Troops company, led by three AMLs, followed by a reinforced infantry column along the causeway in the direction of the ridge.

At first, the attackers came forward quite well: unknown to them, the FAPLA officers had ordered their troops to hold their fire

The livery of four Britannia 318s still operated by Cubana de Aviacion as of 1975 was generally the same: top and upper sides of the fuselage were painted in white, while the rest of the aircraft was left in bare metal overall. Format and size of that airline's insignia as applied on the fin were often different, and at least one aircraft wore them applied in entirely different fashion (compare with photo on p.). Although not entirely suited for the task, the type proved superior to any other transport aircraft available to Cuba at the time, and delivered the first few – crucial – groups of Cuban advisers to Angola. (Artwork by Tom Cooper)

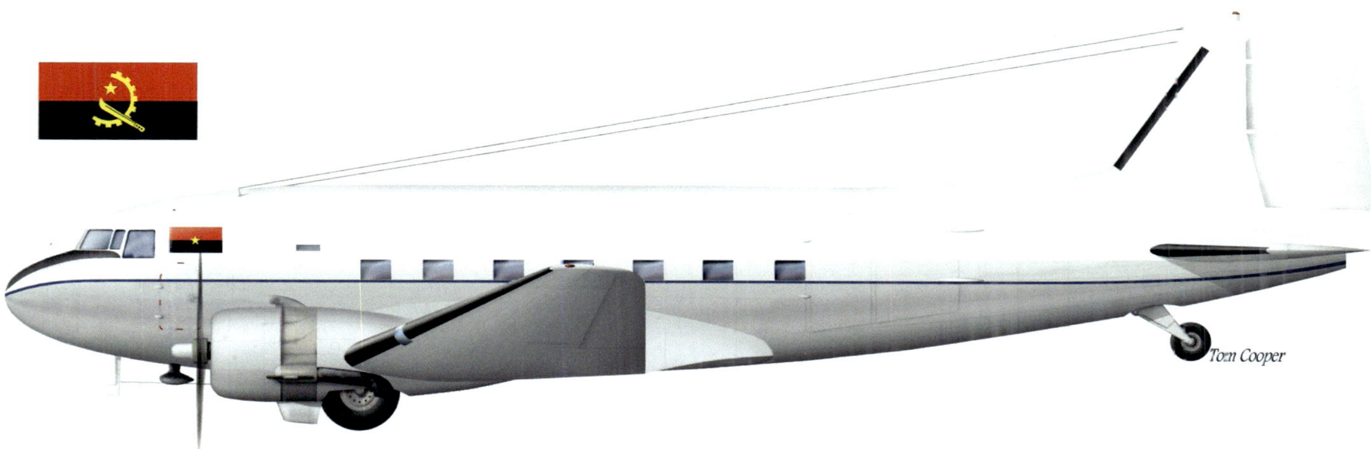

At least four C-47/DC-3s are known to have been inherited by the FAPA/DAA when that air force came into being in January 1976. At least two of these were former mounts of the Portuguese Air Force (including the former serial 6164). Both were left in their original livery, with the top of the fuselage in white, and the rest of the aircraft in aluminium colour. Whether any serials or registrations were applied as of January 1976 remains unknown: it is possible a civilian registration was applied on the front lower part of the fin. (Artwork by Tom Cooper)

Based on a still from a rather poor-quality documentary movie aired in Cuba, this is a reconstruction of one of six ex-Diamang Alouette IIIs that the Cuban troops found at Luanda IAP in November 1975. The helicopter seems to have had its top surfaces and sides painted in green, and the lower surfaces (including those of the boom) either in white, or a very light shade of blue or grey. No national markings were visible, but it is possible that they had received small codes or serials in yellow, half-way down the boom. No national markings are known to have been applied, although the two SA.315B Lamas found on the same occasion are known to have worn early FAPA/DAA roundels. (Artwork by Tom Cooper)

Theoretically, the first jet aircraft with combat capability in service with the FAPA/DAA was the sole MiG-15UTI delivered to Luanda in early January 1976. The aircraft was painted in light admiralty grey (BS381C/697) overall, and initially wore the serial C31, as shown here: this was subsequently changed to I11. Instead of the new national flag of Angola or a fin flash, it had the lower half of the ruder painted in Angolan national colours: this was to become typical for all Cuban-flown MiG-17s and MiG-21s of the FAPA/DAA. Inset is shown the crest of the Angolan air force. (Artwork by Tom Cooper)

The first – and only – batch of MiG-17Fs to enter service with the FAPA/DAA were nine examples delivered in January 1976. Serialed C20 to C28, they were all initially painted in the same light admiralty grey as the sole MiG-15UTI. Angolan national colours were applied on the ruder, but it remains unclear if roundels were applied in four or only two positions on the wing. According to the recollections of Cuban pilots, all had their maintenance stencils applied in French, indicating that Angola was not their original destination. Armed with S-5 57mm unguided rockets and internal cannons, they saw sporadic combat service between February and June 1976, primarily in south-eastern Angola. (Artwork by Tom Cooper)

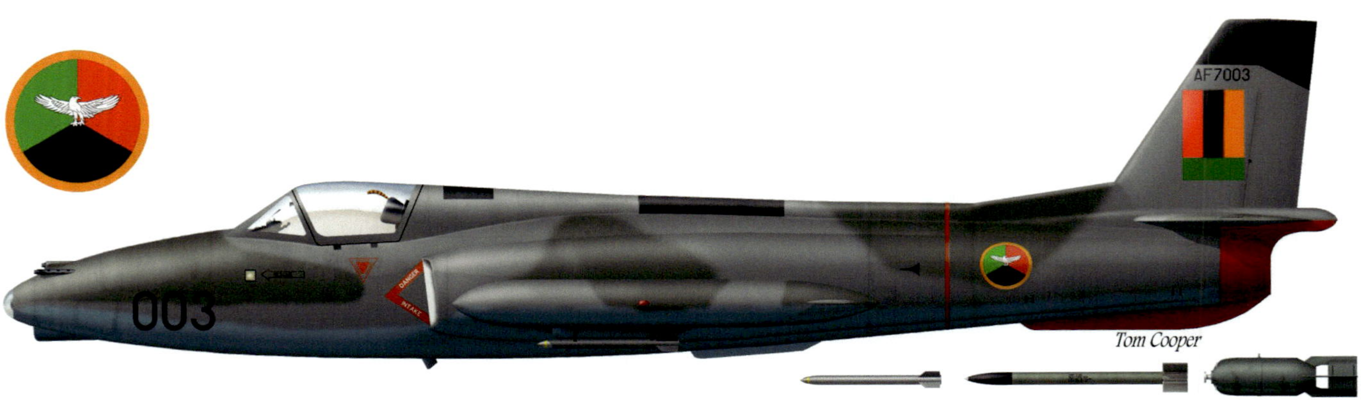

The least-well-known type that saw combat service in Angola during the period covered in this book were the SOKO G-2A Galebs (two-seaters) and J-21 Jastrebs (single-seaters) of the Zambian Air Force. Zambia was the launching customer for both of these light jets of Yugoslav design: it should have received 15 G-2A two-seat jet trainers and 18 J-21s light strikers, starting in 1971, but it remains unknown if all of these were delivered. It is certain that J-21s received serials in the range AF7001 upwards, and G-2As serials in the range AF8001 upwards, of which the 'last three' (on J-21s) or the 'last two' (on G-2As) were repeated on the forward fuselage. The standardised camouflage pattern on both variants consisted of RAF Dark Sea Grey (FS26152) and RAF Dark Green (FS24079) on top surfaces, and light blue (FS25107) on undersurfaces. Armament consisted of three internal 12.7mm machine guns, up to two 100-250 kilogram bombs, and either six HVAR-5 127mm unguided rockets, or up to 24 57mm S-5 rockets. (Artwork by Tom Cooper)

C40 was the first of 12 MiG-21MFs delivered to Angola in January 1976. All were newly-manufactured, and camouflaged in different variants of what should have been (but rarely was) a standardised camouflage pattern, consisting of beige (BS381C/388), and either grey-green (BS381C/283) or olive drab (BS381C/437) on upper surfaces and sides, and light admiralty grey (BS381C/697) on undersurfaces. The aircraft are not known to have worn any kind of roundels: only Angolan national colours over the full ruder. (Artwork by Tom Cooper)

As of early 1976, the primary armament of Cuban-flown, Angolan-owned MiG-21MFs consisted of UB-16-57 rocket pods for S-5 57mm unguided rockets, S-24 240mm unguided rockets, and FAB-250M-62 250 kilogram bombs. However, on his last combat mission in the country, del Pino flew the C-41 loaded with two of the rather unusual UB-32-57 pods for S-5 rockets installed under outboard underwing pylons. (Artwork by Tom Cooper)

The last new type to enter service with the FAPA/DAA as of early 1976 were four Mil Mi-8MT helicopters. Delivered from the USSR, they were left in their dark olive green overall colour (bottom surfaces were painted in light admiralty grey). Large serials H01 to H04 were applied in yellow on the top centre of the cabin, roundels on the rear fuselage, and national colours on the fin. Flown by Cuban crews for the first few years of service, three of them were written off: the fourth example was brought to Cuba, but found in such poor condition that it was beyond repair. Although primarily used for transport and liaison purposes, they were nearly always armed, usually with a pair of UB-16-57 rocket pods. (Artwork by Tom Cooper)

The first armoured vehicle in service with the FAPLA was the BRDM-2 armoured car, more than 100 of which were delivered from the USSR by March 1976. Each was armed with a single, turret-mounted 14.5mm heavy machine gun, and a co-axial 7.62mm machine gun (with manual traverse and elevation). In a rush to press as many of them into service as possible, and then deploy them on the battlefield, most of them received no markings at all: very few vehicles were seen marked with a single red star on the hull side. (Artwork by David Bocquelet)

The next armoured vehicle to enter service with the FAPLA was the BTR-152: the first Soviet armoured personnel carrier to enter mass production. The type proved highly popular in Angola, especially because of its capability to inflate or deflate its tyres, adapting to the ground for better grip and traction. Armament usually consisted of a single SGMB 7.62mm light machine gun installed in front of the troop compartment. Illustrated is the BTR-152K variant, which had armour plating over the top of its troop compartment: most of BTR-152s delivered to Angola remained open-topped. (Artwork by David Bocquelet)

The first tanks to officially enter service with FAPLA were 22 T-34/85s ordered for the 9th BRIM. However, it seems that the T-34/85s of a single company assigned to the Third Motorised Infantry Battalion FAR (3 Bon IM) saw action at around the same time. All seem to have been left in their dark green livery, applied before delivery, and are not known to have worn any kind of markings. (Artwork by David Bocquelet)

Although not cited in any of the published Cuban sources of reference, one of the FAR units deployed in Luanda, and then in northern Angola as of late 1975 and early 1976 had also a company of PT-76 amphibious tanks attached. As usual, these were left in their dark green overall livery, and wore no other markings. (Artwork by David Bocquelet)

The primary armoured personnel carriers of the 3 Bon IM were 30 BTR-60s. Delivered form Soviet stocks, all were left in their original dark green overall livery. Very few are known to have worn any kind of markings: this example has received the number 100, possibly indicating one of two vehicles assigned to the company commander. The BTR-60 was armed with the same turret as that mounted on the BRDM-2, and containing a 14.5mm heavy machine gun and a 7.62mm light machine gun. (Artwork by David Bocquelet)

Theoretically, the first direct equivalent to the FAPLA-operated BRDM-2s should have been Panhard AML-90 armoured cars from Zairean stocks, donated to the FNLA. All of these were left in their dark green livery, as painted before delivery. Designed on basis of experiences from the Algerian War, these fast, cheap, and simple to maintain and operate vehicles have proven highly popular in service. While not as mobile cross-country as the BRDM-2, their Giat F1 gun made them vastly superior in firepower. However, the FNLA and its allies made very little effective use of them, whether in northern Angola, or in the Cabinda enclave. (Artwork by David Bocquelet).

The Panhard M3 was a small, wheeled armoured personnel carrier with amphibious capability, that was widely exported in the 1970s, about 60 of which were sold to Zaire – which in turn provided several to the FNLA. Very little is known about their service with Holden Roberto: apparently left in their dark green overall colour applied before delivery, nearly all – if not most – were operated by foreign mercenaries, and at least a handful were knocked out in combat operations. Their armament usually consisted of a single FN MAG 7.62mm machine gun. (Artwork by David Bocquelet)

The primary armoured car deployed by the SADF during Operation Savannah was the Eland Mk.7. Originally a version of the AML-90, externally, it looked almost the same, though it consisted of components made in South Africa. Nevertheless, it did include a number of minor improvements, including a dome-shaped commander's cupola, making it weigh slightly more than the original. The primary weapon was the low-velocity Denel GT-2 90mm cannon: while still highly effective during the fighting in 1975 and 1976, this was to prove barely sufficient in following years. (Artwork by David Bocquelet)

The Eland 60 was the South African variant of the AML-60 – a vehicle armed with a breech-loading 60mm mortar instead of the 90mm cannon. Like the Eland Mk.7, it earned itself a fearful reputation early during Operation Savannah, where Elands became known as 'Red Ants' – because of the unorthodox, but highly effective tactics of combining their high mobility with swarming of the enemy. On the negative side, their low clearance over the ground made them susceptible to getting struck in thick bush, they lacked amphibious capability, and their low silhouettes made sighting difficult. (Artwork by David Bocquelet)

Map of Angola, showing major directions of the FNLA's advance from the north, and the South African Operation Savannah, in the south. (Map by Tom Cooper)

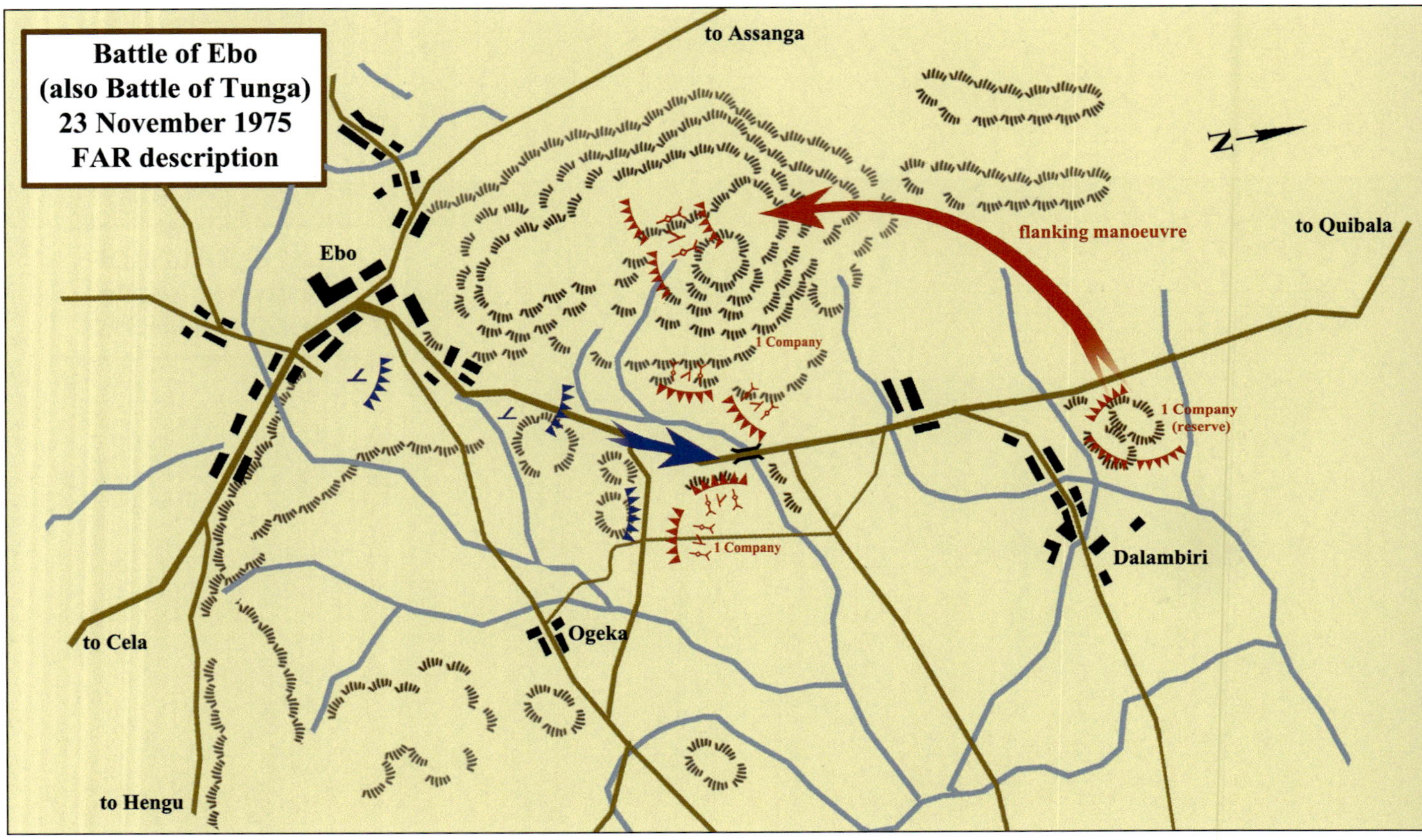

Map of the Battle of Ebo (also known as the Battle of Tunga to the Angolans and Cubans), in the course of which a combined Angolan-Cuban task force stopped the advance of Battle Group Foxbat over the Mabassa River on 23 November 1975. (Map by Tom Cooper)

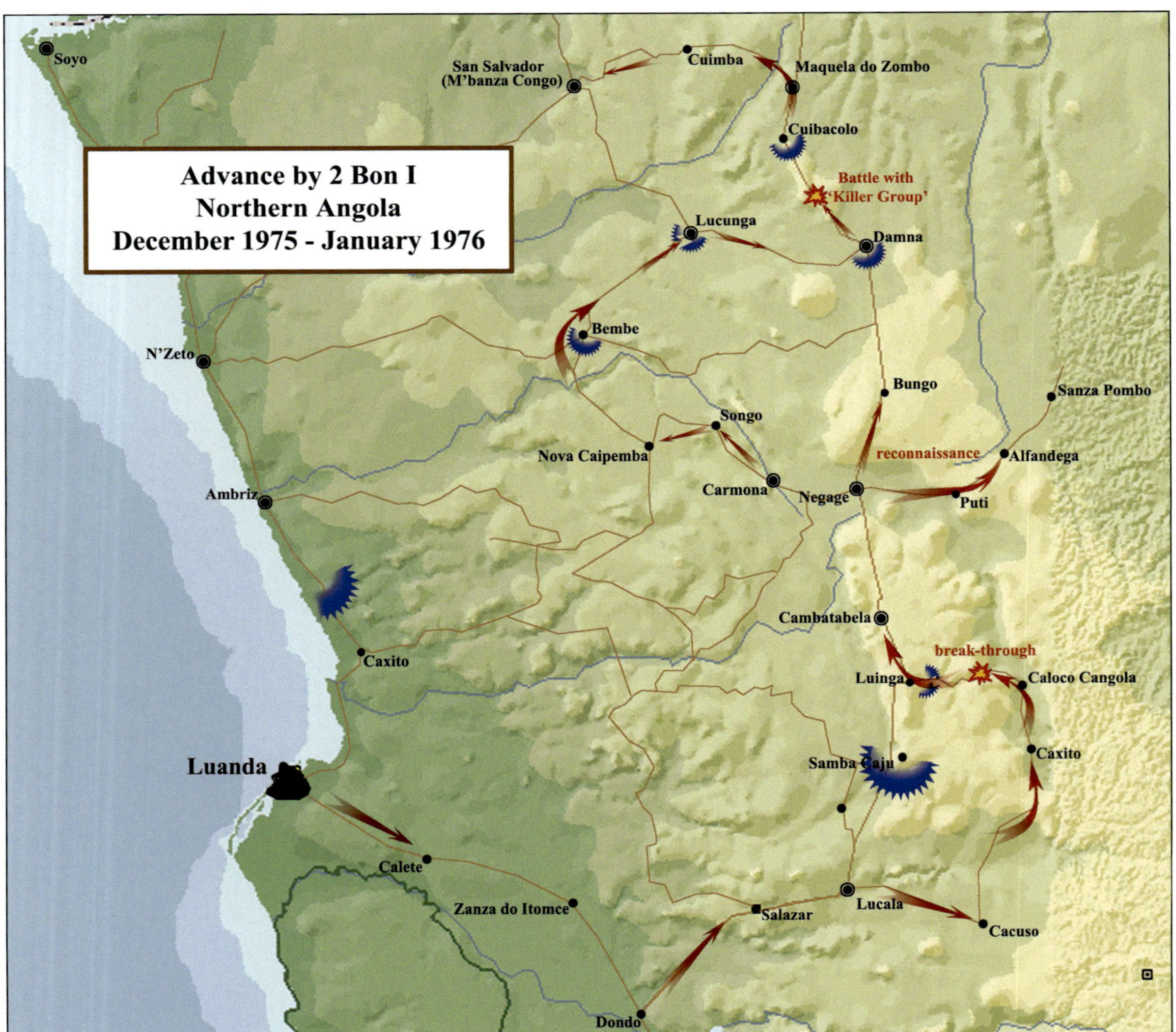

A reconstruction of the advance by the 2 Bon I of the FAPLA into northern Angola, between December 1975 and March 1976 – an operation run along the methods of Auftragstaktik, and in the best traditions of manoeuvring warfare, even if at a much-reduced pace. (Map by Tom Cooper)

A Cuban mortar team setting up their 120mm tube, outside Quifangondo, in November 1975. (Albert Grandolini Collection)

and wait for the enemy to close the range. The battle thus began when the ELNA-FAZ column was only a hundred metres from the forward Angolan position. All a sudden, it was subjected to the concentrated fire of multiple recoilless rifles, ZPUs, machine guns and mortars that promptly disabled one AML-90 and one AML-60 each. The ELNA infantry suffered heavy losses, while the Zairian commandos were pinned down. Worse yet, the SADF's artillery battery found itself on the receiving end of a volley of BM-21s, some of which exploded close enough to wound one of the gunners. Thus, forced to change position, the South Africans were out of the game for a while. The next volley of BM-21s then targeted a chicken farm where an ELNA unit was grouping before following the advancing column. Finally, the Cuban battery re-adjusted its fire to plaster the column scattered down the road with volleys of 20 rockets at a time. A few hours later, after between 700 and 2,000 rockets were fired, the ELNA-FAZ offensive was converted into a rout, with the uncontrollable mob fleeing in the direction of Morro da Cal and Caxito. More than 120 were killed, while around 200 dazed survivors were taken prisoners of war. The FAPLA and its Cuban allies lost exactly one killed and five wounded (including two Cubans).[119]

Quifangondo proved a decisive battle in northern Angola, because it destroyed any hope of the FNLA to seize Luanda before the independence day. Furthermore, it ruined the morale of the ELNA and FAZ troops, and ended the South African involvement on this frontline: the SADF gunners withdrew all the way to Ambriz, abandoned their guns to the care of the ELNA (that had

The victorious crew of the Cuban BM-21 battery that proved crucial during the battle on the Death Road on 10 November 1975. (Albert Grandolini Collection)

A group of ELNA combatants captured by the FAPLA during the fighting in the Quifangondo area in November 1975. (Albert Grandolini Collection)

to haul them all the way back to Zaire), and evacuated aboard the frigate SAS *President Styen*.

That Strategically Important Enclave …

Renowned for its opulent sources of crude oil, Cabinda – the area covered by dense tropical forests which the Portuguese unilaterally joined with their overseas territory of Angola despite its own history and separation by Zaire – attracted the attention of multiple local, regional and international powers of the mid-1970s. The primary local actor was the Front for the Liberation of the Enclave of Cabinda (*Frente para a Libertação do Enclave de Cabinda*, FLEC): a movement seeking the independence of this enclave – from Portugal, but also from Angola – established on 4 August 1963 through the fusion of diverse autonomist groups. Over time, the FLEC gained support of several foreign powers, such as France, then Zaire, but also the USA and Congo-Brazzaville. Clearly, this had deleterious effects on the movement's cohesiveness, and resulted in the emergence of several rival factions. By 1967, the FLEC was already split into a group led by Ranque Franque, based in Kinshasa, and another group, led by Henriques Tiago Nzita, based in Brazzaville (and, reportedly, supported by Paris). Quarrels between them had a clearly detrimental effect upon the FLEC's effectiveness on the battlefield, and by the early 1970s its activities inside Cabinda were still very limited.[120]

Following the Carnation Revolution, the local Portuguese authorities granted permission for the FLEC to establish its own bases and, by mid-1974, the movement created its armed wing, the Cabinda Armed Forces (*Forcas Armadas Cabindesas*, FAC), which was massively reinforced through the recruitment of several

French mercenaries and FAZ officers during a conference prior to the invasion of Cabinda. (Albert Grandolini Collection)

hundreds of the former Special Troops of the Portuguese army. However, in October 1974, the Portuguese changed their opinion and began supporting the MPLA instead: insisting on Cabinda remaining a part of Angola, regardless of its non-related history and backgrounds, this brought Neto's movement on a collision course with the FLEC. Indeed, on 1 November 1974, the MPLA suddenly brought all the vital installations in Cabinda City under its control, and expelled – almost without any fighting – the surprised FLEC out of the Enclave.[121]

Despite its weakness, and a very limited (if any) presence, the FLEC subsequently established relations with France, USA and Zaire – all of which were more than keen to prevent the 'Marxist' MPLA from establishing itself in control of Cabinda. That's where all the common interests of the three Western allies were ended: the French were eager to help their companies breach the US monopoly on the enclave's oil resources, Mobutu sought to establish a rich puppet state, while the Americans were sympathetic to the ambitions of what they perceived as their closest ally in this part of Africa. The US Secretary of Defence, James Schlesinger was once quoted:

> We might wish to encourage the disintegration of Angola. Cabinda in the clutches of Mobutu would mean far greater security of the petroleum resources.[122]

Correspondingly, Washington began supporting Zairian designs in regards of support for the Ranque Franque's faction of the FLEC through training of a force of between 800 and 2,000 in several camps close to Tshela. In September 1975, Mobutu further asserted his control over the FLEC by replacing Franque with Tiago Nzita, who was appointed the president of the movement and the commander of its armed wing. The FAC was immediately purged, and around 20 of its cadres – mostly former NCOs in the Portuguese army – were demoted and jailed.[123] Meanwhile, the Zairians exploited their close ties to the External Documentation and Counter-Intelligence Service (*Service de documentation Extérieure et de contre-espionnage*, SDECE) of France, with a request for additional support. The SDECE quickly brought the famous mercenary Bob Denard into the game – despite his history of opposition to Mobutu. Indeed, a few weeks later, a team of ten mercenaries (led by René Dulac, alias Lieutenant-Colonel Victor, and including Guy Cardinal, René Renzi, Serge Bréaud, Paul Bessy, Roger Caillon, and Raymond Thomann) arrived in Zaire with the objective of training the FAC insurgents, most of the weapons for which were provided from sources in the USA (from the budget for the FNLA).[124]

The result of this cooperation was a plan along which the FAC – organised into three battalions, and led by the ten French mercenaries – would cross the border, dash for Cabinda City, and quickly seize the same in a matter of one day, at most. Following several postponements, this operation was initiated on 2 November 1975, when the insurgents and mercenaries moved in the direction of the border, reinforced by a battalion of Zairian troops from the Kamanoyla Division.[125]

Bracing for the Onslaught

For the MPLA and the Cubans, Cabinda was of crucial importance. Correspondingly, nearly half of the original MMCA was deployed there to man one of four CIRs – the No.4 in Cabinda. The commander of the Cuban detachment in the enclave, Commander Ramón Espinosa Martín, arrived in early September 1975, and was followed by 142 out of 192 Cuban troops that arrived aboard two charter flights on 4 October. Shipments of weapons (including one battery of M-30 122mm howitzers, two batteries of 120mm mortars, two batteries of 14.5mm ZPU-4 anti-aircraft machine guns, and two platoons of 75mm recoilless rifles), ammunition, supplies and vehicles followed on board the ships *La Plata* and *Coral Island* on 14 and 22 October 1975, respectively, and 39 additional weapons specialists had arrived by early November. With the help of these troops and armaments, the Cubans planned to train and equip a FAPLA battalion at the CIR 4. Correspondingly, the Cubans established a training camp within the former Portuguese army base at Dinge, on the road connecting Lãndana with Buco Zau, about 80 kilometres (50 miles) from Cabinda City, on 27 September. Training of FAPLA recruits – primarily those already deployed within Cabinda – began almost immediately. Furthermore, on 15 October, CIR 4 opened a new training facility at Lãndana with intention of establishing a second battalion with recruits sent in from Benguela and Lobito. Thus, out of 231 Cuban officers and other ranks deployed in Cabinda as of the time, 8 were attached to the HQ of the CIR 4, 85 to the training section, 90 to the first battalion, 43 to the second battalion, and five to the medical post, as detailed in Table 8.[126]

Table 8: CIR No 4, Cuban Order of Battle, 1 November 1975

Unit	Number of MMCA personnel attached
Headquarters	8
2 infantry battalions	76
Engineer company	3
Support company	38
Medical post	6
Two mortar batteries 120mm	25
Two mortar batteries 82mm	8
Two ZPU-4 batteries	25
Howitzer battery	32
Four heavy machine gun platoons	4
Two platoons of 75mm recoilless rifles	6

However, towards late October 1975, the MMCA and the FAPLA received intelligence about two 'brigade-sized' forces of the FAC and the FAZ deploying near the border and preparing to launch an invasion. According to the information provided, the two units in question included more than 1,000 FAC combatants organized into

Troops of the first of two FAPLA battalions trained by the CIR 4 during the graduation ceremony from their basic training. (Albert Grandolini Collection)

three battalions, around 1,000 FAZ troops and 150 mercenaries, all lavishly armed and supported – including a full squadron of AML armoured cars, several batteries of 81mm and 106mm mortars, one battery of 105mm howitzers, and one 'tank company'. As can be seen from the description in the previous sub-chapter, this assessment was quite precise, even if the available firepower of the combined FAC/FAZ force was slightly overestimated: after all, it included all the heavy weapons the Zairians had in the west of their country at the time.

Having 210 kilometres (130 miles) of border to defend, but very few troops on hand, the FAR Commander Ramón Espinosa Martín, in cooperation with FAPLA commanders Zacarías Pinto ('Bolingó') and Pedro Bera Lima ('Fogotao') had developed a contingency plan. The first FAPLA battalion trained by CIR 4 was mobilised – although having compled only a part of its basic training – and reinforced by Cuban advisors. Furthermore, Espinosa Martín received reinforcement in the form of several FAPLA squadrons experienced in guerrilla warfare, reinforced with Grad-1P launchers delivered directly to the MPLA. Martín thus deployed his units for defence in depth. He distributed several platoon-sized detachments of lightly armed FAPLA guerrillas along the border to Zaire, with the task of monitoring the most likely enemy routes of advance – of which, due to the rugged local terrain and dense jungle – there were not many (indeed, the most obvious one was the 24 kilometres [15 miles] long road connecting Cabinda City with Iema, on the border to Zaire). The task of these units was to slow down a potential invader and report to the MMCA command, so that the latter could identify the main enemy axis of advance. To ease their task, Cuban engineers and the guerrillas deployed several minefields – combining about 500 anti-personnel and anti-tank mines across the expected crossing points.

The first FAPLA battalion – the unit that had recently graduated from basic training – was deployed in the N'To area. Positioned to block the road from Iema to Cobinda City, its first two companies established well-concealed lines of trenches atop a small hill near the village of Buca. Decoy positions – all still well-camouflaged – were laid in front of the same, to attract enemy fire. The third company

A ZPU-1 heavy machine gun mounted on a Unimog chassis, seen on the streets of Luanda before deployment to northern Angola in November 1975. (Albert Grandolini Collection)

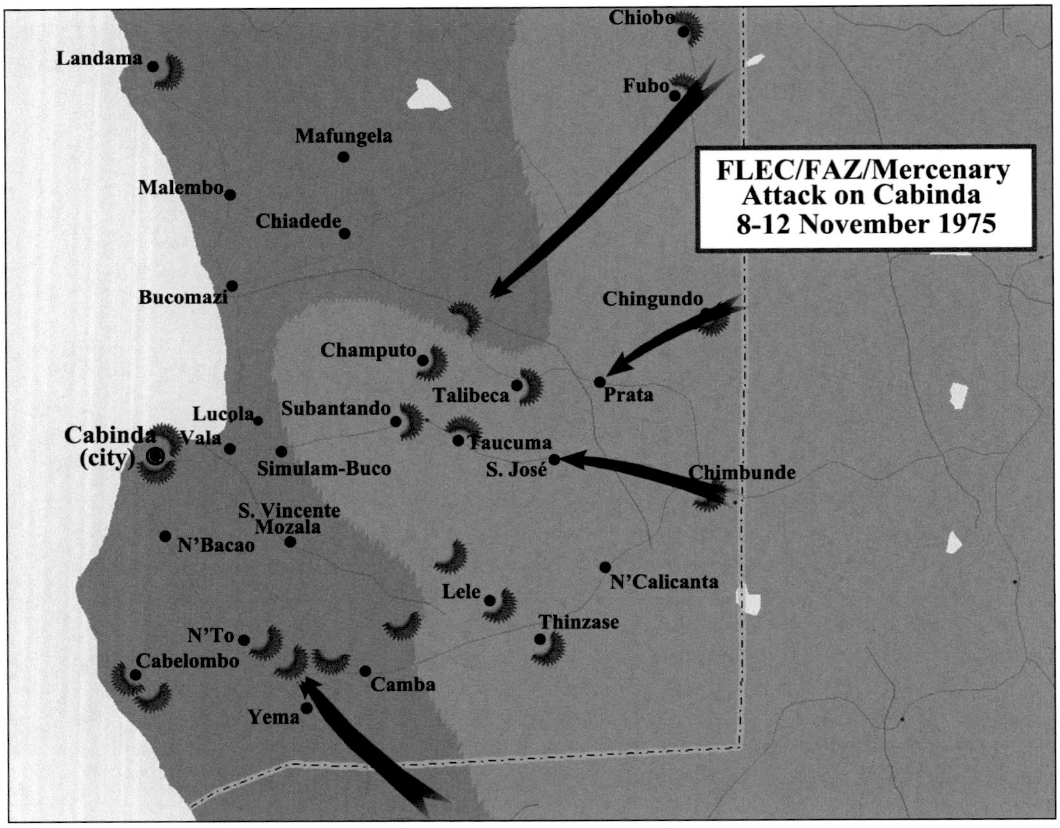

Map showing primary positions of the combined MMCA/FAPLA forces in the Cabinda enclave, diversionary attacks of the combined FLEC/FAZ/mercenary forces in the north, and direction of the major attack from the south. (Map by Tom Cooper)

held the second line of defences, while one of its platoons was held back in reserve. Essentially, this was a text-book trap, because the battalion could call upon massive volumes of support fire. In addition to its organic 82mm mortar battery, 75mm recoilless guns, and heavy machine guns, it was supported by one battery of M-30 howitzers, one battery of 120mm mortars, and one battery of ZPU-4s, all of which were attached to it.

The second FAPLA-battalion, which did not even complete its basic training, was meanwhile re-deployed to Dinge: while continuing its training, it was reinforced by the other mortar platoon and the second ZPU-4 battery of the MMCA, while held back as strategic reserve that could, if necessary, be re-deployed to either reinforce the first battalion, or to meet an enemy advance from the east, along the two tracks connecting the border villages of Chingundo and Chimbuande with Baca. This option was of particular importance, because an advance of the enemy through Subantando and Dingo would virtually cut off the first battalion from Cabinda City. Finally, and although this was the least-expected option, the second battalion was in a good position to move on Buco Zau, in the case of any enemy advance from Kimongo. Finally, a small FAPLA-detachment equipped with two ZPU-1s and two recoilless guns was ordered to entrench in Lãndana, with the task of preventing any amphibious landing in that area.[127]

Even so, the defence of the enclave that was considered a 'strategic asset' was effectively depending on 1,000 troops at most, the majority of which was anything other than 'combat ready'. To add salt to injury, the MMCA command then ordered a re-deployment of 40 Cuban artillerists – including one battery of heavy mortars and one battery of ZPU-4s – to Luanda, from where they were deployed to reinforce the Quifongondo front.[128]

The Four-Days Campaign

The combined offensive of the FAC and the FAZ was initiated on the morning of 8 November 1975, when its first troops crossed the border into the Cabinda Enclave and – exactly as foreseen by Martín – launched a multi-pronged attack from south and east. In the east, the invaders easily reached Chingundo and Chimbunde: although the minefields slowed down their advance, they annihilated the local FAPLA platoon while forcing others to withdraw towards Subantando. Setting his plan into motion, Martín reacted by deploying one company of the second FAPLA-battalion towards Chingundo, and another to Chimbunde, to reinforce allies deployed there. The third company remained in Dinge, to cover their rear. This triggered two days of confused fighting: the company sent to reinforce Chimbunde was ambushed during the night of 8 to 9 November, lost three fighters and fell back in disorder, leaving two 82mm mortars behind it.

By the morning, the Cubans helped settle their panicked allies, and organized a new defensive line, five kilometres (three miles) east of Buca, protected by mines, and a platoon each of ZPU-4s and Grad-1Ps. Several small platoons were sent into reconnaissance: although one of these was ambushed, they provided enough timely warning of the FAC's general attack on the defences of Buka, launched on the morning of 10 November 1975. Waiting patiently until the enemy approached their defence line, the Cubans and Angolans then opened a devastating barrage that combined the fast-firing ZPU-4s and Grad-1Ps. Severely shaken, the insurgents reorganized enough to launch few half-hearted efforts, later on and on the next morning, but none of these was seriously threatening for the defenders. Meanwhile, Martín deployed elements from the second FAPLA-battalion and some of the guerrillas into small-scale counter-attacks on enemy flanks. While resulting in a very fluid situation in which each side attempted to ambush the other, they provided very unsettling for his enemy, which was additionally subjected to constant mortar barrages.[129]

Satisfied with the way things were developing, on the morning of 11 November Martín concentrated the second FAPLA-battalion for a counter-attack on Chingundo and Chimbunde. Because of very dense vegetation, he deployed it into two company-sized task forces. Each of these was preceded by one infantry platoon, followed by the other two advancing on either side in the rear. ZPU-4s were usually 300-400 metres in the rear and – whenever necessary – rushed to a distance of 50-100 metres behind their own infantry, before opening fire. Finally, mortar-teams followed 600-800 metres behind. Correspondingly, any enemy position detected was nearly instantly subjected to a hail of fire from small-arms, heavy machine guns and then mortar barrage. These tactics proved highly effective against an already demoralized enemy. Indeed, on several occasion a few mortar bombs proved more than enough to force the FAC and the FAZ to run away. Unsurprisingly, by the evening of 11 November, the second FAPLA-battalion in Cabinda advanced all the way to the border, and established itself in control of Chingundo and Chimbunde.

However, the main blow of the FAC came from the south, where a battalion of insurgents advancing from Lema was supported by a battalion of the FAZ, the bulk of the French mercenaries, a squadron of AML-60s and AML-90s, at least one mortar battery, and a battery of 105mm howitzers. Nevertheless, things quickly went awry: the initial advance was stopped by heavy rain, which caused most of the vehicles to become bogged down in the mud. When the column started moving again, it ran into an ambush set up by small FAPLA units that were screening the border. Although the Angolans were quickly dispersed into the jungle, this fire-fight alerted the commander of the first FAPLA-battalion. At 0600hrs, he dispatched a mixed Angolan-Cuban patrol to investigate. The latter found the opposition soon afterwards: it set up an ambush and killed – amongst others – Roger Caillon, one of the French mercenaries. Worse was to follow: the withdrawal of the Angolans and Cubans left the mercenaries, the FAC, and the FAZ with the impression that they had just won a major battle against the bulk of the FAPLA in Cabinda, and made them overconfident. Correspondingly, their column resumed its advance up the road without any further reconnaissance or other usual precautions. Unsurprisingly, they drove straight into the deadly trap set by Martín: bunched together within what was a very small area, upon which the Cubans and Angolans poured immense volumes of pre-registered fire. After the first AML was knocked out by a shell from a 75mm recoilless gun from only a few dozens of metres, the Cabindan and Zairian troops were virtually massacred by fire from multiple ZPU-4s. Despite this blow, the survivors reorganized and launched an attack on the flank of the Angolan-Cuban position. Despite support from their mortars and howitzers, this proved a futile exercise due to the massive volumes of defensive fire. Furthermore, the Cuban team operating six M-30 howitzers – commanded by 1st Lieutenant Fray Delgado – began targeting enemy artillery: it not only silenced two mortar positions, but even one of the enemy artillery spotters. After enduring this for several hours, the attacking force was decimated: according to one of the survivors of this catastrophe, the French mercenary René Dulac, 280 Cabindans and Zairians were either killed or wounded in this clash. The survivors were thus left without a choice but to retreat into Zaire. Some of their casualties were evacuated by helicopters of the FAZA, while the Cubans and Angolans subsequently claimed the destruction of four AMLs, and the capture of two 81mm mortars, and a jeep mounting a heavy machine gun. In turn, 2 Cubans and 63 Angolans were killed in action during all of these engagements.[130]

Finally, and also as expected by Espinosa Martín, the FAC did launch a small-scale amphibious landing at Lândana with the help of a flotilla of small boats. However, this quickly collapsed when one of the boats was damaged by a lucky hit from a Grad-1P.

In retrospect, the combined invasion of Cabindan, Zairian, and mercenary forces was a reasonably well-planned affair, including a diversionary blow on Buca, followed immediately by a major advance from Iema to Cabinda city, in turn helped by an amphibious landing on the enemy rear. However, it was based on insufficient reconnaissance and it failed to take into consideration the comparatively massive firepower delivered by the Soviets to the enclave, and the presence of Cuban advisors and artillerymen – who knew how to use their arms efficiently. On the other hand, the blunders committed by the FAC/FAZ force and the French mercenaries can at least be partly explained by the mutual distrust between their officers. Indeed, according to René Dulac, the failure came first and foremost because of the 'hopelessness' of the FAC fighters. In turn, many of the latter suspected that the French mercenaries were Cuban spies and gave away all the positions and plans in advance, and blamed the foreigners for failing to exploit their early successes decisively by ordering them to delay their advance. Unsurprisingly, the mercenaries were later to blame the FAC for their insistence on assaulting a stronger enemy. In the end, and although the Cabinda battle was relatively short and limited, it proved to be a decisive victory because – by retaining control over its precious resources – the MPLA kept the means to wage the war in the longer term.

CHAPTER 7
CRISIS IN THE SOUTH

Following the seizure of Lobito, Task Force Zulu of the SADF had reached all the original objectives defined by Pretoria. For a while at least, the government of South Africa had considered withdrawing its troops, but the increasing Cuban presence made it obvious that both the FNLA and UNITA would be unable to hold the ground they had secured so far. The latter issue became of particular significance considering the announcement by the OAU to decide which government – one run by the MPLA, or the one run by the FNLA-UNITA alliance – it would endorse as legitimate in January 1976. However, what the SADF expected to achieve by re-launching its advance towards north remained 'sketchy', to put it mildly: while both Angolan and Cuban historiography usually consider Luanda as the ultimate South African objective, there are no clear statements in this regard from the other side. Certain is only that it took the politicians and top military commanders in South Africa several days to discuss what to do next, and issue orders for the next phase of the Operation Savannah. Also certain is that the resumption of the advance by TFZ was to see this moving northwards along the coast to seize Nova Redondo (renamed Sumbe), and Porto Amboim. Meanwhile, Task Force Foxbat was to leave the coastal areas and resume its primary duty further inland.

Meeting Engagement

TFZ moved north, with Battle Group Alpha in front, on 10 November 1975. Initially, the advance was rapid and flawless, encountering only a few minor FAPLA ambushes along the road to Sumbe. However, the days-long lull had allowed the mauled FAPLA-MMCA forces from the Benguela CIR to reorganize themselves, get reinforced and establish new defence positions further north. In particular, a mixed force of Cuban advisors and FAPLA troops led by Commandante Eustaquio Nodarse Bonet prepared a carefully camouflaged position just behind a bridge on the Quicombo River, around 19 kilometres (11 miles) south of Sumbe. While this was an expertly chosen site, on a place where the road made an S-turn right into the local pass, it cannot be denied that the defenders made a mistake when failing to destroy the bridge – thus losing the chance of stopping the enemy for quite a while.

Early on the morning of 11 November, Battle Group Alpha – preceded by an Eland troop – arrived at the bridge, but failed to detect any enemy presence nearby. Correspondingly, it continued the advance. The ambushers left the armoured cars to approach and enter the S-turn, before opening fire and quickly knocking out two armoured cars. BGA's mortar platoon quickly reacted with fire-action, but did so in full view of the FAPLA-MMCA position and was promptly targeted by multiple mortars. One bomb fell right in the middle of the South African position, injuring 18 troops – of whom one subsequently died. Commandant Lindford was thus left without a choice but to order a withdrawal, and then regroup one kilometre south of the bridge.

Next, the SADF attempted to approach the ambush position in methodical fashion. A troop of four 25-Pdrs under Captain Chris Bouwer began plastering enemy position with airburst shells. When his troops began suffering losses, and concluding he had completed his mission, Nodarse Bonet thus ordered a withdrawal at dusk. The next morning, Battle Group Bravo took the lead, and seized Sumbe without encountering any significant resistance – until Kassanje, the local Political Commissar of the MPLA, rallied several dozens of retreating soldiers and launched a counterattack. Unsurprisingly, lightly armed and inexperienced Angolans were decimated by South African artillery and the commissar paid the ultimate price for his bravery.[131]

Unknown to all involved parties, the fall of Sumbe marked the high tide of Operation Savannah. Namely, as soon as the northern threat to Luanda had been dealt with, the Cubans rushed all available reinforcements in the southern direction. On 11 November, the 1st Company of the MININT Special Force was deployed in direction of Porto Amboim, followed by the 2nd Company a day later, and then the 3rd. To accelerate their march, some of these troops were flown directly from Luanda IAP on board FAPLA's C-47s. The Cuban BM-21 battery reached Porto Amboim around the same time. Furthermore, the N'Dalantando CIR had dispatched a Cuban-led battalion to protect Quibala: commanded by Prima Commandante Eulister Estrada, this unit was reinforced to a total of five infantry companies by 11 November.

After reconnoitring the area, Cuban commanders decided to use the Queve River – swollen by the rainy season, and having its banks surrounded by high ground and cliffs – as a new line of defence. Unknown to them was the fact that this was to make the Queve a formidable obstacle, simply because advancing SADF units carried no bridging equipment with them. Correspondingly, while Special Troops of the MMCA rushed to blow up all the bridges, thus cutting the roads connecting Suambe with Porto Amboim and Gabela, other units hurriedly constructed extensive and well-concealed fortifications. Overall, by mid-November 1975, the FAR, MMCA and FAPLA troops had established a cohesive frontline, running nearly 160 kilometres (100 miles) along the Queve River, from Porto Amboim to Quibala. This was occupied by a full battalion of the MININT, the combined Angolan-Cuban battalion of the N'Dalatando CIR, mixed remnants of the Benguela CIR, and at least five FAPLA squadrons, supported by the BM-21 battery, several platoons equipped with 82mm and 120mm mortars calibre, multiple batteries of Grad-1P launchers, one battery of 76mm ZiS-3 gun, and a handful of BRDM-2s. Overall commander was Diaz Argüelles, who acted in coordination with FAPLA's Commander Mundo Real.[132]

While controlling a 160 kilometre-long frontline with only 3,000 troops might appear 'impossible', the fact is that the combined Angolan-Cuban forces were greatly helped by the local geography and climate. As well as swelling rivers, heavy rains had transformed most of the open areas into mud fields, forcing the South African motorised columns to stick to the roads. Therefore, Angolan and Cuban commanders had it easy to predict enemy avenues of advance. Furthermore, they were able to rely on aerial reconnaissance provided by light aircraft and helicopters of the

Burned out wreckage of a FAPLA-operated Land Rover, shot-up by the SADF during one of the clashes around Bridge 14. (Albert Grandolini Collection)

A worn-out Eland-90 receiving some much-needed maintenance. Notable is the much lighter camouflage pattern applied by the time of battles in November 1975. (Albert Grandolini Collection)

FAPLA troops entrenching themselves in November 1975. (Albert Grandolini Collection)

TAAG, and could expect their numbers to grow through the arrival of first large Cuban troop contingents – and their fire-power to be greatly enhanced through additional arms deliveries from the USSR, expected in December 1975.[133]

SADF's Reorganisation

Ironically, and as so often before and after, the Cuban involvement was followed in fashion by the South Africans. During November 1975, the SADF greatly expanded its involvement in Angola. A new operational-level headquarters – Task Force 101 commanded by Major-General Andre van Deventer – was established to oversee all the operations in this country. Furthermore, additional task forces and battle groups were assembled and deployed on the battlefield:

- Battle Group Beaver was activated in late November, in the area between Lubango, Benguela, and Lobito, with the aim of acting as a strategic reserve;
- Battle Group Orange (one FALA battalion, one infantry company and one Eland squadron of the SADF) was established on 12 December, with the aim of advancing along the road from Kuito to Malenje;
- Battle Group X-Ray (one FALA battalion, reinforced by diverse elements of the SADF, including one Eland squadron) was established in early December, with the task of protecting the eastern part of the Benguela Railway and seizing Luso (renamed to Luena).

Furthermore, Task Force Zulu was reorganized, put in control of Battle Groups Bravo and Foxbat, and deployed to the area between Cela and Quibala. A new formation, Task Force Delta (which included Battle Groups Alpha and Beaver) was put in charge of the coastal frontlines and the rear areas, while Battle Groups Orange and X-Ray were to operate independently. Moreover, concluding their troops required much more artillery support in order to overcome the defences ahead of them, the SADF had reinforced its artillery assets in Angola. A troop of four 25-Pdrs had been airlifted to Benguela on 10 November. This was followed by additional troops – some equipped with 25-Pdrs, others with 5.5-In guns – over the next few weeks.[134] By early December 1975, at least five troops of SADF artillery were attached to the different task forces and battle groups. Finally, concluding that the ELNA and FALA infantry was rather unsteady when on the receiving end of enemy fire, the South Africans felt forced to reinforce most of their units through additional companies of their own motorised infantry (mainly deployed to protect their artillery units). Overall, by mid-December 1975, the SADF thus had 3,000 troops inside Angola.[135]

Shift to the Centre

The South Africans resumed their advance on 14 November 1975, when Task Force Zulu dispatched its Battle Group Bravo along the coast towards Porto Amboim. However, the column was forced to stop when reaching the Queve River, at a point 15 kilometres (9 miles) short of its objective. As described above, the bridge was destroyed, and the South Africans detected the presence of enemy troops on the other bank. Therefore, they brought their 25-Pdr troop into action and this pounded the Angolan-Cuban positions – until targeted by a volley of BM-21s, and forced to withdraw. Unable to do more, BGB thus returned to Sumbe before driving along the road for Gabela in an attempt to cross the Queve further inland. With similar results: the Caxoeiras bridge was blown up, and the potential crossing site well-defended. In the light of these experiences, the SADF gave up the idea of advancing along the coast, and re-routed most of their units. While Battle Group Alpha remained to cover Sumbe, BGB was dispatched to reinforce Battle Group Foxbat in Cela, where it arrived on 23 November.[136]

Battle Group Foxbat (BGF) initially concentrated in the area of Santa Comba and Cela (renamed Waku-Kungo) on 10 November, and then – exploiting the still 'fluid' nature of the situation in this part of Angola – crossed not only the Queve, but several additional rivers, too. With both sides rushing reinforcements into this area, several skirmishes occurred over the following days. On 11 November, a detachment of BGF, including two FALA companies supported by SADF Elands and mortars, ran into a FAPLA platoon equipped with one Grad-1P launcher, one ZPU-1 heavy machine gun, and several SPG-9 recoilless rifles, around 15 kilometres (9 miles) north of Waku-Kungo. The Angolans were well-entrenched on the high-ground, separated from the road by muddy fields or marshes, which tied the South African armour to the road. Thus, they managed to block the further advance of BGF until dusk – when the SADF decided to withdraw. A day later, one of the FALA companies returned to the site, only to find it deserted, together with two heavy weapons that were abandoned: the Angolans had left their position during the night. Therefore, when Battle Group Foxbat resumed its advance, its Elands ran straight into returning FAPLA troops, mounted on two trucks and two Land Rovers – and quickly destroyed them, killing about a dozen. A few hours later, BGF found the bridge over the Nhia River – subsequently known

Cuban gunners operating an M-30 gun in December 1975. (Albert Grandolini Collection)

A still from a video showing two of the Cuban commanders involved in the battle of Ebo on 23 November 1975. (Mark Lepko Collection)

One of two Eland armoured cars of Battle Group Foxbat left behind and captured by the Cubans during the battle for Ebo. (Albert Grandolini Collection)

One of the – probably Cuban-crewed – BRDM-2s knocked out by the SADF. (Albert Grandolini Collection)

as 'Bridge 14' – destroyed, and decided to withdraw while sending patrols along secondary roads in the hope of finding another suitable crossing site, and thus the way to Quibala. On 13 November, one of its elements had reached Ebo, about 30 kilometres (18 miles) from Waku-Kungo, and briefly seized it, before being forced to withdraw. On 15 November, another patrol including two Eland troops (supported by two mortars), returned to Ebo, but found itself exposed to the volleys of Grads and RPGs, and in the process of being outflanked by enemy infantry. With this, even this patrol was forced to withdraw.

Foxbat Defeated

Realizing he was facing significant enemy reinforcements, the new commander of Battle Group Foxbat, Lieutenant-Colonel George Kruys (who had relieved Lieutenant-Colonel Webb on 15 November), reorganized his units – reinforced through the second Eland squadron and a troop of 25-Pdrs – and went on the offensive again. While the bulk of his battle group advanced along a secondary road to Bridge 14 (which had been reported as 'intact' by FALA patrols), another element – including an Eland squadron, FALA infantry and a mortar platoon – returned to the Ebo area with the intention of diverting enemy attention. Unsurprisingly, the main force quickly realized that the reports about Bridge 14 were incorrect. Meanwhile, the diversion element ran into a convoy of three FAPLA trucks loaded with supplies and quickly destroyed it. However, because this action was expected to alert the enemy, it withdrew to Waku-Kungo, only to run into a full FAPLA company entrenched around a road junction it had crossed few hours before. Although the following clash was fought in a rather confusing fashion at short range, the South Africans quickly overpowered the enemy.

Two days later, on 17 November, Cuban-operated Alouette IIIs went into action in the Ebo area for the first time. One of them was meanwhile equipped for the deployment of Soviet-made 9M14 Malyutka (AT-3 Sagger) ATGMs, and put several of these to good use.[137] This happened because Kruys was trying his luck again – this time by deploying the bulk of BGF to seize Ebo and then advance straight on Quibala. Expecting this crucial crossroad to be heavily protected, the South Africans advanced very cautiously, reaching their first objective only on 22 November. Clearly, this offered the Angolans and Cubans plenty of time to reinforce their position through entrenching two companies of FAPLA infantry, half a company of MININT Special troops, a battery of BM-21s, at least one ZiS-3 gun, two BRDM-2s, and one platoon each of 120mm mortars and Grad-1Ps. As usual, the Cubans did not defend Ebo itself, but picked a position on the high ground two kilometres (slightly over one mile) north of the agglomeration, just behind the bridge over the Mabassa River. There, the defenders constructed multiple, well-camouflaged, mutually protecting positions above their selected killing zone. To make matters more complex, heavy rains transformed the area surrounding the roads into mud fields.[138]

At 0900hrs on 23 November, the vanguard of BGF – including Elands, an ELNA company, and a FALA-manned platoon of 4.2-In mortars – passed through Ebo and reached the bridge. Expecting enemy presence in the area, this column was supported by a single Cessna 185, which flew reconnaissance ahead of it. Its crew sighted several vehicles leaving the area, but failed to detect the enemy positions. To make sure, the South Africans ordered the mortar platoon into fire action, and this bombarded the area where vehicle movement had been reported. The ELNA infantry then started crossing the river, covered by Elands. Exactly at that point in time, the Angolan-Cuban force opened a fierce barrage. The first 76mm round blew up an Eland. A hail of 73mm and 76mm shells, and RPG-rounds targeted the armour, while volleys from automatic weapons, rockets, and mortar bombs plastered the infantry. In a matter of two minutes, two other armoured cars – hopelessly trapped on the road – were knocked out; the ELNA company was decimated; the mortar platoon was bracketed by enemy ranging shots, and narrowly skirted by a volley of BM-21s (which killed one SADF soldier), while the South African troop of 25-Pdrs failed to provide effective support: grid references provided to its crews by the Cessna 185 turned out to be wrong. Finally, another BM-21 salvo devastated the FALA infantry platoon positioned next to the mortar platoon, killing 7 and wounding 19. Panicked, the Angolans ran away and refused to engage in the battle again.

Realising the developing disaster, the HQ of Battle Group Foxbat rushed reinforcements to the scene. Supported by Elands, these managed to recover three of the damaged armoured cars, and cover

Cuban crews of 120mm mortars in action during the fighting for Bridge 14. (Albert Grandolini Collection)

the withdrawal of survivors, while destroying the ZiS-3. However, that was about all the SADF was capable of doing in Ebo. By the time the battle was over, the South Africans lost 5 troops killed and 11 wounded, and had five armoured cars knocked out, while their Angolan allies lost 41 killed and dozens of wounded. In return, one Cuban was killed and five wounded, while FAPLA's casualties remain unknown. The Angolan-Cuban force not only remained in full control of their positions, but subsequently recovered two of the Elands abandoned in the mud, thus scoring a major propaganda victory. Moreover, on 25 November, the Cubans claimed a Cessna 185 of the SAAF as shot down over Ebo. Flown by 2nd Lieutenants Keith Williamson and Eric Bryan Thompson, the aircraft carried Captain Daniel Jacob Taljaard (SADF) into reconnaissance. All three on board were killed in the crash.[139]

Bloody Bridge 14

Following the defeat at Ebo, Task Force Zulu – meanwhile under the command of Colonel Blackie Swart, and including Battle Groups Bravo and Foxbat – shifted its attention on the main road from Waku-Kungo and Quibala. This axis thus became the focus point of Operation Savannah during the first week of December 1975. The task force was significantly reinforced before being sent into the battle again, and meanwhile included 723 SADF personnel and 44 Elands. These were supported by at least two troops of 5.5-In guns, another of 25-Pdrs, and a battery of 20mm anti-aircraft artillery. The latter was protecting the airstrip in Waku-Kungo, which the SAAF used to airlift the bulk of supplies.

Starting on 29 November, BGB and BGF deployed multiple reconnaissance detachments towards the high ground (named 'Top Hat') north of Bridge 14. Following several skirmishes, the SADF established itself in control of this location, and set up an observation post atop of it. Meanwhile, BGF and two artillery troops took a position near, but out of sight of the FAPLA positions on the northern side of the Nhia River. The latter suffered extensive casualties – especially while trying to recover Top Hat, when they found themselves exposed to South African artillery – but were in the process of being reinforced. Thus, except for the weakened FAPLA company entrenched north of Bridge 14, at least one full battalion of Angolan troops and one MININT Special Troops company took positions on the plain separating the Nhia River and Catofe River. These were supported by one BM-21 battery, one battery of 120mm mortars, and one platoon each of ZiS-3s, ZPU-4s, Grad-1Ps, and 82mm mortars. Finally, the Angolan and Cuban infantry were reinforced by a number of RPG-7 launchers, and at least one team equipped with AT-3 Sagger ATGMs.

For a while the battle between these two forces was dominated by an artillery duel – in which the South Africans gained the upper hand, despite the better range of the Cuban BM-21s. The primary reasons for this were the ideally positioned observation post at Top Hat, but also the very aggressive deployment of their artillery – which was often positioned extremely close to the forward line of contact. Indeed, by 9 December 1975, the FAPLA infantry deployed next to the bridge was forced to withdraw after suffering heavy casualties. Furthermore, the Cuban artillery proved unable to disturb the work of SADF's gunners and forward artillery observers – although their and the FAPLA infantry did intercept and engage some of the reconnaissance patrols that had crossed the Nhia River. Ultimately, the South Africans found themselves in the position to deploy a team of combat engineers to repair the Bridge 14, and clear enemy mines on the northern bank of the river, on 10 December.

Repeatedly interrupted by volleys of BM-21s, engineers completed their work by the evening of 11 December, and cleared the bridge for use by the Elands, even if not by truck-towed artillery pieces. Correspondingly, BGF received the order to cross the river in force, on the next morning, and finally break through the enemy positions. Throughout these two days, the Cuban-manned support weapons found themselves constantly on the receiving end of effective counter-battery fire, because the South Africans had meanwhile pre-registered all of their positions: contrary to the South Africans, who frequently changed their positions, the

A 75mm recoilless rifle mounted on an Unimog truck, and its FAPLA crew, in November 1975. (Albert Grandolini collection)

Cuban artillery operated in a much more rigid fashion, using the same network of pre-arranged positions all the time. Even highly-mobile BM-21s would only withdraw to reload their rockets, before returning to exactly the same place to fire again. Unsurprisingly, by 12 December, only one BM-21 launcher was still operational. Furthermore, the Angolan-Cuban chain of command fell into disorder after Commandant Diaz Argülles was killed, on 9 December 1975, when his BRDM-2 either drove over a mine, or was hit by a South African artillery shell.

At 0700hrs in the morning of 12 December, following a lengthy artillery preparation, a column of 12 Elands, followed by infantry, crossed Bridge 14, and then split into two to outflank enemy anti-tank positions – all of which were orientated down the main road. Already in the process of preparing a withdrawal, the Angolans and the Cubans proved unable to offer any coordinated resistance. Moving at high speed, the Elands roamed the battlefield by 1200hrs, inflicting severe casualties upon a completely disorganised opponent. At one point, one of the armoured cars destroyed – at point-blank range – a truck full of Cuban troops that had mistaken it for an allied vehicle. In another case, the SADF artillery annihilated an entire convoy of 12 vehicles.[140]

Meanwhile, Commandant Abelardo Colomé Ibarra – who had taken control following Argülles' death – had arrived in the combat zone together with several fresh units, including a Cuban tank company equipped with T-34/85s, and two FAPLA companies. All were rushed to the bridge spanning the Catofe River – the last significant obstacle before Quibala. Arriving there around 1300hrs, the troops started digging in. However, contrary to what Ibarra expected, no 'last ditch battle' took place: heavy rain all but stopped the further advance of Battle Group Foxbat. Furthermore, the South Africans wanted to reorganize their scattered units, and bring forward their artillery that was still stuck on the southern bank of the Nhia. None of this was ever to happen: an order from Pretoria – issued shortly after BGF had launched its attack over Bridge 14 – forced Task Force Zulu to call off further attacks. Instead, although mauling its opponents while losing four of their own killed in action, and prompting Angolan and Cuban commanders in this part of Angola into becoming extremely reluctant to engage the South Africans again, the SADF's advance was decisively stopped.[141]

During the fighting for Bridge 14, the South Africans claimed to have killed about 400 enemy troops, half of these Cubans. They further claimed the capture of five BM-21s (one of these in intact condition), 10 ZiS-3 guns, and 22 diverse mortars.[142]

Battle Group Orange

Battle Group Orange (BGO) was established through the concentration of one FALA battalion, one infantry company from the 2nd South African Infantry Regiment, one Eland squadron, and one artillery battery with eight 5.5-In guns, in early December 1975. Initially, it advanced along the 200 kilometre (124 miles) long road from Kuito to Mussande, and reached the latter town on 14 December. After finding the local bridge blown up by the retreating enemy, it turned west and advanced on Cariango, thus threatening the eastern flank of the FAPLA and FAR forces defending Quibala from Task Force Zulu. However, once BGO reached Cariango – a mere 30 kilometres (less than 19 miles) from Quibala, on 15 December 1975, it found out that the only bridge spanning the Pombuigi River in this region, was blown up, too. Battle Group Orange thus withdrew and dispatched multiple reconnaissance parties with the task of identifying possible fording points.

The crew of a BRMD-2 and a group of FAPLA troops taking a break during the long mach in the southern direction, at the end of which they reinforced positions (Albert Grandolini collection)

Meanwhile, the FAPLA and the FAR rushed reinforcements to this area, resulting in the first ever clash between the Cuban and South African-operated armour. On 18 December, a section of three T-34/85s underway near the destroyed bridge was engaged by Elands positioned on the other side of the Pombuigi River. Despite their low velocity guns, the South Africans managed to disable one of the Cuban tanks, and forced the other two to withdraw. Nevertheless, their attempt to deploy infantry over the destroyed bridge and establish a bridgehead failed: the Cuban-operated BM-21s and D-44 85mm guns positioned on the high ground further north, subjected the area to heavy volumes of artillery fire.

The front lines in this part of Angola remained static until 20 December, when the FAPLA and the FAR increased the intensiveness of their barrage, and then deployed their infantry to infiltrate the southern bank of the Pombuigi River. Three days later, Cuban counter-battery fire hit one of the SADF's positions, killing two gunners, while the FAPLA began concentrating troops in the Mussande area, threatening to attack the rear of Battle Group Orange, while also building up the pressure in the Cariango area. An Alouette III of the SAAF was shot down while on a CASEVAC mission in the Catofe area, on 23 December, while the SADF artillery reported coming under attack by 'enemy fighter jets', a day later. In return, an AeroCommander 500 flown by a Cuban crew was hit by 20mm cannon fire from South African positions while flying reconnaissance along the road from Cariango to Mussande, on 24 December. The hit blew the cabin roof off, injuring the crew and instantly killing the intelligence officer (Major Fonseca) that sat in the rear, but the pilot managed to return to his base. A day later, as the Angolans and Cubans continued to shell the positions of Battle Group Orange, a South African patrol moving in the rear of their unit was reportedly strafed by an 'enemy fighter jet'. Indeed, on 26 December 1975, one of the SADF's observation posts reported being strafed by a 'single MiG-17', too.[143] All of this eventually drove the South Africans into the realisation that the position of Battle Group Orange was unsustainable, and to order its withdrawal towards Mussande. This, however, was completed only after one of the Angolan infantry patrols captured a South African ENTAC ATGM-team of three, together with their Land Rover-mounted weapon.[144]

The Monster of Luso

The last major South African advance into Angola of 1975 took place in the east, along the Benguela Railway, whith the intention of seizing Luso (meanwhile renamed Luena). The Katangese Tigers defending the town had been successful in repulsing several FALA attacks and had been reinforced by a small team of MMCA instructors. However, this garrison remained isolated and was only supported by a few B-10 recoilless guns and a handful of Grad-1Ps. To obtain as least some armoured capability, its troops converted two Land Rovers and a bulldozer into improvised armoured vehicles, by welding iron plates and mounting machine guns and B-10s atop of them, in the local railway workshop. Eventually, this armoured bulldozer became known as the 'Monster of Luso' to the South Africans.

The SADF's involvement in this part of Angola began with the advance of Battle Group X-Ray – by road and by train – on Munhango, on 28 November, and then on Cangumbe, on 3 December 1975. This part of the operation went nearly unopposed, except for a brief encounter with some FAPLA infantry supported by a BRDM-2 on 30 November. Thus, a week later, on 6 December, X-Ray approached Luena and even launched its first attempt to invest the town. It was at this point in time that this enterprise suffered a disaster: one of the FALA companies involved had established an ambush position without informing the other units. Correspondingly, it was misidentified as FAPLA, promptly subjected to the attention of the SADF artillery, and its survivors forced to withdraw, leaving the Katangese Tigers and the MMCA in control of Luena.

On the next day, the SADF artillery opened up against enemy positions in the town, supported by a SAAF Cessna that acted as an airborne forward controller, while the FALA infantry – supported by Elands – mounted a new attack. However, the infantry of UNITA fled as soon as it found itself under fire from the Katangese Tigers. On 10 December, X-Ray opted for a flanking move along the western side of Luena, before rushing straight for the airport. The first Eland barely reached the latter, when it found itself confronted by the improvised 'armour' operated by the Tigers: the 'Monster of Luso' and one of the armoured Land Rovers. Certainly enough, the latter was quickly dealt with, and the supporting enemy infantry forced to withdraw, but – to no little surprise of the South Africans – it took five 90mm shells to stop the 'Monster'. With this, the defenders had concluded that the situation was hopeless and decided to withdraw: because the FALA-company deployed to block their retreat route had been forced away from its position days earlier, they did so in good order. Indeed, after blowing up the same, the Katangan Tigers and Cubans entrenched themselves behind the Buçaco bridge.

Emboldened, the FALA launched an advance along the roads connecting Luena with Luau and Saurimo, while the FAPLA rushed reinforcements, all of which – together with the surviving Katangese Tigers – were put under the command of the MMCA. By early January 1976, two FAPLA battalions – both commanded by the Cuban cadre, and reinforced by artillery and tanks – were in position, together with a mixed Angolan-Cuban company flown in from Cabinda. While these reinforcements were capable of stopping the FALA advance cold, the Cubans in Luau took no chances and blew up the bridge connecting the town with Zaire, thus pre-empting any attacks from that side.[145]

Operation First Congress

Meanwhile a new round of fighting was in the process of development on the central front, in the Catofe area. On 17 December, the Cubans managed to seize the Tongo Hills, provoking two days of fierce artillery duels. During this action, several light aircraft of the FAPA/DAA were reported as in action over South African positions, attempting to pinpoint the SADF's artillery. Without a clear task on hand, the SADF stopped its attempts at further advance, in turn significantly increasing the confidence of Angolan and Cuban commanders. The FAR meanwhile had more troops deployed in Angola than the SADF, and was in the process of infiltrating multiple FAPLA detachments behind enemy lines, with the intention of collecting intelligence, but also of harassing enemy supply links. Not wasting any time, and knowing that significant reinforcements were underway from Cuba, the MMCA came to the idea to open the planning for its first major counter-offensive, Operation First Congress.

Despite its bombastic designation, this enterprise remained a rather limited affair. On 31 December 1975, MININT Special Troops assaulted and seized the Medunda Hills on the road connecting Quibala with Waku-Kungo, and established an important observation post – a pre-requisite for any further advance on Cela. As expected, Task Force Zulu reacted with several vicious counter-attacks in the following days: these recovered one of the two hills, and came close to overrunning the Cuban platoon entrenched on the second. However, at the last moment the Cuban commander requested the supporting BM-21 battery to open fire on his own position: this desperate measure worked better than expected, because the Cuban troops were sheltered in a cave, while the assaulting enemy was exposed in the open. The surviving SADF-FALA troops were forced to retreat.[146]

The Decisive Front

Ultimately, it was neither the ebb nor flow of the battles in Angola that proved decisive for the outcome. On the contrary: once it became known how deeply the South Africans were involved, the country found itself exposed to fierce accusations on the international scene. Considered a stop-gap measure all the time, Operation Savannah depended on secrecy and speed for exercising only enough pressure upon the MPLA, to enable the FNLA and UNITA a negotiated settlement. Initially at least, the expectation that the OAU might impose a new solution drawn at least roughly along the lines of the Alvor Accord – and thus preserve the political influence of the FNLA and UNITA in Luanda – appeared realistic. For example, during the congress of 11 November 1975, only 9 out of 46 members of the Organisation of African Unity recognized the MPLA as the legal government of Angola. However, the FNLA and UNITA proved unable to overwhelm the FAPLA and the growing number of its Cuban allies on their own before the next OAU meeting, on 10 January 1976, and thus forced the South Africans to extend their involvement – although time was not on their side. On 22 November, Fred Bridgland, the first journalist to obtain evidence of the SADF's involvement in Angola, published his findings in the Washington Post. All of a sudden, the 'whole World' knew about Apartheid-ruled South Africa being secretly engaged in a war against the MPLA. As John Stockwell, the CIA officer in charge of the IAFEATURE concluded:

> The propaganda and political war was lost in that stroke. There was nothing the Lusaka station could invent that would be as damaging to the other side as our alliance with the hated South Africans was to our cause.[147]

Five days later, the government of Nigeria – which had so far supported a negotiated settlement – switched its position: it not only recognized the MPLA, but also granted it a US$20 million loan. Tanzania followed in kind, just a day later. Moreover, on 19 December, the US Congress disavowed the allocation of another US$7 million to the IAFEATURE program – authorised by President Ford on 27 November 1975 – through voting for the Clark Amendment. With this, the provision of any further help to FNLA and UNITA by the US government was prohibited. Pretoria thus found its position in Angola not only fully exposed, but also untenable, and there was nothing its diplomacy could to do – even more so considering how fragile the FNLA-UNITA alliance proved to be (as obvious from their mutual clash in Huambo, on 25 December, when several dozens were killed). When the OAU then meet in Addis Ababa, on 10 January, 22 of its members voted in support of the MPLA government, while 'only' 22 still supported an accord. However, Ethiopia and Uganda – which restrained from voting – then changed their positions in favour of Neto's movement. With this, the die was cast: during a meeting in Waku-Kungo on 16 January 1976, two high-ranking SADF officers announced to Jonas Savimbi, Holden Roberto and Daniel Chipenda that the South Africans had decided to withdraw from Angola.[148]

CHAPTER 8
COUNTER-OFFENSIVE IN THE NORTH

Following their victory against the ELNA and Zairians at Quifangondo, the Angolan and Cuban commanders did not feel in a position to exploit the opportunity and launch a pursuit because of the South African threat in the south. Thus, they offered their enemies in northern Angola plenty of time and opportunities to recover. However, as the Cuban reinforcements and Soviet arms continued converging on Luanda, the MMCA and the FAPLA felt encouraged to start planning an operation aimed to finish off not only the ELNA, but indeed the FNLA. The operation in question was envisaged to have two phases: the first included the seizure of Caxito, Ambrizete (renamed N'Zeto) and Carmona (renamed Uíge). The capture of these towns and the local airport was in turn to enable the second phase, during which an advance all the way up to the Zairian border was planned. Even then, this plan had to wait for a suitable opportunity, then for much of November and December 1975, the MMCA and the FAPLA were preoccupied with the crisis in southern and central Angola, caused by the South African invasion. One the local frontlines stabilised, the Angolan and Cuban commanders immediately turned their attention back towards the north.

Northern Front

By early December 1975, the 9th BRIM had finally received its full complement of heavy weapons, including a battery of BM-21s and a tank company of T-34/85s – all manned by the Cubans. Correspondingly, it became a full brigade including 100 Cuban and 1,200 Angolan troops, organized as listed in Table 9. Parallel with the build-up of the 9th BRIM, a new command structure was developed for the Northern Front: under the overall command of Commander Víctor Schueg Colás, this now included the 9th BRIM and several Cuban-trained FAPLA battalions, numbered in the sequence in which they became operational, each was 450 strong, and included a battery of 82mm mortars, and a platoon each of 75mm recoilless guns and heavy machine guns. The first two of the units in question, 1 Bon I, and 2 Bon I, were grouped into a task force that included numerous supporting units, including a battery operating ZiS-3s, one mortar battery (82mm), one BM-21 battery, one ZPU-4 platoon, and a platoon with five Grad-1Ps. With an initial strength of about 250 Cubans and 1,050 Angolans, and subsequently reinforced through the addition of the 4 Bon I, this formation almost matched in size the 9th BRIM. Finally, in early January 1976, the Northern Front was reinforced through a small, but very powerful unit of the FAR: the 3rd Bon IM, equipped with BTR-60s. Led by Commandant Raúl Fernández Marrero, this battalion disembarked from the merchant *Jigüe* in Luanda on 16 December, and was initially deployed in the Catumbela area, before being re-routed towards north. In addition to one company of T-34/85 tanks, it included a platoon of ZPU-4s, a mortar company (120mm), a battery of M-30s, one BM-21 platoon, and two SA-7 teams. Overall, as of early January 1976, the Northern Front FAR/FAPLA was organized as listed in Table 10.

On the basis of their intelligence reports, the Cuban and Angolan commanders assessed the total strength of the ELNA at about 2,000 well-armed, and reasonably well-trained men, both Angolan and Portuguese, organized into several combined-arms battalions equipped with AMLs, mortars, and jeep-mounted recoilless rifles. They also assessed that the FAZ still had three battalions inside northern Angola (although all of these were meanwhile withdrawn, looting anything they could take with them as they went). Finally, their intelligence informed them that the ELNA was expecting an advance from Caxito directly towards Uige – the 'capital' of the FNLA and its primary logistic hub – and thus had blown up all

A Cuban-operated PT-76 as seen on a street in Luanda in November 1975: although not mentioned by any of the available Cuban sources, about a company-worth of these was subsequently seen during the counter-offensive on the FNLA/ELNA. (Albert Grandolini Collection)

BTR-60s of the 3 Bon IM on advance towards Ambrizete in early February 1976. (Albert Grandolini Collection)

Cuban and Angolan troops of the 1 Bon I inspecting large stocks of ammunition during the seizure of Caxito. (Albert Grandolini Collection)

FAPLA troops with M79 grenade launcher of US origin, captured from the FNLA. (Albert Grandolini Collection)

the bridges in between. Correspondingly, the decision was taken to first let the 9th BRIM advance on Toto (renamed Xamindele) and to Nambuangongo, before turning west and attacking Ambrizete. Meanwhile, the Task Force including the 1, 2, and 4 Bon I, and then the 3 Bon IM, was to follow the central road linking N'Dalantando with Negage.[149]

Table 9: 9th BRIM, late December 1975, early January 1976

Unit	Heavy Equipment
HQ Company	
Communications Company	
3x Infantry Battalion	BTR-152
Engineer Company	
Two Commando companies	BTR-152
Tank company	T-34/85s
Mortar battery	120mm
Artillery group	ZiS-3 guns
Anti-Aircraft Group	ZPU-4s & Dushkas
MRL battery	BM-21
Launcher group	Grad-1P

Table 10: Northern Front FAR/FAPLA, early January 1976

Unit	Commander
	Víctor Schueg Colás
9th BRIM	Commandant N'Dalu
1 Bon I	Major Ibraim Dinmajamad Arias
2 Bon I	Major Gonzalo del valle Céspedes
3 Bon IM	Commandant Raúl Fernández Marrero
4 Bon I	Commandant Luis Evelio Vega Romero

Auftragstaktik

While there has been plenty of discussion of, and publications about, the amazing advances of the SADF into southern Angola in October 1975, there are next to no publications pointing out that – due to the huge size of the area where the counter-offensive of the Northern Front was to be undertaken, and rather insufficient means of communication – the Cuban commander decided to operate along what is known as '*Auftragstaktik*' in military technical jargon. This is a form of command originally developed by the German military before and during WWI and refined early during WWII. In this way of commanding military units, the commander only assigns objectives to his subordinate officers, while leaving it to them to decide how they are to complete their tasks. Similarly, various support units were deployed very flexibly. Colás' sole advice to his officers was to always carefully reconnoitre their routes of advance in order to avoid ambushes, and to make use of their

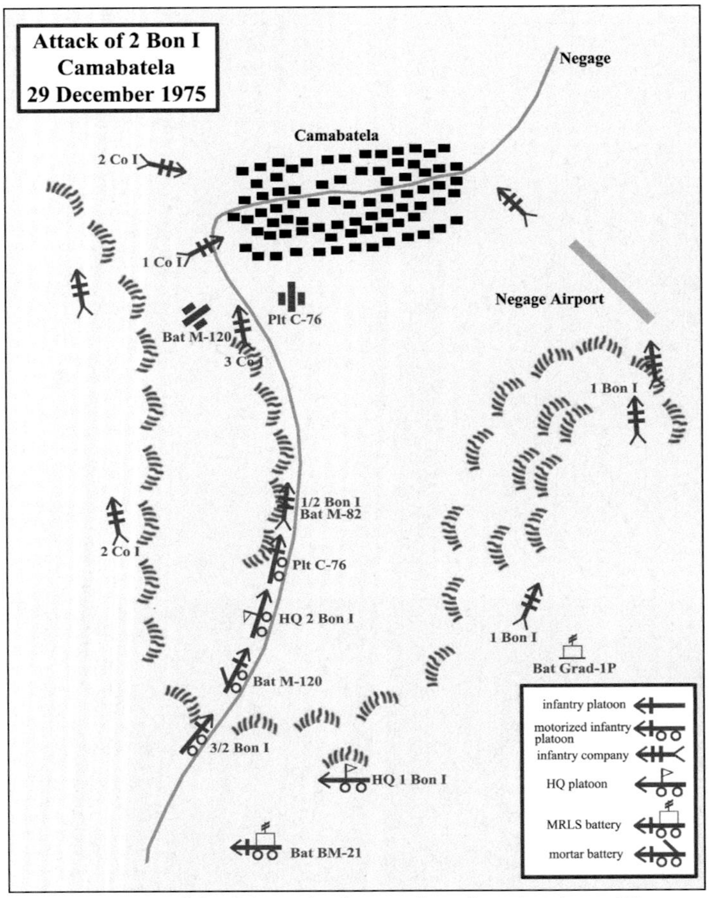

A reconstruction of the Cuban plan for attack on Camabatela, on 29 December 1975. (Map by Tom Cooper)

The local population greeting FAR/FAPLA troops on the streets of Uige on 29 December 1975. (Albert Grandolini Collection)

One of the T-34s from the 9th BRIM passing a pontoon bridge over the M'Bridege River on 5 February 1975. (Mark Lepko Collection)

support weapons only once specific targets were clearly identified. These two pieces of advice were also the sole reasons why the FAR-led advance proceeded at a slower pace than that of Task Force Zulu's 'reconnaissance by fire' through southern Angola, two months earlier: the fact was that due to its supply lines being at least 12,000 kilometres long, the Cuban military simply couldn't afford extensive expenditure of ammunition and other supplies.[150]

Fall of Carmona

With one of the FAPLA commando units recovering Morro da Cal already on 21 November 1975, the first move of the Northern Front's big counter-offensive took place between 3 and 5 December 1975, when the 1 Bon I attacked Caxito, while the 2 Bon I covered flanks and the rear. The desultory resistance of the demoralised ELNA was quickly overrun: the Cubans and Angolans not only seized a large stock of arms and ammunition, but also rounded up around 150 prisoners. As planned, the 9th BRIM then took over and dashed along the coastal road towards Ambriz and Ambrizete, slowed down only by several destroyed bridges. Meanwhile, the 1 Bon I and the 2 Bon I were grouped into the North Western Task Force, before launching their advance on Luinga. On 12 December, 1 Bon I quickly seized the neighbouring village of Cateco Cangola, capturing around 80 prisoners, 500 M1 carbines, and Uzi and Sten sub machine guns in the process. This move triggered a strong reaction from the ELNA: on the next day, this counter-attacked with two companies supported by mortars and a pair of AML-90s. However, this was quickly repulsed: emboldened, the Angolans launched a pursuit – only to run into an ambush, which took them by surprise and scattered the better part of the 1 Bon I in panic. The 2 Bon I thus couldn't count on support when running into difficulties while attacking the town: slowed down by minefields and long-range fire from jeep-mounted recoilless rifles of the ELNA, it was forced to stop, reorganize and establish defence positions south-west of Luinga. The final attack on this town was launched only after comprehensive preparations, and once the insurgents withdrew, following a loss – according to Angolan-Cuban estimates – of about 30 killed and 80 captured.

Ten days later, the North Western Task Force reached the area of Camabatela, estimated as defended by two ELNA battalions, special commandos of the ELP, AML armoured cars and heavy mortars. This time, the Cuban commander took no chances and set up a methodical attack: 2 Bon I provided supportive fire while the 1 Bon I manoeuvred around the eastern flank: although one vehicle was destroyed by mines, the two units reached their starting positions by the evening of 28 December. Their pincer attack was opened at 0800hrs the next day, when 1 Bon I advanced for the airport, while the 2 Bon I went attacked from the west before going for the centre of the town – only to find itself stopped by heavy resistance, a mortar barrage from the north-east, and heavy rain. Thick haze completely blanked the battlefield, making it impossible for the Cubans to silence enemy mortars: even Alouette helicopters – that provided plenty of aid by that point in time – couldn't fly reconnaissance. By the afternoon, 2 Bon I was still tied in a deadly battle, and meanwhile short on ammunition. The deadlock was broken only after the 2 Bon I secured the airfield and then hit the flank of the

An AML-90 knocked out during the Cuban advance on Ambrizete. (Albert Grandolini Collection)

Mercenaries from the group led by 'Colonel Callan' in a requisitioned civilian car, which had its roof removed and received an elaborate coat of camouflage colour, in January 1976. (Mark Lepko Collection)

An ELP Portuguese fighter that served with the FNLA, as seen in northern Angola of early 1976. (Albert Grandolini Collection)

enemy troops facing its sister unit in the town. The ELNA finally fell back, though only temporary: after bringing reinforcements from the north, it attempted to counterattack. This time it was the battery of Grad-1Ps and recoilless rifles that broke the insurgent momentum: at 1900hrs, after the fiercest battle of the offensive by this point in time, Camabatela was finally secured, and about 200 ELNA combatants taken captive.

After being reinforced by the 3 Bon IM, the North Western Task Force advanced on Negage, expecting to find it as fiercely defended as Camabatela. The investment began on 3 January 1976, early in the morning, and following exactly the same plan as during the last battle, but with the 3 Bon IM making the frontal attack along the main town. The defenders engaged the approaching BTR-60s and T-34/85s, but the FAR unleashed all of its firepower: after four hours of fighting back, the remaining ELNA troops broke and fled. Even so, at least 400 were captured, including six Portuguese and eight Zairians, and a large haul of arms and ammunition.

Opting not to wait this time, the North Western Task Force proceeded for Uige reaching the point barely eight kilometres (5 miles) short of the town the same evening. At 0900hrs of 29 December 1975, following an hour-long artillery preparation, 1 Bon I attacked along the main road, while 3 Bon IM made a flanking move towards the airport, where a Fokker F.27 was claimed as destroyed by artillery fire (while still on the ground).[151] However the motorised battalion then took the wrong turn and realised this only after finding out that the road led straight into dense forest. Turning around, the unit returned to its starting point to find the 1 Bon I there – and then, finally, attacked Uige. The ELNA fought back, early on, until the massive firepower clearly shifted the balance of power: the defence of the FNLA's 'capital' collapsed once the Angolans and Cubans reached the local military base, which prompted their surviving enemy to run away. Coming just a day before the OAU's session during which it finally shifted its support to the MPLA, this was a massive blow for Holden Roberto.[152]

Free Advance

With the Phase I of the northern offensive complete, 3 Bon IM was ordered to continue for Ambrizete along the road from Carmon via Songo and Toto (renamed Xamindele), where it arrived on 11 January. Toto had not only a former Portuguese army base, but a good airstrip nearby too. On the next day, the unit was reinforced by the 9th BRIM, which advanced inland from Caxito and then to Nambuangongo. The two units then launched a methodical attack, well-supported by artillery guided by Alouette helicopters that served as forward observers. After holding out for a few hours, the ELNA fall back behind the M'Bridege River, and blew up the bridge: only the latter act stopped further Angolan-Cuban advance, because 3 Bon IM and the 9th BRIM simply lacked bridging equipment. The latter arrived only in early February. Following several days of skirmishing and multiple artillery exchanges, the 9th BRIM crossed M'Bridege River on 5 February and then pushed along the coast towards Santo Antonio de Zaire (renamed Soyo), reaching this town two days later without encountering serious resistance, but finding a large minefield. Although 'corseted' by foreign mercenaries, the ELNA fell back, and one of the foreigners – James Baker – was captured

Group of 'Colonel Callan's' mercenaries with one of the AML-90s donated by Zaire. (Albert Grandolini Collection)

alive, while another escaped to Zaire. On 8 February, another of the Angolan-Cuban battalions had secured Tomboco, where it captured three AML-90s and large quantities of ammunition.

With the ELNA offering only light resistance, all the units of the Northern Front pushed their advance very hard during the following days, stopping only due to ever more problematic roads, and an increasing number of mines. The North Western Task Force went from Carmona straight for the Zairian border with 2 Bon I – which requisitioned a civilian bulldozer in order to ease the work of the attached engineers – took Bembe (190 kilometres/118 miles from Negage!) on 18 January and Demba three days later. At this point in time, 1 Bon I left the main column (it was replaced by 4 Bon I) and opened the advance on San Salvador do Congo (renamed Mbanza-Kongo) – but was stopped early by a destroyed bridge on the M'Bridege River.[153]

Dogs of War

It was at this point in time that the North Western Task Force encountered an entirely new kind of enemy: British and US-sponsored 'soldiers of fortune'. Upon the catastrophe at Quifandongo, the CIA had concluded that – as well as continuing provision of weapons through Operation IAFEATURE – the battered ELNA could only be supported through recruitment of mercenaries. With the agency's traditional source of the same – such as anti-Castro Cubans – not being an option, it attempted to cooperate with France. However, Bob Denard's group was already involved in supporting the FLEC and UNITA, and not numerous enough to detach any of its experienced cadre for the third operation at the same time. Therefore, in early December 1975 the CIA opened negotiations with the Portuguese Colonel Santos y Casto, leader of the ELP. The latter promised to – provided with the necessary funding – recruit 300 Portuguese army veterans. However, and despite relatively high wages offered, this plan collapsed on its own: only a single Portuguese sergeant turned up in Kinshasa by 1 January 1976, followed by a group of 12 – 27 days later! Thus, the CIA cancelled this operation and sent everybody home. Meanwhile, Roberto Holden requested his representative in Great Britain, Donald Belford, to recruit mercenaries. In turn, the latter contracted the owner of the British private military company (PMC) Security Advisory Services ("SAS"), John Bank, to recruit mercenaries with experience from serving in the British army, and organise their transfer to Zaire. The first four men contracted by the "SAS" turned up in Zaire in early December 1975. They were promptly embedded into the ELNA, and appointed officer positions – although none of them had reached a rank superior to that of a sergeant: Costas Georgiou, a Greek Cypriot, was even given the rank of a full colonel, in which he took part already during the battle for Negage. The other men – most of them Greek Cypriots and Portuguese, but also several British, a few Irishmen, and several French, arrived in Kinshasa by 5 January 1976, and were then taken to Sao Salvador do Congo (renamed to Mbanza-Kongo).[154]

Meanwhile, the "SAS" had increased its recruitment efforts in Great Britain and managed to collect a group of 19 mercenaries, mostly ex-paratroopers and commandos. This had reached Kinshasa on 18 January 1978. By this time, Banks felt he had exhausted the pool of qualified soldiers and thus decided to lower the recruitment standards. Correspondingly, the next group of 90 men he had sent to Zaire included several men with no military experience at all, while a few had served on submarines of the Royal Navy. However, this became known only by the time all the mercenaries had already reached Angola, in late January 1976 – by when it also became clear that the group would have a de-facto desperate task: its leaders not only lacked insight, but experienced leaders too, and some – like 'Colonel Callan', as Christos Georgiou was nicknamed – turned out to be true psychopaths, behaving erratically. They not only terrorised their ELNA allies, imposing capital punishments even for the smallest of mistakes, but the local civilian population, too. Soon after their arrival, 23 of the mercenaries were declared as unfit for combat and ordered to stay in Maguela do Zombo, where they served as guards only. To say that they caused more problems than good would be an understatement: in one case they opened fire at a column of mercenaries returning to the base unannounced, then panicked and fled. When the 'crisis' was sorted out, 14 of the 23 were summarily executed. Overall, the entire enterprise proved to be a failure: there was no way to use the remaining mercenaries to retrain the ELNA or combine the two the way the MMCA's instructors and FAR troops were combined with the FAPLA. Furthermore, because of Callan's overbearing role, it proved impossible for the group to run multiple operations at the same time – which was of particular importance considering ELNA's situation: as of early February 1976, Holden's movement was flush with US-supplied weapons, but desperately short on trained troops and cohesive military units: a core of experienced combat leaders and advisors could thus have made much possible.[155]

Killers at Quibocolo

The first significant clash between the North Western Task Force and the mercenaries took place near Demba, on 24 January 1976, when a small party led by Callan attacked an Angolan reconnaissance party from the 4 Bon I. The latter lost at least 21 troops killed and retreated in panic, while the commander of the unit reacted by opening fire from all of his heavy weapons at the estimated enemy position – and missed.[156] Unimpressed by performance of its 'green' unit, the North Western Task Force resumed its advance on Quibocolo, with 2 Bon I in the lead. Correspondingly, Callan gathered around 80 mercenaries at Maquela do Zombo, and then departed in a column of 10 vehicles carrying two M40 recoilless guns. Underway to Quibocolo one of the vehicles ran over a mine that blew it away, killed three and injured several mercenaries. Since the injured had to be evacuated, Callan's 'Killer Group' reached the battlefield with only five Land Rovers and 48 men – and then ran straight into the vanguard of 2 Bon I (for an order of battle of the latter unit as of early February 1976, see the Table 11). According to their own testimonies, the mercenaries 'routed' the enemy, destroyed 'four tanks' with their recoilless rifles and LAWs, killed and wounded between 160 and 200 enemy troops, in exchange for three wounded and the loss of the Land Rover carrying the ammunition. Furthermore, the high tide of the battle apparently occurred when a single 'T-54' charged at them, impervious to nine hits from 106mm recoilless guns, before it was knocked out by a LAW rocket fired from near point-blank range.

What actually happened was that the mercenaries ran into a combined, Angolan-Cuban reconnaissance patrol, which had detected them early, but over-reported their column as consisting of 20 vehicles including two AML-90s. Correspondingly, 2 Bon I quickly took defensive positions on either side of the road, and laid several mines to protect its frontline – consisting of one infantry company, supported by two T-34s and recoilless guns. Certainly enough, the Cuban commander of the unit, Gonzalo del Valle Céspedes, over-claimed at least as much:

> ...the crews of recoilless guns opened fire seconds before the enemy tanks reached our minefield. The fight began, and the adversaries avoided our fire by stopping, making a 180-degree turn and retreating. ...One of our tanks hit the vehicle carrying 106mm rounds. The car immediately caught fire and projectiles exploded, some flying around in circles before exploding in mid-air, like fireworks. The mercenaries on foot shot at us with all their weapons, attacking and trying to break our positions at all costs.... we responded with all the means at our disposal, including 76mm cannons that hit their flank; we shot them with tanks, mortars, and all infantry weapons. I ordered the BM-21 battery to aim his pieces on the enemy formation, too.
>
> Inexplicably, one of our tanks rushed towards the enemy...I am completely convinced it was no error or indiscipline, but anger at the heat of intense combat and desire to kill the enemy... They stumbled upon one of our mines, whose explosion stopped the tank and critically injured the driver, who died later. Under great difficulties, the crew of the tank jumped out, taking with them the wounded comrade....Then they all returned to the immobilised tank and continued fighting without abandoning it, even after receiving a hit from a Bazooka rocket, which penetrated the turret. The mercenaries, trying to annihilate the crew...began surrounding it at close range...unable to hit them with tanks' weapons our comrades...opened the hatches, threw hand grenades at them, and forced them to withdraw.
>
> The rumble of the battle was tremendous...the mercenaries did everything possible to defeat us...but not one of our soldiers took a step back or stopped firing...It was then that the BM-21 battery, under the command of 1st Lieutenant Abel Olivera Iraola, was ordered into action and...poured a devastating salvo into the enemy ranks, without any projectile hurting any of our troops, which were in direct contact. That barrage was irresistible ...[157]

Actually, it seems that most of the BM-21 rockets and other indirect fire weapons – the three ZiS-3s are known to have fired 93 rounds within one hour – failed to hit the enemy. Nevertheless, the mercenaries withdrew – even if without delivering anything like the massive blow they thought they had. Similarly, while claiming to have killed 27 and injured 16, the Cubans remarked that the enemies evacuated their casualties. Correspondingly, the only soldier definitely confirmed as killed in this 'battle' was the unlucky driver of the T-34/85 tank.[158]

The North Western Task Force resumed its advance on Quibocolo a few hours later. Meanwhile, Callan quickly reorganized what was left of his 'Killer Force', and then led the remaining 23 mercenaries into a new action. On 3 February, this group set up three ambushes, always using the same tactics: the troops took positions near the road, waited for an appropriate target, and opened fire before advancing to contact, forcing their enemies to retreat. Eventually, they claimed to have killed no less than 200 Angolan and Cuban soldiers, destroyed four additional tanks and several other vehicles. By early evening, Callan ordered them into action for the fourth time, just as a small convoy of soft-skinned vehicles approached, including a jeep and several trucks. The first volley of fire killed the Cuban Major

Some of the foreign mercenaries captured during the battle for Quibocolo, as seen during their trial in Luanda, in June 1976. (Albert Grandolini Collection)

'Colonel Callan' – actually a Greek Cypriot Costas Georgiou – during the trial. He was sentenced to death and executed on 10 July 1976. (Albert Grandolini Collection)

Cornelio Dúran Castillo and soldier Camilo Hernández Carmona, next to him, while another officer was injured. As usual, Callan then led his men into a frontal assault on the remaining vehicles, and fired a LAW rocket on a GAZ-66 truck. Unknown to him, the latter hauled more than 1,000 kilograms of explosives – which enthusiastically detonated. The massive explosion wrecked several other vehicles and stunned everybody nearby, including Callan and another man from his group, both of whom were seriously injured. FAPLA troops rushed to the scene, and killed another mercenary, dispersing the rest: only five stayed with Callan, and attempted to evacuate him. They managed to evade several enemy patrols over the next few days, before being captured by troops of 2 Bon I, on 6 February. Without their 'leader', the remaining dogs of war fled to Zaire in whatever fashion they could. Some even hijacked a Fokker F.27 at Maquela do Zombo and forced the pilot to fly them directly to Kinshasa. Ironically, Roberto then dealt the mortal blow to the entire enterprise: he ordered the execution of one of the few remaining officers, and demoted another as a punishment for the summary execution of 14 others, mentioned above. Thus, the ambushes from 3 February 1976 proved to be the last significant clash involving European mercenaries in this conflict.[159]

To say that the entire affair was an outright disaster for the FNLA, would be an understatement. Not only that the mercenaries failed to reverse the flow of the war, but they delivered a major propaganda coup straight into the hands of the MPLA. At least 20 of the Europeans had been killed, while 13 – including nine British and four Americans – were captured. Starting with 11 June 1976, the Angolan government ran a highly publicised trial in Luanda, in the course of which four – including Callan – were condemned to death (they were executed on 10 July 1976), while others were sentenced to long prison terms.

Table 11: 2 Bon I Order of Battle, early February 1976[160]

Unit	Commander
	Gonzalo Del Valle Céspedes
	Fabio González Guethón (Chief of Staff)
1st Infantry Company	Major Erálides Pérez Leblanche
2nd Infantry Company	Major Sergio Vega Ramirez
3rd Infantry Company	Captain Pablo Pineda Núnez
Mortar Battery (82mm)	Hornedo Vega de los Santos
Recoilless Gun Platoon (75mm)	?
Heavy Machine Gun Platoon	Hermes Agüero Kindelán
Reconnaissance Platoon	?
Engineer Platoon	Rafael Reina Duquesne
Logistics Platoon	Rafael Brito

Aerial Action

The losses the mercenaries claimed to have caused to the Angolan-Cuban units in the Quibocolo area did not prevent the fall of that town on 5 February 1976. Nevertheless, the Cuban officers remained cautious when approaching the town: the assault launched on the next day with two infantry platoons in front, with the third and mortars in the rear, was supported by a reinforced battery of M-30s and T-34s, as well as engineers that removed plenty of mines.

Upon reaching the outskirts of Quibocolo the infantry found itself pinned down. As usual, the Cuban officers sought for less well-defended sectors to infiltrate, but ELNA's resistance was such that there was no room for manoeuvre. Correspondingly, all the artillery fire was concentrated against one spot of enemy positions, which was pounded until there was no return fire. The infantry finally broke through, and by 1600hrs Quibocolo was under the control of the FAR and the FAPLA, which claimed over 100 enemies killed. On the next morning, one of 2 Bon I's companies advanced for another five kilometres, until running into a minefield. The FAPLA took two hours to overwhelm the resistance of a single ELNA detachment, claiming to have caused 30 casualties to the enemy.[161]

Next, 2 Bon I – followed by 1 Bon I, which had received the order to give up its attempts to cross the M'Bridege River, and by 4 Bon I – then resumed its advance inland, in the direction of Sao Salvador do Congo. This was supported by all the available transport aircraft and helicopters – whether flown by Angolans or Cubans. However, due to the ban on combat operations imposed by Fidel Castro, the MiGs remained at Luanda – at least according to Cuban sources, and despite reports about two air strikes on the SADF's Task Force Orange, from 25 and 26 December, mentioned earlier. This ban was lifted on 1 February 1976, when permission was granted for light aircraft and helicopters to re-deploy to the airport of M'banza-Kongo. Unintentionally, this led to the only recorded 'air combat' of this campaign.[162] On 7 February 1976, the Alouette III flown by a pilot known only as 'Fedor' and tasked for reconnaissance of the road from Quibocolo to Saurimo, encountered one of the CIA-operated Cessnas. Neither the Alouette nor the aircraft were armed, but their crews carried multiple firearms with them, and began

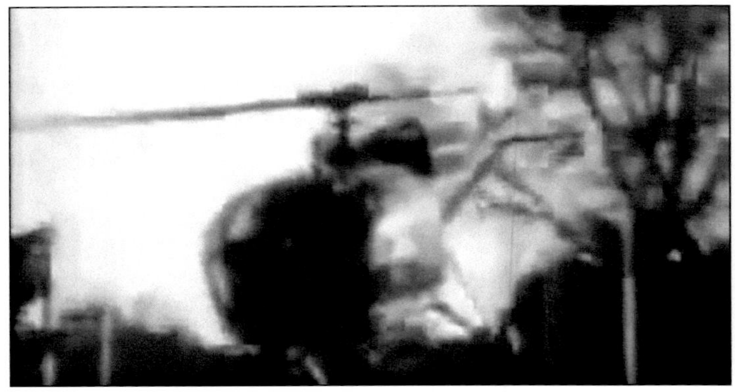

A still from a video showing one of the Cuban-operated Alouette III helicopters in action during the hunt for Portuguese and British mercenaries. The helicopter appears to have been painted in dark green overall on top surfaces and sides, and light grey or even white on the underside. Sadly, no national or other markings are recognizable. (Tom Cooper Collection)

CIA-recruited mercenaries continued flying supply sorties for the FNLA to the bitter end. The left wing-tip of this Auster was visibly damaged during a landing on a rather unsuitable site in northern Angola, in late January 1976. (Albert Grandolini Collection)

shooting at each other through the open windows of their aircraft. Fortunately for everybody involved, all the bullets missed and there was no damage.[163]

Unsurprisingly, considering exaggerated reports about clashes with foreign mercenaries, in combination with the lack of coordination between top FAR and MMCA commanders, and despite success of the Northern Front, the clashes with foreign mercenaries had negative consequences for what some of the Cuban officers intended to become the first combat deployment of the FAPA/DAA – i.e. its Cuban fighter-pilots and their Angolan MiG-21s. Rafael del Pino and his MiG pilots longed for action, but were still excluded from it. Thus, as soon as the South Africans withdrew from Waku-Kungo, the daunting Cuban came to the decision to re-deploy his jets to the airport of Cela – which used to have the only sufficiently long (2,000m/6,600ft) and metalled runway for 'his' MiGs in western central Angola. However, the South Africans had sabotaged the runway on their withdrawal by cratering it in dozens of places. Lacking equipment and troops for necessary repair works, and in emergency, the Cubans collected some of the cattle from nearby farms abandoned by the Portuguese, and offered this to the locals in exchange for their services. In reaction to such an offer, over 2,000 civilians gathered at the airport on the morning of 28 January 1976. Although using the most primitive methods imaginable, guided by the Cuban military engineer Echabasal, they helped repair the runway. The ground equipment – including fuel trucks, vehicles carrying auxiliary power units and other equipment necessary to operate combat aircraft – followed in the form of a big convoy which arrived safely on 2 February. Because the Soviets flatly refused to deliver more than one vehicle with compressed air for the brake system of Angolan MiGs, the Cubans were forced to improvise: they loaded a stock of compressed-air bottles on to one of the vehicles, and then a similar stock of high-pressure tyres for their MiGs into another. However, as soon as this convoy had reached the airport of Cela, and on order from deputy commander MMCA, General Rochelio Asevedo, it was re-routed to Negage – more than 800 kilometres (497 miles) away! As with so many other 'army' officers, Asevedo was ignorant of the necessities related to operating modern combat aircraft, and thus astonished at 'all the advanced equipment' deployed at Cela – and this at the time he knew that his ground forces were fighting foreign mercenaries that caused lots of trouble in northern Angola. Thus, acting spontaneously and without asking any questions, he destroyed the planning and work of dozens of involved officers and technicians in a matter of minutes. It is almost unnecessary to add that it took the officers of the DAA/FAR contingent days to recover at least some of the equipment in question and even longer to bring it back to working order. Of course, the MiGs remained at Luanda IAP.[164]

Destruction of the FNLA

That such, and many other precautions, of Cuban commanders proved unnecessary became obvious by 10 February 1976, when 2 Bon I reached M'banza Kongo, encountering only mines underway. The following assault was executed in – the meanwhile – usual fashion: while the artillery pounded enemy positions, starting at 1400hrs, the first infantry company, supported by T-34s, attacked along the main road, while the second made a flanking move to attack from the south-east, and the third was held in reserve. Although M'banza Kongo was easily defendable, the ELNA garrison quickly folded and withdrew.

The 1 Bon I and 4 Bon I exploited this opportunity to press their attack and launched a pursuit. On 13 February 1976, they overwhelmed ELNA elements that staged a last-ditch attempt at Cuimba. With the town under their control, the vanguard of the Angolan-Cuban units then caught an enemy reconnaissance party killing two mercenaries and two ELNA soldiers, while capturing another European. Cuimba was secured on 14 February, with which all the objectives of the offensive were achieved: for all practical purposes the ELNA – and thus the FNLA – was destroyed as a fighting force, and its survivors scattered or forced to leave Angola. Therefore, the Northern Front subsequently re-deployed some of its units – including the 3 Bon IM – to the Southern Front.[165]

CHAPTER 9
INVISIBLE HEDGE

By the end of January 1976, the balance of power in Angola had decisively shifted in favour of the Angola-Cuba alliance. On one hand, reinforced by 11,000 Cuban troops, FAPLA was in the process of crushing the FNLA in the north. On the other, UNITA was massively weakened by South African withdrawal. Although Jonas Savimbi claimed to have as many as '50,000 armed men' by that time, the FALA could at most rely on – at most – two dozen well-trained and reasonably-experienced infantry battalions – and it had to expect the onslaught of its enemy. To make matters worse, a new bout of fighting between UNITA and FNLA erupted in Huambo on 27 January 1976, on the eve on the FAPLA-FAR general offensive. Unsurprisingly, the CIA concluded on 26 January:

> In sum, as the situation now stands, there is little to prevent the MPLA side from winning a conventional military victory, and in fairly short order.[166]

Indeed, the MMCA officers were already neck-deep into planning a general offensive towards the south and east. Code-named Operación General Antonio Maceo, this was to involve multiple, simultaneous thrusts in different directions. During the first phase of this offensive, the primary axis of advance was to see the involvement of a full motorised brigade of the FAR, equipped with T-34/85s, BTR-60s and plentiful artillery support from Waku-Kungo to Alto Hama and Huambo. On the coast, a battalion-sized task force centred on a FAPLA battalion commanded by the Cubans, supported by a battery each of Grad-1Ps and ZiS-3s, and a single BM-21, was to advance from Porto Amboim on Sumbe, then Lobito, and Benguela, before following the Benguela Railway on Huambo. Another FAPLA force, supported by Cuban armour, was to advance from Mussande on Kuito (HQ of the FALA), while in the east two columns combined from FAR, FAPLA, and Katangese Tigers, supported by armour and artillery, were to advance from Saurimo and Luau on Luso.

Two Cuban-operated T-34/85s (or 'T-34M' in Cuban military parlance) on the streets of Huambo in February 1976. As usual, neither was wearing any kind of visible markings. (Albert Grandolini Collection)

During the second phase, which was to be initiated after securing the Benguela Railway, the Cubans intended to emulate the 'blitzkrieg' conducted by Task Force Zulu through advancing to secure one objective before stopping for a few days to rest, reorganize, resupply, and reconnoitre the route to the next objective. Furthermore, knowing that most of the bridges were destroyed, they expected that this would slow down their operation. Finally, they were not keen to catch up with the withdrawing SADF and suffer any unnecessary casualties as a result.[167]

Table 12: Cuban Commanders of Operación General Antonio Maceo

Position	Name
Commander MMCA	Abelardo Colomé Ibarra
Commander, Southern Front	Leopoldo Centra Frías
Commander, Eastern Front	Carlos Fernández Gondín

Rolling Southwards

On the coastal plain, Operation General Antonio Maceo was launched on 23 January, with the advancing Cuban column attacking several battalions of the ELNA and FALA defending Sumbe. As usual, BM-21s proved highly effective: the ELNA unit dispersed, and when the FALA attempted to rush in reinforcements, these were outflanked by two FAPLA companies that advanced around Ngunza, before striking into the rear of the enemy. The Angolans later claimed to have killed around 80 enemy combatants. With the insurgent resistance broken, the column entered Sumbe on 25 January and drove straight through for Lobito, its first main objective. Destroyed bridges and several FALA ambushes delayed its further advance, and the Cuban-commanded FAPLA-battalion only reached the town on 9 February, instead of 4 February as originally planned. However, the FALA did not attempt to defend the harbour, and this was seized the next day, followed by Benguela. From there the Angolan unit commanded by the Cubans launched the advance on Huambo along the Benguela Railway, easily dispersing enemy units on several occasions.[168]

On the central front, the Cuban motorised brigade quickly overran Waku-Kungo, on 26 January, and the nearby airfield. The FALA did attempt to defend, but suffered heavy losses to the infiltrated FAPLA infantry, which also sized the high ground in the enemy rear, thus blocking the main withdrawal route. Many of the insurgents that attempted to evade into the marshes drowned as a result. After stopping for a few days to enable Cuban engineers to prepare several crossing points over the Queve River, and Alouette helicopters to deploy reconnaissance parties in the enemy's rear, the Angolan-Cuban formation resumed its advance on 31 January. After crossing the Queve at Massongo, it seized Alto Hama a day later. The two FALA-battalions – about 1,600-strong in total – fought back fiercely but suffered more than 600 casualties. Unsurprisingly, when the Angolan-Cuban units re-launched their advance, they met only weak resistance before reaching Huambo. Expecting UNITA to defend its self-proclaimed capital, the FAPLA and the FAR made extensive preparations before investing the town, including an extensive barrage of the local airport. However, the FALA understood that resistance was futile and thus ordered all the 5,000 combatants it claimed to have in the area to withdraw. Huambo was thus secured on 9 February, without much fighting. A week later, the FAPLA battalion that cleared the railroad between Lobito and Huambo then joined the main force, before being sent in the direction of Lubango and Namibe, secured on 16 and 17 February 1976, respectively. Meanwhile, the main column marched on Kuito, which was defended by a FALA battalion fresh from completing its training. Contrary to what happened at Huambo, UNITA this time attempted to repulse the FAPLA and the FAR, and thus triggered fierce fighting in which the Cubans made extensive use of their artillery. After suffering heavy losses UNITA/FALA were left without a choice but to evacuate the town: on 10 February. Jonas Savimbi fled in the direction of Luso on board a Fokker F.27. Kuito was secured by the Angolans and Cubans on 12 February 1976.[169]

According to unofficial reports, the threat of an Angolan-Cuban assault on UNITA in eastern Angola prompted the Zambian president Kenneth Kaunda – an ally of Jonas Savimbi – to order an air strike by four SOKO J-21 Jastreb jets of the Zambia Air Force (ZAF) on FAR/FAPLA-positions in the Luau area on 28 January 1976. While the results of this attack remain unknown, word is that one of the involved jets was shot down by a Cuban-fired SA-7. When ordered to launch the second strike, not only the Zambian pilots, but also the commander of the ZAF, Air Commodore Peter

The first P-18 (ASCC-code 'Spoon Rest') early warning radar acquired by the FAPA/DAA, installed by the Soviets, and operated by the Cubans at Luanda IAP starting in January 1976. At the time, Cubans were particularly concerned about the possibility of air strikes by recently-delivered Zairian Mirage M5s. (Albert Grandolini Collection)

Cuban officers with two MiG-21MFs (serials C43 and C45) and a Mi-8M (serial H08) at Huambo airport in early March 1976. (Albert Grandolini Collection)

A Soviet An-12 transport unloading ground equipment for the 'MiG-21 Squadron' of the FAPA/DAA at Huambo airport. (Albert Grandolini Collection)

In addition to Cuban-flown MiGs, the FAPA/DAA was heavily reliant on a group of Portuguese and a few Cuban pilots that operated miscellaneous light aircraft – like this Beech 55 Baron. By March 1976, most of these had received camouflage colours applied in diverse patterns, but also a full set of national markings on the fin. (Albert Grandolini Collection)

Zuze, refused to 'fight for UNITA' – in turn provoking a fire-fight with loyalists at the Lusaka IAP, in which seven were killed. In attempt to recover the control over the air force later the same year, Kaunda stripped the ZAF of its independent status, and merged it into the unitary command of the Zambian military.[170]

What is certain is that on 4 February 1976, the two eastern columns of the FAPLA and the FAR had initiated their advance from Saurimo and from Luau. Only a day later, the Luau-column encountered determined resistance of the FALA near Lumenje, and had to fight bitterly for days before being able to break through, to meet the Saurimo-column at Bussaco. On 10 February, the combined force was confronted with defensive positions anchored on the southern bank of the Luxia River: these were collapsed only by the heliborne deployment of a commando unit in the enemy's rear. A day later, infantry, tanks and artillery of the Angolans and the Cubans began approaching Luena. Although having around 3,000 combatants in the area, Savimbi decided not to fight but to withdraw towards Gago Coutinho (meanwhile renamed Lumbala). Luena was thus seized on 14 February 1976. Three days later, two reinforced battalions resumed the advance in the direction of Lumbala – meanwhile the last stronghold of UNITA. This operation was slowed down by blown-up bridges and a series of ambushes and minefields. Thus, it took the Angolans and Cubans until 14 March to reach their objective. By then, most of between 2,000 and 4,000 FALA combatants fled the town – together with most of the local population – though not before they executed 17 Cubans captured during earlier fighting. What was left of UNITA then began a long trek towards a new – and remote – area where Savimbi intended to reorganize his movement and re-launch a guerrilla war 'from the scratch'. This proved anything other than easy, survivors of his battered organisation were subjected to merciless and relentless pursuit by what were now the government forces of Angola. All the time suffering heavy losses, the insurgent leader was finally forced to scatter his forces in mid-1976. In turn, declining to approach the border with South West Africa, the FAR and the FAPLA remained keen to let the South Africans complete their withdrawal – on 27 March 1976 – unobstructed. More was not necessary then; from the standpoint of the government in Luanda, UNITA and the FALA were finished.

MiG-21s in Action

Meanwhile, FAPA/DAA's MiGs were still at Luanda IAP. For a while at least, pilots of the MiG-21 Squadron busied themselves studying potential targets and developing plans for air strikes on Kitona AB and the Inga Dam, in western Zaire – should such prove necessary. It was only on 8 February 1976 that an emergency on the Southern Front prompted del Pino to launch an action over that part of Angola – entirely at his own discretion, and contrary to the still valid order from Fidel Castro. The emergency in question was caused when a 16-man strong team of Cuban special forces, led by Lieutenant Artemio Rodriguez Cuza, deployed by Alouettes 55 kilometres south of the Queve River, six days earlier, found itself cut off by the FALA, encircled and short on ammunition. Upon hearing about this problem during his visit to the newly-established HQ of the Southern Front, Del Pino quickly organized a rescue operation. On the next day (9 February 1976) he flew in a single MiG-21MF armed with two UB-16-57 rocket pods all the way from Luanda to provide top cover for a pair of Alouettes. Because of fierce ground fire, the helicopters could not land and pick up the troops. Operating in a great hurry because he was critically short on fuel, del Pino delivered just one attack, first unleashing all 32 of his rockets, and then spending all the ammunition from his internal 23mm cannon. This proved more than enough to scatter the opponents, and the Cuban special forces managed to escape on their own. It is almost unnecessary to say that the Cuban pilot returned to Luanda with only a memory of fuel in the tanks of his MiG-21MF.[171] Del Pino found himself facing fierce critique from his superiors, as recalled by González Sarría:

> Combat operations were still strictly prohibited. Rafael del Pino violated that order and was almost stripped of his wings by the chief of the MMCA, and put under house arrest until further notice.

Eventually, the dauntless Cuban flier was saved from being demoted and subjected to a military court martial through the personal intervention of Raul Castro, who stressed his earlier merits. Nevertheless, henceforth there were no end of reports about 'MiG strikes' from other parts of Angola. For example, on 10 February 1976, FALA troops reported a jet fighter high in the sky over Luena, and later during the afternoon, 'MiG strikes' on UNITA/FALA positions in this town, too. Whether these were genuine MiGs of the FAPA/DAA, propaganda-motivated claims by UNITA, or perhaps Zambian G-2s, remains unclear to this day: available Cuban sources deny having flown any kind of combat sorties before mid-February.[172]

On 19 February 1976 a pair of MiG-21MFs flown by Umberto Trujillo and Alexandro Morchon were forward deployed to the airport of Huambo. To avoid any kind of possible misunderstanding with army commanders, this time all the ground crews and support equipment were re-deployed on board one of TAAG's C-47s and a Soviet An-12. By the end of the month, the entire 'MiG-21 Squadron' was based at this airport, and on 20, 21, and 26 February Trujillo flew a series of visual-reconnaissance sorties along the Benguela Railway.[173] Deliveries of additional equipment – foremost drop tanks – and fuel enabled 26 further reconnaissance sorties over southern Angola, sometimes all the way to the border with South West Africa, by the end of the month. Meanwhile, the unit was 'reinforced' through the addition of a Cessna Skymaster, formerly owned by Cuca Brewery: this aircraft was deployed as a 'squadron hack' – for liaison, but sometimes also for reconnaissance purposes. Eduardo González Sarría recalled about the type of sorties flown by him and his comrades from Huambo in March 1976 as follows:

> We mostly escorted truck convoys, but also visual reconnaissance (carrying three drop tanks), combat air patrols (carrying four R-3S air-to-air missiles) and so on. Our armament consisted of up to four UB-16-57 rocket pods, each for 16 57mm rockets.

Wreckage of the Fokker F.27 destroyed by Cuban-flown MiG-21MFs of the FAPA/DAA at Lumbala airport on 13 March 1976. (Albert Grandolini Collection)

Unfortunately, only blurred videos and photographs too poor for reproduction of early Angolan MiG-21MFs are available. This one shows the example with serial 'C40' returning from a combat sortie from Huambo airport, in 1976, with two UB-16-57 rocket pods under its wings. At that time, FAPA/DAA's MiGs were still exclusively flown by Cuban pilots. (Mark Lepko Collection)

> Alternatively, our aircraft could carry two 500kg bombs, if operating from air bases on the sea level, or less heavier ones when operating from "hot and high" runways, like in Huambo. Another weapon we deployed in Angola were S-24 240mm rockets. That was a very tricky weapon able to flame out the engine when fired.

Operation New Shoes

On 8 March 1976, the MMCA ordered the re-deployment of four MiG-21MFs (flown by Benigno González Cortes, Emer Juan Bita, Alvio Cordova Mantecon, and Arhelio Cordero Rayes) to the airport of Luena. Ground crews and support equipment were transported by one of the Noratlases, while the fighter-bombers were supported by a single Alouette III (flown by Ases Ramos), and a Beech-18 (flown by del Pino). Once in Luena, the Cubans were informed about Savimbi planning to meet his top commanders in a church about one kilometre from the airport of Lumbala. They promptly prepared a corresponding air strike, code-named Operation New Shoes. Originally planned for the morning of 9 March, this was spoiled by two factors. The Beech-18 – this time flown by Modesto Conception Puna – which was to establish the precise position of the church and then guide MiG pilots into the attack, was forced into a hurried withdrawal by several SA-7s fired at it. Subsequently, the target zone was subjected to torrential rain, which lasted for four days. Correspondingly, a new attempt was initiated on 13 March. This time, the Beech-18 was late in reaching the target zone due to massive clouds. Thus, the first pair of MiG-21MFs – flown by del Pino and Cortes, and armed with two S-24 heavy unguided 240mm rockets each – descended out of the overcast skies about 2,000 metres (6,561ft) above Luena, only to find a Fokker F.27 transport of Air Zaire (registration 9Q-CLO) parked at the local airport and in the process of unloading food supplies from Rhodesia. Forgetting about his original target, del Pino dove to attack, exploiting the fact that his supersonic MiG couldn't be heard by those on the ground before it was too late. He unleashed both of his S-24s at the Fokker, followed by Cortes: their rockets not only obliterated the F.27, but also ruined the main terminal of the airport. The next two MiG-21MFs – flown by Bita and Cordoba – then bombed the runway and the main terminal. Between two and six SA-7s fired by FALA troops in return all missed the rapidly distancing fighter-bombers.[174]

The MiGs were hardly away when the belated Beech-18 finally appeared over Luena. After its crew found out that the actual target remained untouched, it observed another F.27 in the process of landing at the local airport. The pilot of the Beech called for MiG pilots to return and shoot the transport down, but these responded that they were out of munitions and on the way back to Luena. Therefore, the flight mechanic positioned his 7.62mm RPK machine gun into the open door while the pilot steered in the direction of the approaching Fokker. However, the mercenary pilot recognized the approaching threat, pushed his throttles and accelerated away. Two hours later, the four MiG-21MFs returned to crater the runway at Lumbala with four FAB-250 bombs, and hit the positions of a FALA mortar platoon near the Lufute River north of the airfield with four additional S-24s. The third attack on the airport of Lumbala took place on the morning of 14 March: better coordinated with the Beech-18 than before, two of the Cubans then cratered the runway with four additional 250kg bombs, while the other two plastered a nearby FALA camp with a total of 128 57mm S-5 rockets. Heavy rain precluded further attacks – enabling Savimbi to escape the wrath of

Two BTR-152s of the combined FAR-FAPLA forces involved in fighting in southern Angola, towards what many of the involved Cubans expected would have been the final episode of the war in Angola, in March 1976. (Mark Lepko Collection)

Cuban MiG pilots – until del Pino decided to take off regardless of the weather, this time flying the MiG-21MF with serial C41, armed with two UB-32-57 rocket pods. Once airborne, he lost direction in massive clouds, and eventually ran out of fuel before making an emergency landing on an airstrip outside Munhango, only recently secured by a company of FAPLA. Protected by a troop of Cuban troops flown in by two Alouettes, del Pino's MiG was refuelled and flown out by Umberto Trujillo with help of SPRD-99 rocket-boosters brought in from Cuba for this purpose, on 23 March. However, visibly shaken by his experiences in Angola, del Pino was subsequently taken off flying and then sent back to Cuba: he was never to fly combat again. Thus ended Operation New Shoes, in the course of which the 'MiG-21 Squadron' flew a total of 13 combat sorties, dropped 12 FAB-250 bombs, and fired 8 S-24 and 192 S-5 rockets, to destroy a single F.27, ruin the airport of Gago-Cutinio, and cause up to 100 casualties to the FALA.[175]

The End

By this time, the first regular DAA/FAR helicopter squadron had arrived in Angola. Initially equipped with four (later at least a dozen more) Mil Mi-8s – delivered from the USSR in mid-May 1976 – this saw plenty of action in the form of transporting top commanders, but also hauling reinforcements and supplies around the country. With one squadron each of Mi-8s, MiG-17Fs and MiG-21s in the country, the DAA/FAR formalized the status of these units in the form of an 'Air Group'. The commander of the same was Commandante Enrique Carreras, with Deputy Commandate Raúl P James. One of first tasks of Carreras' officers was to repair the abandoned airfield of Cabinda. Following various necessary works, this became the home-base of the MiG-17 and Mi-8 squadrons. MiG-17Fs of this unit flew their first combat operations against the FLEC on 1 May 1976.[176]

The rapid advance of the FAR and the FAPLA into southern Angola was followed by the DAA/FAR contingent, too. As soon as Menongue was secured, in early April 1976, the Cubans deployed a pair each of MiG-21MFs and MiG-17Fs there. These flew their first combat sortie on 7 April, when Umberto Trujillo led an attack on the FALA HQ and radio station in Tempue. In the course of this action, Trujillo hit the selected building with S-5 rockets first, after which one of MiG-17Fs deployed its internal 23mm and 37mm cannons. A few hits from these caused the local fuel depot to catch fire, which then spread to the nearby wood depot – resulting in a huge conflagration. In another attack, the MiGs hit two FALA camps outside Cuito Cuanavale, and in the third, the last remaining enemy concentrations in Cangombe and Muie. UNITA attempted to hit back through raiding Menongue airport during the night of 11 to 12 April, but not only missed its target: the following morning, all the MiGs were flown out to Mocamedes. This phase of the war in southern Angola ended with Cubans flying additional reconnaissance sorties along the border to South West Africa, and a cease-fire negotiated between Havana and Pretoria.

Overall, the multi-pronged offensive of the FAR and the FAPLA shattered the FALA – and, indeed, all there was of UNITA as of early 1976 – in a matter of a few weeks. Not only that it had reached all of its major objectives and recovered all the major towns, but it resulted in the virtual destruction of Savimbi's organisation. For example, out of around 5,000 insurgents that had retreated from Huambo between 8 and 9 February 1976, only around 300 were left a month later: the rest were either killed, captured, or simply dropped their weapons and went home. As such, Savimbi's order for his combatants to disperse and reverse to guerrilla warfare had come much too late to avoid crippling blows and only resulted in a chaos. His subsequent explanation that the CIA lured him into believing that new weapons – including ATGM-armed helicopters – were about to be delivered and to reverse the flow of the battle, appears to have been a rather cheap excuse. The truth was that many of his commanders insisted on retaining control over diverse towns: there is no reason to doubt the UNITA leader's keen interest in attempting something of that kind.[177]

Within something like 18 months, and thanks to the military intervention of Cuba, the MPLA not only secured itself in control of Luanda, but virtually all of Angola too. The Angolan Civil War thus appeared to have ended almost as soon as it began. Tragically, little did any of those involved know about how much longer, and how much bloodier this conflict was to become.

SELECTED BIBLIOGRAPHY

Abeli Meitho, Kisukula, *La désintégration de l'armée congolaise de Mobutu à Kabila*, (Paris: L'Harmattan, 2001). ISBN 9782747586931

Allport, Richard, *The Battle of Bridge 14* (online article), rhodesia.nl

Ardanuy, S., Manuel F., *Reconversión de Ejército Rebelde a Éjercito Regular al Servicio de la República de Cuba (1956-1970)* (Sevilla: Universidad Pablo Olavidé, 2012) ISBN 978-84-616-0546-0

Baines, Gary, 'The Saga of South African POWS in Angola 1975-82', *Scientia Militaria* (vol 40, no 2, 2012)

Baxter, Peter, *SAAF's Border War: The South African Air Force in Combat 1966-89* (Solihull: Helion and Company, 2012). ISBN 978-1908916235

Bell, Kelly, 'Operation Savannah: Task Force Zulu & the Rommel of Angola', (Modern War Magazine, Number 4)

Borges Coelho, João Paulo, 'African Troops in the Portuguese Colonial Army, 1961-1974: Angola, Guinea-Bissau and Mozambique', *Portuguese Studies Review* (10 (1) (2002))

Braeckman, Colette, *Le Dinosaure, le Zaïre de Mobutu* (Fayard, 1992) ISBN 978-2213028637

Breytenbach, Jan, *Forged in Battle; The birth and growth of 32 Battalion from former enemies and terrorists into decorated soldiers* (Pretoria: Protea Book House, 2014) ISBN 978-1-4853-0044-1

Bridgland, F, *Jonas Savimbi, A Key to Africa; The Story behind the Battle for Angola* (New York, Paragon House Publishers, 1987) ISBN 0-913729-33-7

Bruyère-Ostells, W., *Dans l'ombre de Bob Denard, les mercenaries francais de 1960 à 1989* (Noveau Monde Èditions) ISBN 978-2-36942-390-4

Butler, Shannon Rae, *Into the Storm: American Covert Involvement in the Angolan Civil War, 1974-1975*, (Dissertation, The University of Arizona, 2008)

Byangoy, Dieu Merci, *Le role de l'Armée dans la pacification des nations, Cas de la RDC et du Rwanda* (Université de Lubumbashi, 2011)

Cann, John P., *Counterinsurgency in Africa, The Portuguese Way of War 1961-1974* (Solihull: Helion & Company, 2012). ISBN 978-1-907677-73-1

Capita, B , *Cabindan National Movement, Cabinda, an African People and Nation Betrayed by U.S.A.* (Bern, 2017)

Carreras Rolas, E., *Por El Dominio del Aire: Memorias de un piloto de combate, 1943-1988* (Havana, Editora Politica, 2008) ISBN 978-959-01-0789-4

Castro, F., *Speech at the 15th Anniversary of the Founding of the MININT*, Karl Marx Theatre, Havana, 6 June 1976 (transcription posted at lanic.utexas.edu)

Castro, R., *Speech at the Ministry of the Revolutionary Armed Forces*, Mangos de Baragua (Santiago de Cuba province), 16 February 1977 (posted at lanic.utexas.edu)

Cooper, T., Weinert, P, Hinz, F., & Lepko, M., *African MiGs; MiGs and Sukhois in Service in Sub-Saharan Africa; Volume 1, Angola to Ivory Coast* (Houston, Harpia Publishing, 2010) ISBN 978-0982553954

Cooper, T., *Great Lakes Holocaust: First Congo War, 1996-1997* (Africa@War Volume 13), (Solihull, Helion & Co., 2013) ISBN 978-1909384651

Cooper, T., *Wings over Ogaden: The Ethiopian-Somali War, 1978-1979* (Africa@War Volume 18), (Solihull, Helion & Co., 2015) ISBN 978-1909982383

Cooper, T., *Hot Skies over Yemen, Volume 1: Aerial Warfare Over the Southern Arabian Peninsula, 1962-1994* (Middle East@War Volume 11), (Solihull, Helion & Co., 2017) ISBN 978-1912174232

Cosma, Wilungula B., *Fizi 1967-1986; le Maquis Kabila* (Paris, L'Harmattan,1997). ISBN 2-7384-5961-7

Del Pino, Rafael, *The African Adventure – A Cuban perspective of Air Operations in Angola* (online document, including English translation of del Pino's book 'Proa a Libertad')

Del Valle Céspedes, Gonzalo, *Angola; Memorias de un internacionalista cubano* (La Havana : Editorial Capitán San Luis, 2012). ISBN 978-959-211-407-4

Denard, B., Corsaire de la République (*orbspatrianostra.com*)

Le Colonel Kasongo 'Kava' répond aux reactions des lecteurs (I): la création de la Division Kamanyola ne fut pas une mauvaise idée', *desc-wondo.org*, 24 September 2013

Diario los Americas, '800 tanquistas Cubanos pelearon en Siria en 1974 contra Israel', 23 October 1998

Martin, E., R., *La batalla de Cabinda* (La Havana: Casa Editorial Verde Olivo, 2012) ISBN 978-959-224-309-5

Martin, F., J., *Histoire d'une guérilla fantôme, Le(s) Front(s) de libération de l'enclave du Cabinda* (Paris: Ifri, 2017) ISBN 978-2-36567-668-7

Fitzsimmons, S., *Mercenaries in Asymmetric Conflicts* (New York: Cambridge University Press, 2013) ISBN 978-1-107-67977-1

George, E., *The Cuban Intervention in Angola, 1965-1991. From Che Guevara to Cuito Cuanavale* (Oxon: Frank Cass, 2005) ISBN 0-415-35015-8

Gleijese, P., *Havana's Policy in Africa, 1959-76: New Evidence from Cuban Archives* (Cold War International History Project, Bulletin 5)

Gleijese, P., *Conflicting Missions, Havana, Washington and Africa 1959-1976* (The University of North Carolina Press, 2002) ISBN 0-8078-2647-2

Guevara y Moyano, I., *Latin American Fighters: A History of Fighter Jets in Service with Latin American Air Arms* (Houston, Harpia Publishing, 2009) ISBN 978-0982553909

Harmse, K. & Dunstan, S., *South African Armour of the Border War 1975-89* (Oxford: Osprey Publishing, 2017). ISBN: 978 1 4728 1743 3

Heitman, H-R., *South African War Machine* (Greenwich: Bison Books Corp., 1985) ISBN 0-8317-7929-2

Isaev, S., 'The 32nd Guards Air Fighter Regiment in Cuba (1962-1963)', (online book at airforce.ru)

Junior, M., *Popular Armed Forces for the Liberation of Angola; First National Army and the War* (1975-1992) (Bloomington: Authorhouse, 2015) ISBN 978-1-5049-4126-6

Junior, M., *Angola; the Failure of Operation Savannah 1975* (Bloomington: AuthorHouse, 2015) ISBN 978-1-5049-4129-7

Junior, M., *Angola; The Battle of Kifangondo 1975* (Bloomington: AuthorHouse, 2017) ISBN 978-1-5462-8341-6

Kasongo, Col., Le Colonel Kasongo 'Kava' répond aux reactions de lecteurs (I): la creation de la Division Kamanyola ne fut pas une mauvaise idée (Desc-wondo.org, 24 September 2013)

Kennes, E. & Larmer M., *The Katangese Gendarmes and War in Central Africa* (Bloomington, Indiana University Press, 2016) ISBN 9780253021304

Klepak, H., *Cuba's military 1990-2005, Revolutionary Soldiers During Counter-Revolutionary Times* (New York: Palgrave Macmillan, 2005) CH 978-1349533367

Labuschagne B., *South Africa's Intervention in Angola : Before Cuito Cuanavale and Thereafter*, (Thesis, Stellenbosch University, 2009)

Liebenberg, I., Risquet, J., & Shubin, V., *A Far-Away War; Angola 1975-1989* (Sun Press, 2015) ISBN 978-1-920689-72-8

Loiseau, Y. & de Roux, P.-G., *Portrait d'un révolutionnaire en général: Jonas Savimbi* (Paris: La Table Ronde, 1987) ISBN 2-7103-0330-2

Marcum, J., *The Angolan revolution, Vol.2, Exile Politics and Guerrilla Warfare 1962-1976* (Cambridge: Massachusetts Institute of Technology Press, 1978)

Martínez H. E., Kalimantán-2. Cronología de las armas (online article at monografias.com/)

Matos, J., 'La psychose des MiG dans la guerre de Guinée' *Airmagazine*, (No. 61, April-May 2014)

Matos, J., Cooper, T., 'Ginas über Afrika', *Fliegerrevue Extra Vol.24*

Meitho, Col. Kisukula Abeli, *La disintegration de l'armée congolaise de Mobutu à Kabila* (L'Harmattan, 2001)

Méndez, L. S., *Angola Frente Norte* (La Havana; Casa Editorial Olivo, 2015) ISBN 978-959-224-358-3

Miller, Jamie, Yes, Minister: Reassessing South Africa's Intervention in the Angolan Civil War, 1975-1976*Journal of Cold War Studies* (Volume 15, Number 3, Summer 2013)

Moorcraft Paul L., *African Nemesis; War and Revolution in Southern Africa 1945-2010* (London: Brassey's, 1990) ISBN 0 08 036715 1

Mos, Robert, *How did it come about that South African unconventional units, which were successful in many battles, were unable to turn their victories into political success during the South African Border War 1966 – 1989?* (Thesis, Univseriteit Leiden, 2013)

Nouzille, Vincent, *Les tueurs de la république; Assassinats et opérations spéciales des services secrets* (J'ai lu, 2016) ISBN 978-2290122129

Péan, Pierre, *Affaires africaines* (Fayard, 1983) ISBN 978-2213013244

Ramón Perez Cabrera, *La historia cubana en África*, (July 2013) ISBN 9781447502203

Rivas, S., *Playa Girón: the Cuban Exiles' Invasion at the Bay of Pigs, 1961* (Latin America@War Volume 2), (Solihull, Helion & Co, 2017) ISBN 978-1911096023

Scherman, J-P., *Ambush at Ebo: The Darkest Day in SAAC History*, (Staff Paper on Battle of Ebo, 2015)

Scholtz, L., *The SADF in the Border War 1966-1989* (Solihull: Helion & Company, 2015) ISBN 978 1 909982 76 5

Shubin, V., *The Hot 'Cold War': the USSR in Southern Africa* (London: Pluto Press, 2008) ISBN 978 0 7453 2472 2

Stapleton, T. J., *A military history of South Africa: from the Dutch-Khoi wars to the end of Apartheid* (Santa Barbara; Praeger, 2010) ISBN 978-0313365898

Stockwell, J., *In Search of Enemies; A CIA Story*, (W W Norton & Company Inc, New York, 1978) ISBN 978-0-393-00926-2

Telepneva, N., *Our Sacred Duty: The Soviet Union, the Liberation Movements in the Portuguese Colonies, and the Cold War, 1961-1975*, (Thesis, the London School of Economics, 2014)

Tickler, P., *The Modern Mercenary; Dog of War, or Soldier of Honour?* (Book Club Associates, 1987)

Toperczer, I., *MiG-17 and MiG-19 units of the Vietnam War* (Oxford: Osprey Publishing, 2001) ISBN 978-1841761626

Trujillo, H. H., *Trueno Justiciero, Mis campañas en cielo angolano* (La Havana, Ediciones Verde Olivo, 2005) ISBN 959-224-169-4

Uys, I., *Bushmen Soldiers; the History of 31, 201 & 203 Battalions during the Border War 1974-1990* (Solihull; Helion & Company, 2014) ISBN 978-1-909384-58-3

Van der Waals, W.S, *Portugal's War in Angola* (Pretoria: Protea Book House, 2011) ISBN 978-1-86919-351-5

Venter, Al. J, *Battle for Angola; the End of the Cold War in Africa 1975-89* (Solihull, Helion & Company Limited, 2017) ISBN 978-1-911096-41-2

Venter, Al. J, *Portugal's Guerrilla Wars in Africa; Lisbon's Three Wars in Angola, Mozambique and Portuguese Guinea 1961-1974* (Solihull: Helion & Company, 2013) ISBN 978-1-909384-57-1

Warwick, Rodney, 'Operation Savannah: A Measure of SADF Decline, Resourcefulness and Modernisation', *Scientia Militaria* (Vol. 40, no 3, 2012)

Waters, M-A., *Cuba & Angola; Fighting for Africa's Freedom and Our Own* (Pathfinder Press, 2013) ISBN 978-1-60488-046-5

Weigert, S. L., *Angola A Modern Military History, 1961-2002* (New York: Palgrave Macmillan) ISBN 978-0-230-11777-8

Wilsworth, C., *First in Last Out; The South African Artillery in Action 1975-1988* (Brixton: 30 Degrees South Publishers, 2010) ISBN 978-1-920143-40-4

Wolfers, M., Bergerol, J., *Angola in the Frontline* (London, Zed Press, 1983) ISBN 0-86232-106-9

NOTES

1 The Cabinda Enclave is a part of Angola separated from the rest of the country by the DR Congo's coast to the Atlantic Ocean. The area actually had its own history in form of the Cabindan kingdoms of N'Goyo, Kakongo, and Loango, until the Portuguese invasion of 1883. Sometimes called the 'Portuguese Congo', it was declared a protectorate in the Treaty of Simulambuco, in 1885, but experienced next to no developmental work during 87 years of the Portuguese rule. In 1956, the area was placed under direct administration of the Portuguese Governor-General of Luanda (see Martin, 2017, pp9-11). Subsequently, the area gained in importance because of discovery of oil sources. By 1973, its population grew to about 100,000, of whom around 25,000 were living in its capital (Cabinda City), while a year later the American Gulf Oil company is known to have been extracting about 140,000 barrels of crude a day – royalties for which reached US$550 million in that year, or about 70% of the Angolan income from foreign trade.

2 Van der Waals, pp. 62-72, 110-118 & Venter, 2013, pp. 132-133.

3 Van der Waals, pp. 78-82 & Venter, 2013, p. 138.

4 Van der Waals, pp. 114-119, 178-182; Stockwell, p. 48; Cann, 2015, pp. 41, 44; Venter, 2013, pp. 141 & 143; Guerra Colonial (www.guerracolonial.org), 'UPA/FNLA', extracted 24 April 2017 (henceforth, 'Guerra Colonial').

5 Van der Waals, pp. 179, 193 & Guerra Colonial, 'UPA/FLNA', extracted 24 April 2017. Notable is that various estimates of ELNA's strength for the period 1972-1974 vary widely, ranging from around 6,000 up to 12,000, or even 25,000. However, the most often available estimate – apparently based on an unknown CIA report – is for about 6,200 combatants (see Abbott, 1988, p9 or Van der Waals, pp84, 179, 193).

6 Van den Waals, pp. 68, 70-71, 77-78 & Cann, p. 38.

7 Van der Waals, pp. 121-123; Georg, p. 9 & Cann, p. 38.

8 Telepneva, p. 83, 119, 121; Georg, pp. 10-11; Gleijeses, 2002, p. 82; Cann, 2012, p. 38; Van der Walle, pp. 109, 113.

9 Junior, 2015, pp. 160-161; Venter, 2013, pp. 129, 134, 140-141; Van der Waal, p. 172 & Guerra Colonial. Notable is that some Mauser rifles received by the MPLA early on were original, German-made Mauser 98Ks, stocks of which were captured during World War II. The reason was that – at least initially – the Soviets attempted to hide their support for this movement.

10 Van der Waals, pp. 126, 160-162, 165, 169-178, 201-204, 214; Miguel Junior, 2015, pp. 167-169; George, pp. 46-46; Gleijeses, 2002, pp. 177-178; Venter, 2013, p. 341 & Guerra Colonial.

11 Shubin, pp. 7-9, 17, 27; George, p. 22; Telepneva, pp. 68, 74, 76-80; Weigert, p. 243.

12 Weigert, p. 243.

13 Van der Waals, pp. 125-126, 160; Telepneva, pp. 110, 121, 131-134, 145; Shubin, p. 19; Georg, pp. 47, 53.

14 Georg, pp. 22, 25-28, 32; Gleijeses, 2002, pp. 161-163, 166.

15 As a punishment, the advisors in question were subsequently forced to

go back and recover their weapons. For details see Georg, pp. 27-29 & Gleijeses, pp. 175-177.
16 Cuban sources always cite a 'Column'. However, the unit in question was a 'Squadron' in EPLA's parlance (see Junior, 2015).
17 Georg, pp. 36-39; Gleijeses, pp. 180-181.
18 Georg, pp. 39-41; Gleijeses, pp. 182-184.
19 Bridgland, pp. 85, 91.
20 Cann, 2012, pp. 40; Van der Waals, pp. 119, 127-129; Bridgland, pp. 58, 66-70, 89, 118; Loiseau & de Roux, pp. 137-138; 153, 184 & Guerra Colonial.
21 The figure of 25 killed is as provided by Savimbi; other sources cite up to 300 killed and injured FALA insurgents.
22 Van der Waals, p. 185; Brigland, pp. 71-73.
23 Van der Waals, pp. 129, 186, 189-190; Bridgland, pp. 71, 91; Loiseau & deRoux, pp. 143, 147, 154.
24 Bridgland, pp. 80, 84, 95 99; Van der Waals, pp. 185-187, 191-192; Loiseau & de Roux, p. 173; Guerra Colonial.
25 Coelho, pp. 136-137.
26 Cann, 2012, pp. 107-108; Coelho, pp. 140, 146.
27 Cann, 2012, pp. 108-113; Coelho, pp. 141-146.
28 Cann, 2012, pp. 110-11; Kennes & Larmer, pp. 78-83, 95; Coelho, p. 142.
29 CIA, 'Cuba, A Country Study', CIA/FOIA/ERR; Klepak, 2005, p. 42; cubadefensa.cu.
30 Rivas, 2016, pp. 23-24; cubadefensa.cu; Raul Castro, 1977; Ardanuy, p.239.
31 Ardanuy, pp.541-542.
32 Cubadefensa.cu. Notable is that all the Cuban units were significantly smaller than even their Soviet counterparts. For example, a standard tank battalion included three companies, each of which included one command tank and three two-tank platoons each, only, plus the tank of the battalion-commander – for a total of only 22 vehicles, or approximately the same number of vehicles as a single tank company of the US Army. Only the artillery units tended to follow the traditional pattern of six guns per battery, and three batteries per battalion (or a 'group'), even though some of these had only four-gun batteries. Another distinction of the Cuban military were its unit designations, designed to create confusion. According to this system of nomenclature in use in most Eastern countries, the designation of each unit starts with the prefix 'UM' – short of Military Unit (*Unidad Militar*) – followed by a four-digit number, which usually indicates their size and geographic location. Traditional military designations are used too, but frequently remain unknown. Furthermore, some of units have commemorative designations. For example, the UM1011 was also known as the 'Managua Tank Unit' or the tank unit '*Rescate de Sanguily*'. Similarly, Tank Brigades UM2600, UM1688, and UM1448 were also known as the 1st, 3rd, and 10th Tank Brigades, respectively. For further details, see, CIA, Handbook on the Cuban Armed Forces, April 1979, CIA/FOIA/ERR.
33 CIA, 'Military Deliveries to Cuba in 1974' & 'Cuba, a Country Study', 2002; DIA, 'Handbook on the Cuban Armed Forces', April 1979, CIA/FOIA/ERR.
34 DIA, 'Handbook on the Cuban Armed Forces', 1979; Fidel Castro, 6 June 1976.
35 Ardanuy, pp. 230-232; CIA, 'Cuba, A Country Study', 2002 & Guevara y Moyano, p. 112.
36 Isaev, 'The 32nd Guards Air Fighter Regiment in Cuba, 1962-1963' (online book available at airforce.ru); CIA, 'Soviet Military Deliveries to Cuba in 1974'; DIA, 'Handbook on the Cuban Armed Forces', April 1979; Ardanuy, pp. 230-233; Guevara y Moyano, pp. 113-117.
37 Russianships.info; Ardanuy, pp. 233-234, 239.
38 Ardanuy, p. 376; CIA, 'Cuba, a Country Study', 2002.
39 Gleijeses, 2002, pp. 190, 227-228.
40 Ibid, pp. 39-48 & cubadefensa.cu.
41 Gleijeses, 2002, pp. 189-197.
42 Matos et all, 'Ginas über Afrika', *Fliegerrevue Extra*, Vol.24; Eduardo González Sarría (retired Lieutenant-Colonel of DAA/FAR, with several tours of duty on MiG-21s and MiG-23s in Angola), interview, February 2010; Cooper et all, *African MiGs, Volume 1*, pp. 197-200.
43 Ibid.
44 Gleijeses, 2002, p. 226; Toperczer, pp. 53-54; Cooper, Yemen, pp. 38-41.
45 For Cuban involvements in Yemen and Ethiopia, see *Hot Skies over Yemen, Volume 1* and *Wings over Ogaden* (details in Bibliography).
46 Gleijeses, 2002, p. 226; cubadefensa.cu; Diaro Las Americas, 23 October 1998; Cooper, MiG-23, p. 12.
47 CIA, 'Zaire, National Intelligence Survey, 1973', CIA FOIA Electronic Reading Room (henceforth 'CIA/FOIA/ERR'); Dieu Merci Byangoy, 2011; Stockwell, p. 163 & Wilangula P Cosma.
48 Braeckmann, pp. 61, 170, 229 & Dieu Merci Byangoy, 2011.
49 Braeckmann, p. 61; DIA, 'Zaire, Mobutu and the Military, An intelligence Assessment', August 1982; Dieu Merci Byangoy, 2011; Desc-wondo.org, 24 September 2013.
50 CIA, 'Zaire, National Intelligence Survey, 1973', CIA/FOIA/ERR.
51 Ibid; Loi n 75/010 du 25 avril 1975 portant création et organisation de la Force Navale Zaïroise; Colette Braeckmann, p. 229.
52 For further details on chaos within the FAZ, and its poor condition, see Meitho, pp. 25-26; CIA, 'Zaire, National Intelligence Survey 1973', CIA/FOIA/ERR; Stockwell, p. 209. Perhaps the best example for the poor state of the FAZ as of 1975 was the fate of two Swift patrol boats delivered in this year. Both remained operational for only a few weeks, before the lack of maintenance and mishandling by their crews rendered them non-operational.
53 Meitho, p. 7 & CIA, 'Zaire, National Intelligence Survey, 1973 , CIA/FOIA/ERR.
54 Stockwell, p. 102; CIA, 'Zaire, National Intelligence Survey, 1973', CIA/FOIA/ERR; Cooper, 2013, pp. 15-17.
55 Scholtz, 2013, pp. 8, 41-42; Warwick, pp. 359-364, 386-389, 366, Stapleton, pp. 154-158.
56 Baxter, pp. 10-18; Scholtz, 2013, pp. 9-10; Warwick, pp. 361-362; Van der Waals, p. 228; Venter, 2016, pp. 125-127, 134-136.
57 Van der Waals, pp. 263-264, 270-274; Gleijeses, 2002, pp. 233, 241-242; Telepneva, p. 236.
58 Van der Waals, pp. 263-264, 270-274; Georg, p. 50; Gleijeses, 2002, pp. 233, 241-242; Miguel, 2015, p. 132; Junior, 2015, p. 11; Shubin, p. 38; Telepneva, p. 236; Weigert, p. 57.
59 Bridgland, pp. 104, 118; Van der Waals, p. 272; Weigert, pp. 54-56; Gleijeses, 2002, p. 241; Butler, pp. 471-472, 477-478.
60 Stockwell, pp. 67, 155; Brigland, pp. 116, 121; Butler, pp. 383-384; 387, 398-400; Gleijeses, 2002, pp. 238, 250; Telepneva, p. 23; Loiseau & de Roux, p. 188.
61 Georg, p. 56.
62 Not only because of his political and organisational work in Luanda, but also because he remained in Angola all the time, Nito Alves – probably the best qualified political figure in the MPLA – gained immense popularity in the country. Considered a 'radical leftist' by many, Alves subsequently enjoyed ever stronger support from the USSR. Ultimately, this led him on a collision course with Neto: their differences were to culminate in a coup attempt instigated by Alves in May 1977, which was crushed with help of the Cuban military.
63 The figures provided here are medians of those provided by all available sources. Actual military strength of the three Angolan nationalist movements as of the first half of 1975 remains a sort of a mystery. On one side, not one of the available estimates for the MPLA/FAPLA is precise in regards of whether it includes only the FAPLA, or the Poder Popular units, too. Similarly, while the coordinated Sino-Zairian training programme for the ELNA, launched in mid-1974, was supposed to build-up a force of 15,000 – nobody knows how much of the same was ever realised.
64 Junior, 2015, pp. 18-21, 171-172; Shubin, pp. 34-35, 41-44; Gleijeses, 2002, pp. 244, 247-250, 349-350; Marcum, 1978, pp. 253-256; Georg, pp. 54, 61.
65 Georg, pp.56, 58, 63-64; Gleijeses, 2002, pp. 245-250, 254; Kennes & Larmer, pp. 102-116; Junior, 2015 (FAPLA), pp. 16, 22, 171-173. Notably, the number of troops the FNLC brought into the fight remains unclear. Contemporary estimates for its troop-strength varied from 2,100 to 6,000, with authors considering the lower range for 'more credible'.
66 Georg, p. 311; Brigland, pp. 119-120; Marcum, 1978, pp. 258-259; Gleijeses, 2002, pp. 251-252; Weigert, p. 59; Butler, p. 310.
67 Marcum, 1978, pp. 258-259; Junior, 2017, p. 2; Brigland, p. 119; Gleijeses, 2002, p. 252; Georg, p. 59; Shubin, p. 41; Butler, p. 500.
68 According to Brigland, (p. 123) Savimbi cited up to 260 executed recruits, mostly from central Angola.
69 Shubin, p. 47; Marcum, 1978, p. 260; Brigland, pp. 119, 123; Gleijeses, 2002, pp. 252-254; Kennes & Larmer, p. 114.
70 Junior, 2015, p. 10; Junior, 2015, pp. 12-13, 24; Junior, 2017, p. 3; Georg, p. 60; Shubin, p. 47; Brigland, pp. 125-126; Telepnova, p. 251, Liebenberg et all, p. 98. Savimbi later claimed that the convoy carried between 8,000 and 10,000 members of UNITA and FALA, and that most of them were killed in the ambush near Dondo (see Weigert, p. 59).
71 Subsequently, the CIA bought four Alouette IIIs for the FNLA – which were never pressed into service due to the lack of qualified crews – and attempted to acquire two Douglas AC-47 gunships from surplus USAF stocks.
72 Butler, p. 506; Stockwell, pp. 88-90, 124, 206, 265; Bridgland, p. 126; Junior, 2017, pp. 3-4; Gleijeses, 202, p. 257; Telepnova, p. 252.
73 Junior, 2017, pp. 5, 11, 19-22; Stockwell, pp. 121, 130, 135.
74 Waters, 2013, p. 25; Gleijeses, p. 268; Junior, 2015, p. 24.

75 During the battle of 7 September, the FNLA/ELNA claimed a 'Portuguese-flown Fiat G.91R' jet fighter as shot down. However, as described below, none of these were around Angola at the time.

76 Junior, 2015, pp. 21, 24; Stockwell, p. 163; Gleijeses, 2002, p. 269.

77 Bridgland, pp. 126-127; Junior, 2015 (FAPLA), pp. 16, 22-23; Junior, 2015 (Savannah), pp. 37-38; Stockwell, pp. 150-164; Gleijeses, 2002, p. 258; Weigert, p. 59; Marcum, 1978, p. 261.

78 Sources differ in regards of the size of the FALA unit, some mentioning just 'one company'.

79 Stockwell, pp. 151-164; Venter, 2016, pp. 248-249; Junior, 2015 (Savannah), pp. 37-39; Miller, p. 28; Harmse & Dunstan, pp. 10-11; Wolfers & Bergerol, p. 15.

80 Labuschagne, pp. 12-14, 19; Miller pp. 7-12; Warwick p. 356; Gleijeses, 2002, p. 294; Scholz, 2015, pp. 13-14; Venter, 2016, p. 248.

81 Miller, pp. 13-18, 20; Gleijeses, 2002, pp. 276, 294-295; Warwick p. 368.

82 Scholz pp. 17-18; Miller, pp. 21-25, 27-28; Warwick, pp. 356-357, 368, 390; Gleijeses, 2002, pp. 295-296; Breytenbach pp. 11, 13, 16; Venter, 2016, pp. 245-247.

83 Waters 2013 p. 26.

84 Ibid, p. 27.

85 According to an agreement signed in 1965, Cuba was prohibited from delivering weapons provided by the USSR to any third parties – at least without Moscow's approval.

86 Georg, pp. 63-67; Gleijeses, 2002, pp. 259-261, 265; Waters, 2013, pp. 25-28; ecured.cu/BM-21, Lázaro Salgado Méndez pp. 40-42, 57,63-64, 77, 91-92, Gonzalo Del Valle Céspedes pp. 24, 26, Enrique Martínez Hernández extracted 26 March 2018.

87 Céspedes, p. 26.

88 Warwick, p. 370: Miller, pp. 28-30; Uys, pp. 19-20, 27, 34, 36: Breytenbach, pp. 25-26, 30, 39, 49; Wolfers & Bergerol p. 15.

89 Notable is that while the usually available sources of reference tend to cite only the presence of these two task forces and two battle groups, and their operations only, eventually, at least *three* task forces and *seven* battle groups formed from various units of the SADF, and its allies, became involved in Operation Savannah (for details, see the further below).

90 Nick-named the 'Dinky Toy', the Beech Baron in question was armed with a Browning machine gun and flown by SAAF pilot, Major Piet Uys (see Venter, 2016, p. 257).

91 Junior, 2015 (Savannah), p. 43; Warwick, pp. 369-370, 392; Stapleton, p. 170; Harmse & Dunstan pp. 11-12; Uys, pp. 37-38; Breytenbach, pp. 61-64, 66-68; Georg, pp. 71-72; Venter, 2017, pp. 257-259; Wolfers & Bergerol, p. 23; Harmse & Dunstan p. 12.

92 Warwick, p. 370; Georg, pp. 72-73; Junior, 2015 (Savannah), p. 43; Uys, pp. 39-41; Breytenbach, pp. 69-76, 85-86, 93; Harmse & Dunstan, p. 12; Wolfers & Bergerol, pp. 20-23.

93 Céspedes, p. 33. In comparison, Breytenbach (see p. 115) later recalled a position occupied by around 1,000 troops, supported by a large concentration of support weapons, including 15 mortars, additional recoilless guns and heavy machine guns. Here it is important to note that although Céspedes' force was supposed to include two FAPLA battalions, none of the available Angolan or Cuban sources actually cites the participation of more than one of these in the following battle. What exactly happened with the second FAPLA battalion from the CIR 2 prior to this clash remains unknown. The only available detail in this regard is that the FAPLA cited the presence of 'seven (infantry) squadrons' (see Wolfers & Bergerol, p. 24).

94 Ibid, p. 33-35; Gleijeses, 2002, p. 303; Cabrera, pp. 199-204; Breyentbach, pp. 101-115; Georg, pp. 75-76; Uys, pp. 41-42; Junior, 2015 (FAPLA), p. 29; Wolfers & Bergerol, p. 24.

95 Breyentbach, pp. 101-115; Georg, p. 76; Uys, pp. 42-43; Junior, 2015 (Savannah), p. 43; Breytenbach pp. 136-144.

96 The Cubans were already trained on Strela-2s. This advanced variant was delivered by Moscow because of the perceived threat of newly-delivered Dassault Mirage M5s of the FAZA.

97 Originally, this deployment of the Cuban artillerymen was a result of an MPLA request made in September 1975, related to the requirement to train enough Angolan soldiers to man the various heavy weapons which were ordered from the USSR and about to arrive in much larger quantities than ever before. Therefore, it was by sheer accident that the deliveries of Soviet arms coincided with MPLA's desperate plea for help and – apparently – 'prompt' arrival of the Cuban reinforcements. Gleijeses, 2002, pp. 303, 307-308; Georg, pp. 77-78; Ecured, BM-21; Cabrera p. 208.

98 Sublin, p. 59.

99 Unofficial Cuban sources often claim that the first two flights of Britannias to Congo-Brazzaville took place on 1 and 3 October 1975. However, such claims remain unconfirmed.

100 Despite Moscow's refusals to do more, early on, there is no doubt that at least one Soviet officer, Colonel Yuriy Mitin – colloquially known as 'Comrade Yuriy' in Angola – did take part in the battle of Quifangondo, on 10 November 1975. At the time, he was assigned to the 9th BRIM's artillery group (see Shubin, p. 57).

101 Waters, 2013, pp. 127, 130; Villegas p. 44; Georg p. 81; Shubin, pp. 53, 57; Ecured BM-21 Entry; Gleijeses, 1996/1997, pp. 11-15; Gleijeses, 2002, p. 325; CIA, 'The President's Daily Brief', 13 January 1976, CIA/FOIA/ERR

102 The regiment included one group each of M-30 122mm Howitzers, D-44 85mm guns, 120mm mortars and ZPU-4s. Diverse sources mention that these three ships also carried a motorized infantry battalion, as well as tank crews, with a total of 1,253 men (see Georg p. 99; Gleijeses, 2002, p. 317 & Waters, 2013, p. 128).

103 Georg, pp. 82, 99; Gleijeses, 2002, pp. 305-308, 314-317, 320, 325; Cabrera, pp. 208, 246, 278; Ecured Carlota and BM-21 entries.

104 The first recorded sortie by aircraft and pilots associated with the future Angolan air force took place on 7 October, when a light aircraft provided reconnaissance for a FAPLA column in southern Angola.

105 Cooper et all, *African MiGs*, Volume 1, p. 17. Notable is that the acronym TAAG remains in widespread use until today. Another notable fact is that, although now perceived as controlled by a Marxist movement (MPLA), one of first decisions of the TAAG was to place an order for two Boeing 737-200Cs airliners and civilian airport-related equipment in the USA. Although the delivery of the same was embargoed by the US State Department in January 1976 (see Flight International, 'Air Transport', 10 January 1976), the same was eventually lifted, two months later, and both Boeings arrived at Luanda IAP in April (Flight International, 'Air Transport', 24 April 1976). The TAAG continued purchasing US-made aircraft – including more Boeing 737s, at least one Boeing 707, and at least one Lockheed L-100-20 – during the following years, too (Flight International, 'World News', 21 February 1976).

106 Ibid; del Pino, *The African Adventure*, p. 95; Carreras Rolas, p. 214. According to del Pino (p. 95), Jorge Quintana Barbosa and René Corredera Brito were already assigned to the Cuban military mission in Guinea-Bissau before being re-deployed to Angola. Notable is that DIAMANG used to be a 'state within a state', which controlled much of the local economy during the times of the Portuguese rule. The consortium survived until 1986, when it was nationalised by the Angolan government.

107 Cooper et all, *African MiGs*, Volume 1, p. 17 & Gleijeses, 2002, p. 265. According to Shublin (p. 60), the Mozambican government provided not only one Noratlas (which was reportedly in action already during the SADF's assault on Namibe), but also (at least one) 'Dakota' (i.e. C-47 or DC-3), and even the BM-21s used to crush the FNLA/FAZ invasion from the north may have been rushed to Angola from Mozambique. Notable is that for most of the 1970-1990s, there were reports about the FAP leaving behind between 4 and 12 Fiat G.91Rs in Angola. However, subsequent research has shown that all of the related rumours – including those about G.91s being deployed in combat – are unsubstantiated.

108 del Pino, *The Adventure in Africa*, pp. 97-98.

109 Carreras Rolas, p. 215 & del Pino, *The Adventure in Africa*, pp. 94, 99. Notable is that the contemporary US intelligence reports cited an acquisition of MiG-17Fs from Nigeria (see 'Cuban Military Intervention in Angola: Report', Department of State Telegram, Ref. STATE 003167, from 15 January 1976, CIA/FOIA/ERR). Of further interest is that one of the Cuban pilots that arrived in Angola few weeks later, Eduardo González Sarría (interview, February 2010) recalled that the maintenance stencils on MiG-17Fs were applied in the French language – thus indicating that these aircraft were originally planned to be delivered somewhere else.

110 Cooper et all, *African MiGs*, Volume 1, p. 18.

111 As of 1975, the DAA/FAR had no MiG-21MFs in service: it operated the slightly older MiG-21M instead.

112 González Sarría, interview, February 2010. This and all subsequent quotations from González Sarría are based on transcriptions of the same interview.

113 Carreras Rolas, p. 215. In comparison, del Pino (p. 101) recalled the delivery date of the first MiG-21MFs in Angola as 8 January 1976. Notable is that according to del Pino (pp. 111-112), at an unknown date in January 1976 two Portuguese pilots also appeared at Luanda IAP, both supposedly veterans of the FAP. The story was that the Communist Party of Portugal had sent them to Angola to 'help out'. Once in Luanda, they received commendation letters from the MPLA's Minister of Defence, Iko Carreiras, who – desperate for close-air-support – forwarded them straight to the DAA/FAR detachment. Nevertheless, due to orders from Havana banning combat operations of the MiGs, the Cubans never let them anywhere close to 'their' aircraft.

114 Méndez, pp. 71, 77-81, 86, 91-92, 106-107.

115 Wolfers & Bergerol, p. 17.

116 Georg, pp. 73-74, 88; Wilsworth, p. 45-47; Junior, 2017, pp. 5, 19;

Cabrera, pp. 210-215; Angola Working Group Papers pp. 77, 84 & 89.
117 Méndez pp. 71, 77-81, 86, 91-92, 106-107.
118 Shubin, p. 58; Georg, pp. 81, 88; Gleijeses, 2002, p. 310; Ecured BM-21 entry.
119 Georg pp. 89-90, 317; Wilsworth, pp. 30-31, 45-48, 56-57; Stockwell, pp. 213-215; Junior, 2017, pp. 4, 6, 14, 24; terryaspinall.com.
120 Martin, 2017, pp. 13-16.
121 Martin, 2017, pp. 16-18 & Gleijeses, 2002, p. 262.
122 CIA, 'Talking Points for Sec. Kissinger, National Security council Meeting on Angola', 27 June 1975, CIA/FOIA/ERR & Martin, 2017, p. 18.
123 Martin, 2017, p. 18 & Cabindan National Movement, 2017, p. 10.
124 Most of the mercenaries used to serve in the Presidential Guard of the Gabonese President Omar Bongo, which in turn was closely linked to the SDECE within the complex of informal networks generically known as the 'France-Africa' (*Franceafrique*), and proved crucial in enabling Paris to exercise strong influence upon most of its former colonies on that continent (see Péan et all, pp. 164-175 & Denard, orbspatrianostra.com).
125 Cuban sources cite the presence of two FAZ battalions, about 150 mercenaries of French, but also US and Portuguese origin (see ecured.cu) totalling around 2,000. For Western sources, see Stockwell, p. 164; Gleijeses, 2002, p. 312 & Martin, 2017, p. 18.
126 Martin, pp. 37-51, 166-167.
127 Ibid; George, pp. 66-67, 82-83; Junior, 2017 (FAPLA), pp. 19-20, 35; ecured.cu.
128 Martín, pp. 37-51, 166-167.
129 Martín, pp. 47-55, 69-71; George, pp. 83-84; Cabindan National Movement, 2017, pp. 10-11 & ecured.cu.
130 Martín, pp. 63-71; Denard, orbspatrianostra.com; ecured.cu; George, p 84; Bruyère-Ostells, p. 176 & Cabindan National Movement, 2017, pp. 10-11.
131 Scholtz, p. 18; Gleijeses, 2002, p. 313; Cabrera, p. 277; Wilsworth, pp. 51-55; Warwick, p. 370; Georg, p. 94; Uys, pp. 44-46; Breytenbach, pp. 154-163; Junior, 2015 (Savannah), p. 103; Wolfers & Bergerol, p. 27; Scherman, p. 14
132 Subsequently, Mundo Real was appointed the Commander, Southern Front, FAPLA, after Frias took over the MMCA.
133 Cabrera, pp. 278-283; Ecured.cu (Operacion Carlota & BM-21); Gleijeses, 2002, pp. 314-315; Georg, pp. 94-96; Wolfers & Bergerol, p. 27; Junior, 2015 (Savannah), pp. 45, 50, 101.
134 Notable is that in the SADF of the mid-1970s, an artillery troop included four artillery pieces, while an artillery battery included two troops.
135 Scherman, p. 14; Moorcraft, pp. 91-92; Wilsworth, pp. 51-58, 63-67, 74-75, 79; Warwick, pp. 372-375, 380, 394; Heitman, pp. 170-175.
136 Wilsworth, pp. 55-57; Georg p. 96.
137 del Pino, *The African Adventure*, p. 96.
138 Warwick, p. 372; Georg, p. 97 & Scherman, pp. 14-21 (Scherman provided the most detailed account of the following Battle of Ebo).
139 Scherman, pp. 21-28; Cabrera, pp. 289-291; Wolfers & Bergerol, pp. 39-42; Breytenbach, pp. 185-186; Wilsworth, p. 63; Gleijeses, 2002, pp. 317 & 484. Despite reports that two crewmembers of the Cessna 185 survived the downing and were held imprisoned in Luanda, a privately-run investigation 30 years later provided unmistakable evidence for all three South Africans being killed in the crash, and then buried by the locals.
140 Georg, p.103; Allport; Wilsworth, p. 99.
141 Wilsworth, pp. 75-83, 86-89, 98-99, 121; Warwick, pp. 374-375; Harmse & Dunstan, p. 13; Heitman, pp. 172-173; Breytenbach, pp. 198-200; Cabrera, p. 303. For a detailed overview of Bridge 14, see Georg, pp. 102-103 & Allport.
142 All available Angolan and Cuban sources confirm a major setback, but remain elusive about details of this clash in general, and the losses in particular (see Gleijeses, 2002, p. 321).
143 Warwick, pp. 375 & 392; Willsworth, pp. 112 & 119. According to same source, the 'enemy fighter jet' that attacked the SADF's position on 26 December 1975, deployed unguided rockets.
144 Warwick, pp. 375-381, 394; Baines, p. 109; Wilsworth, pp. 77, 110-115; Heitman, p. 173; Junior, 2015 (FAPLA), p. 33; Junior, 2015 (Savannah), pp. 91, 119; Wolfers & Bergerol, pp. 42-43; del Pino, *The African Adventure*, p. 96.
145 Wolfers & Bergerol, pp. 32-33, 46-47; Heitman, p. 173; Wilsworth, pp. 90-97; Cabrera, p. 314
146 Gleijeses, 2002, p. 325; Wilsworth, pp. 112, 119; Wolfer & Bergerol, p. 54; Ecured.cu (BM-21 entry); Georg, pp. 105-106.
147 Stockwell, p. 202.
148 Brigland, pp. 142-143, 149-150, 155, 159, 160-163; Scholtz, pp. 18-20; Stockwell, pp. 202-207. By this time, the SAAF is known to have suffered a particularly painful loss, when a SA.330 Puma helicopter was shot down by SADF anti-aircraft gunners in a blue-on-blue incident on 4 January 1976 (see Warwick, p. 384), killing the crew consisting of Captains F. Immelman and C. D. de Wit, and sergeant G. W. Kellet.
149 Ironically, while the Cuban sources – like Mendez, Cabrera, and Céspedes – describe the flow of subsequent operations in corresponding fashion (see Gleijeses [2002, p. 238], Georg [p. 84] and even contemporary CIA intelligence reports [CIA Weekly Summary, 2 January 1976], describe it in the way the FAPLA/ELNA expected the Cubans and Angolans to advance!
150 Junior, 2015 (FAPLA), pp. 24, 27, 173-174; Cabrera, pp. 237-239, 246; Georg, pp. 106-107; Gleijeses, 2002, p. 338; Mendez, pp. 159-160, 268; Céspedes, pp. 196, 212.
151 González Sarría, interview, February 2010. During the fighting for Negage airport, the Cuban SA-7 team narrowly missed a Fokker F.27 that was taking off. Contemporary rumour was that Holden Roberto was on board of that aircraft.
152 Georg, pp. 107-108; Cabrera, pp. 239-249; Mendez, pp. 141; 162-168; Céspedes, pp. 93-106, 125-131.
153 Tickler, p. 92; Cabrera, pp. 251-257; Mendez, pp. 193-199, 203-204, 211-215, 225; Céspedes, pp. 152-158, 162-163, 169-190
154 Stockwell, pp. 217-223; Tickler, pp. 62-68; Fitzsimmons pp. 109-110.
155 Tickler, pp. 62-63, 69-83; Fitzsimmons, pp. 112, 116, 119, 123, 133.
156 Tickler, pp. 76-78; Fitzsimmons, pp. 123, 131, 138; Céspedes, p. 173; Cabrera, p. 258.
157 Céspedes, pp. 180-182.
158 Ibid, pp. 180-183; Tickler, pp. 87-88; Fitzsimmons, pp. 125-127, 140-149, 159; Cabrera, p. 259.
159 Céspedes, pp. 183-191; Tickler, pp. 90-96; Fitzsimmons, pp. 139-159.
160 Céspedes, pp. 267-268.
161 Céspedes, pp. 192-196.
162 Carreras Rolas, p. 215 & Warwick, p. 375 & 392.
163 González Sarría, interview, February 2010.
164 del Pino, *The African Adventure*, pp. 101-103. To add salt to the injury, most of precious ground equipment from that convoy was subsequently lost. The vehicle carrying the high-pressure tyres was abandoned only 20 kilometres outside Cela. The trailer truck loaded with rockets had an engine burn-out about 10 kilometres outside Quibala. The vehicle carrying the start-up engine drove over a mine near Camabatela and was totally destroyed. Finally, only a part of the column arrived at Negage, while the rest went astray and disappeared.
165 Céspedes, pp. 201-207, 210, 213, 218; Mendez, pp. 227-229; Cabrera, pp. 262-264.
166 CIA, 'Intelligence Memorandum: the Present Military Situation in Angola', 26 January 1976, CIA/FOIA/ERR.
167 Georg, pp. 110-111; Cabrera, pp. 319-322; Wolfers & Bergerol, pp. 55-56; Bridgland, p. 171.
168 Bridgland, p. 171, 175; Wolfers & Bergerol, pp. 54-57; Gleijeses, 2002, p. 340; Cabrera, p. 322.
169 Brigland, p.127, 166-177, 182, 195; Cabrera, pp. 319-323; Wolfers & Bergerol, p. 56; Junion, 2015 (Savannah), p. 136; Del Pino, p. 101; Stockwell, p. 250.
170 Brigland, pp. 187-188.
171 Ibid, pp.105-107. Years later, Cuza finally found an opportunity to meet del Pino and thank him for flying this attack and saving his unit.
172 Bridgland, pp. 196.
173 According to the recollections of various Cuban sources and retired DAA/FAR pilots interviewed over the last ten years, none of the Cuban flying units deployed to Angola ever received any kind of an official designations. Instead, they were known as 'MiG-17 Squadron', 'MiG-21 Squadron' and similar.
174 Carreras Rolas, p. 216 & del Pino, pp. 117-119. The CIA was subsequently forced to pay US$600,000 to Mobutu, who was enraged over the loss of 'his' aircraft in Angola.
175 Del Pino, pp. 120-122.
176 Carreras Rolas, p. 216.
177 Bridgland, pp. 172-200; Loiseau & de Roux, pp. 239-240; Cabrera, pp. 314-316; Junior, 2015 (FAPLA), p. 34; Georg, pp. 111-112; Stockwell, pp. 233-234, 240.

ABOUT THIS BOOK

As of 1975, the decades-long insurgency in Angola appeared to be coming to its conclusion. However, with no fewer than three major insurgent movements fighting for supremacy, the war continued and then South Africa, the USA, the Soviet Union, Zaire and Cuba became involved.

Affairs like the CIA's efforts to destabilise Angola for little else but to recoup its prestige after the catastrophic defeat in South Vietnam, or the South African military intervention in Angola – Operation Savannah – have attracted lots of public attention and are relatively well covered in related publications. However, the final stages of the Portuguese withdrawal, the military build-up of three native insurgent forces, and then the onset of the Cuban military intervention in Angola – Operation Carlotta in 1975 and 1976 – remain largely unknown.

Based on extensive research with help from Angolan and Cuban sources, the 'War of Intervention in Angola, Volume 1' provides a unique insight precisely into the latter topic. It traces the failures of the US-supported FNLA, the growth and reorganization of the MPLA into a conventional army; the Cuban military intervention in Angola, the capabilities and intentions of Angolan and Cuban forces, the performance and experiences of war with South Africans, and the diversity of rival armed nationalist movements.

The volume is illustrated with over 100 rare photographs, half a dozen maps and 18 colour profiles.

ABOUT THE AUTHORS

Adrien Fontanellaz

Adrien Fontanellaz, from Switzerland, is a military history researcher and author. He developed a passion for military history at an early age and has progressively narrowed his studies to modern-day conflicts. He is a member of the Scientific Committee of the Pully-based Centre d'histoire et de prospective militaries (Military History and Prospective Centre), and regularly contributes for the Revue Militaire Suisse and various French military history magazines. He is co-founder and a regular contributor to the French military history website *L'autre coté de la colline*, and this is his sixth title for Helion's '@War' series.

Tom Cooper

Tom Cooper is an Austrian aerial warfare analyst and historian. Following a career in a worldwide transportation business – during which he established a network of contacts in the Middle East and Africa – he moved into narrow-focus analysis and writing on small, little-known air forces and conflicts, about which he has collected extensive archives. This has resulted in specialisation in such Middle Eastern air forces as those of Egypt, Iran, Iraq and Syria, plus various African and Asian air forces. As well as authoring and co-authoring more than 30 books - including an in-depth analysis of major Arab air forces at war with Israel during the period 1955-1973 - and over 1,000 articles, Cooper is a regular correspondent for multiple specialised defence-related publications.